PEACE AND CONFLICT SERIES
RON MILAM, GENERAL EDITOR

Also in this series:

Admirals Under Fire: The US Navy and the Vietnam War
by Edward J. Marolda
The Air War in Vietnam
by Michael E. Weaver
Charging a Tyrant: The Arraignment of Saddam Hussein
by Greg Slavonic
Crooked Bamboo: A Memoir from Inside the Diem Regime
by Nguyen Thai, edited by Justin Simundson
Girls Don't: A Woman's War in Vietnam
by Inette Miller
Memorial Days: Vietnam Stories, 1973–2022
by Wayne Karlin
Rain in Our Hearts: Alpha Company in the Vietnam War
by James Allen Logue and Gary D. Ford

CAPTURING SKUNK ALPHA

A BARRIO SAILOR'S JOURNEY IN VIETNAM

RAÚL HERRERA

TEXAS TECH UNIVERSITY PRESS

This book is typeset in EB Garamond. The paper used in this book meets the minimum requirements of ANSI/NISO Z39.48-1992 (R1997). ⊗

Designed by Hannah Gaskamp
Cover design by Hannah Gaskamp

Library of Congress Cataloging-in-Publication Data

Names: Herrera, Raúl, 1946– author. Title: Capturing Skunk Alpha: A Barrio Sailor's Journey in Vietnam / Raúl Herrera. Other titles: Barrio Sailor's Journey in Vietnam
Description: Lubbock: Texas Tech University Press, [2023] | Series: Peace and Conflict |
Includes index. | Summary: "One deckhand's memoir of Swift Boat life in Vietnam"—Provided by publisher. Identifiers: LCCN 2022050589 (print) | LCCN 2022050590 (ebook) |
ISBN 978-1-68283-173-1 (paperback) | ISBN 978-1-68283-174-8 (ebook)
Subjects: LCSH: Herrera, Raúl, 1946– | Vietnam War, 1961–1975—Riverine operations, American. | Operation Market Time, 1965–1973. | Sailors—United States—Biography. | Mexican Americans—Texas—San Antonio—Biography. | Vietnam War, 1961–1975—Naval operations, American. | Vietnam War, 1961–1975—Personal narratives, American. | United States. Navy—Hispanic Americans. | San Antonio (Tex.)—Biography.
Classification: LCC DS558.7.D35 2017 (print) | LCC DS558.7 (ebook) |
DDC 959.704/345—dc23/eng/20230222
LC record available at https://lccn.loc.gov/2022050589
LC ebook record available at https://lccn.loc.gov/2022050590

23 24 25 26 27 28 29 30 31 / 9 8 7 6 5 4 3 2 1
Texas Tech University Press
Box 41037
Lubbock, Texas 79409-1037 USA
800.832.4042
ttup@ttu.edu
www.ttupress.org

This book is dedicated to the memory of Boatswain's Mate 1st Class Bobby Don Carver, who was killed in action on December 6, 1967, Quảng Ngãi Province, Republic of Vietnam. A Swift Boat hero.

CONTENTS

ILLUSTRATIONS

FOREWORD

My life and that of Raúl Herrera have common origins from the beginning, although we did not know of each other for many years. We were both raised with strong Hispanic roots and were close in age. We graduated from rival Catholic high schools, Central Catholic and Holy Cross, in San Antonio, Texas. From there, by different paths, we each ended up in the United States Navy serving on Swift Boats in faraway Vietnam during the war, over half a century ago.

There are many accounts of war by admirals and politicians, usually with themselves as the centerpiece and heroes of the story. Raúl's book is relatively rare because it is the story of a young sailor who was so close to battle that he could see the terrible carnage of gunfire and witnessed the death of his crew's lead petty officer.

The numerous Swift Boat versus resupply trawler battles during the war—one of which Raúl participated in and describes at length—were likely the only surface-to-surface ship battles of the US Navy in the seventy-five years after World War II. Raúl and his fellow sailors performed courageously in the highest traditions of a naval service whose battles began with *Bonhomme Richard*'s victory over *Serapis* and continued through Midway. But war leaves terrible scars even on the survivors—victors and vanquished alike. Raúl's book is the product of those memories. The death of Bobby Don Carver, his older Navy nemesis and mentor, is one that Raúl remembers daily and whose life he is determined not be forgotten.

Raúl is among the most highly respected of all Swift Boat veterans, serving for many years as president of the Swift Boat Sailors Association. In that capacity, he has assisted veterans of those battles for over forty years and often their survivors. I first spoke to him when he was assisting the relative of a sailor looking for the final story of their brother who died near me many years ago in Vietnam.

It is noteworthy that Raúl was able to write and then publish this remarkable story, which captures the nature and events of very extraordinary naval warfare a half-century later. It is a product of his love for Swift mates whose lives were lost in youth long ago fighting in our country's service. They speak through him. They will always live in Raúl's heart and in mine.

JOHN E. O'NEILL

SWIFT BOAT SKIPPER PCF-53 AND PCF-94

NEW YORK TIMES BESTSELLING AUTHOR

ACKNOWLEDGMENTS

F irst and foremost, I owe the deepest gratitude to our Swift Boat crew lead petty officer, BM1 Bobby Don Carver. "Boats," as we called him, was the driving force in getting this story into print, albeit via a spiritual influence. Promise kept, Boats. . . . We remember.

This literary journey spans four decades. Along the way, I have received assistance and encouragement from countless individuals. I begin by thanking all those not specifically mentioned herein. Your association with my work, both directly and indirectly, will always be appreciated.

Early on, Mamá Sarita, my dear mother Sara Herrera, presented me with two shoeboxes containing all the letters I sent home from Vietnam. The letters and postcards—seventy-nine in all—were instrumental in capturing the personal side of my days in Vietnam.

US Congressman Henry B. González of San Antonio assisted by securing pertinent declassified government documents relating to Operation Market Time and Swift Boats, as well as reports on the North Vietnam aerial campaign.

I knew I had a story to tell. Writing it was a separate issue. In the late '70s, members of the Manuscriptors Guild were there to get me started in shaping my thoughts. I learned that immersing myself in the writing community through critique groups and conferences was a good start. Dawn Ireland, Jeanne Perdue, Mavis Rayburn, and Rita Mills stand out as mentors along the way.

I'm honored to have had the privilege of communicating with and receiving research information from key Operation Market Time participants. I will forever be indebted to Rear Admiral Kenneth L. Veth, commander of Naval Forces Vietnam; Captain

Arthur P. Ismay, commander of Boat Squadron One; and Army 1st Lieutenant James S. Bowers, Helicopter Company, 52nd Aviation Battalion, who was heavily involved in the Vũng Rô Bay incident—the catalyst to the creation of Task Force 115.

A special thank you is extended to the two survivors of the tragic mining of Swift Boat PCF-4: Lieutenant Junior Grade Charles Lloyd and Radioman Third Class Robert Johnson. Their courageous sharing of the disastrous event, as difficult as it may have been for them to recall after fifty-three years, is immensely appreciated. Norman Hatch, crewman on the USS *Krishna* (ARL-38), provided details and dramatic photos of the PCF-4 salvage operation.

From the coastal aerial surveillance unit, Lieutenant Commander Max G. Branscomb, commander of Lockheed P2V-7 Neptune surveillance aircraft YB-10, and Lieutenant Vernon Jones, YB-10 Tactical Coordinator / Navigator, shared eyewitness accounts of how they detected enemy resupply trawler Skunk Alpha, off the Quảng Ngãi Province coast. During the ensuing three-day marathon radar tracking by the USS *Wilhoite* (DE-397), Radarman Second Class Dave Payson and Radarman Third Class John Wayne Bohon provided details of the pursuit.

Lieutenant Victor G. "Pete" Reiling Jr., First Coastal Zone Psychological Operations Officer, shared detailed information about the inclusion of a psychological warfare speaker team in the trawler intercept plan. Providing additional eyewitness accounts of the close-to-shore chase were Lieutenant Junior Grade Norman T. Saunders, skipper of the Coast Guard Cutter *Point Orient* (USCGS 82319), and his executive officer, Lieutenant Junior Grade Kenneth J. Morris.

Supporting the seaborne mission during the trawler intercept were Firebird and Rattler helicopter units from the 71st Assault Helicopter Company, Chu Lai: SP4 Ron Seabolt, Firebird gunship crew chief; WO-1 Dave Ellingsworth and WO-1 Ken Weigand; Captain Rodney Bither, 161st Assault Helicopter Company, Scorpions, Chu Lai; and Major Derald Smith, 14th Aviation Battalion, Task Force Oregon provided information surrounding the organization and supervision of the air assault lift of elements from the Republic of Korea 2nd Marine Brigade at the mouth of the Sa Kỳ River where the trawler was forced aground.

Providing an eyewitness account of disarming the enemy ship's 2,046-pound self-destruct TNT charge placed around the ship's hull was Explosive Ordnance Disposal (EOD) Specialist Gunner's Mate Guns Second Class Eddie Knaup.

My appreciation is extended to Quartermaster Second Class (SS) Dan B. Odenweller, Naval Support Activity (NSA), Da Nang, Vietnam, for providing superb color photographs of the arms cache on display at the awards ceremony held in Da Nang on July 19, 1967.

Chief Engineman Harold Guinn and Boatswain's Mate First Class Leo Pearman provided on-the-ground eyewitness accounts of the South Vietnamese Navy's Coastal Group 16 Junk Base, which was overrun by Viet Cong and North Vietnamese Regulars in retaliation for the capture of the Skunk Alpha trawler.

Assisting with details surrounding Swift Boat capsizing incidents were Seaman Quarter Master John Paul Jones, Skippers Tom Jones, Tony Taylor, and David Wilbourne, and crewmen Stirlin Harris and Tony Snesko. Skipper Mike Tackney coined the term the Tonkin Flyer to describe the fierce Northeastern Monsoon. In his honor, I so named the relevant chapter.

Many who rode the Swift Boats, known in the Navy as Patrol Craft Fast, or PCFs, contributed to the accuracy of what lies between the covers. I continue to insist that although the book is a narrative nonfiction memoir, it is as much theirs as it is mine. Some helped considerably: Robert "Bob" Bolger, Bob Brown, Dan Daly, John English, Virgil Erwin, Hal Griffin, Lou Masterson, Joe Pope, Ray Michilini, Bill Rogers, George Rekow, Eldon Thompson, Viet Truong, Ha Tuong, Michael Turley, Terry Vander Molen, Bruce Wentworth, and James D. Wiggins.

Two internet websites were a treasure trove of Swift Boat research information: Larry J. Wasikowski's *Coastal Squadron One Swift Boat Crew Directory* and Bob Shirley's Patrol Craft Fast website. Both shipmates left their labor of love on the internet, allowing people around the world to find out what it was like to be a Swift Boat sailor during the Vietnam War. . . . Bravo Zulu.

Closer to home are my fellow crewmen who helped immensely by contributing their own recollections of what took place fifty-six years ago in a foreign land. Some reflections were painful, while others brought healing and laughter. My thanks to PCF-79 Skipper Ed Bergin, Gunner Bob Middleton, Engineman Ronald Rinehart, (RIP), Seaman Timothy McNamara (RIP), and Engineman Jim Schneider. A special thanks is extended to the Carver family, who provided stories about our lead petty officer, BM1 Bobby Don "Boats" Carver.

I'm also indebted to members of the Houston Writers Guild Wednesday night critique group members. Helping me improve my work were Alice, Araceli, Beabe, Brett, Carolyn, Connie, Denise, Felicia, Fern, Frank, Karina, Landy, Meg, Melineh, Ollie, and Ron.

My thanks are extended to Jeremy Odell for creating my original website and to Felicia "Mack" Little and Brian Bearden for restoring and rebuilding the original site. Sue Edwards created a memorial tribute video for Bobby Don Carver. Nathan Ryan, my grandson, developed a PowerPoint presentation about Swift Boats and the Skunk Alpha trawler incident. Gabriel Herrera, another grandson, created charts and diagrams for the book. José Cueva, my best friend from high school, supported my endeavor by helping me recall personal details in my story.

Providing helpful marketing ideas were members of the Nonfiction Authors Association, Houston Chapter: Mike Ellerkamp, Mike Kowis, Kate Frank, Katherine Swarts, Red O'Laughlin, Hiett Ives, and Melanie Bragg. Sandy Lawrence, Aimee Ravichandran, and Russell Little were the driving social media force that brought *Capturing Skunk Alpha* to the front line of public awareness. C. J. Peterson provided exceptional development of public relations material. Preparing the way for a great book release event in Houston was my dear Swift Boat shipmate John E. O'Neill. In San Antonio, Richard Ríos and Jerry Galván coordinated the book launch events. Their untiring dedication and support are greatly appreciated.

John Paine's keen editorial eye was crucial in trimming down my manuscript to an acceptable word count. In addition, John shaped the remaining work into a higher level of prose. A special salute goes to Travis Snyder, PhD, and the Texas Tech University Press staff for making my dream of telling the Swift Boat story come to pass. A close friend of the Swift Boat Sailors Association, Vietnam Center and Archive Director Stephen Maxner, added his support to my work.

Throughout the many years this work has been in progress, my family has been most supportive. My children—Odessa, Angela, Anthony, Michael, and Eileen—continually encouraged me to finish the book. I owe a great deal of respect and appreciation to my wife, Luz Analida, for her patience, support, and belief in me to fulfill my promise to the memory of Bobby Don Carver by bringing this literary project to fruition. My wife's daughter and granddaughter, Erika and Camila, gave me refuge after Hurricane Harvey forced us out of our home. Their loving gesture allowed my work on the book to continue.

In closing, I thank everyone who prayed for my safe return from Vietnam fifty-five years ago, enabling me to share this story. And most of all, I thank God for answering their prayers.

INTRODUCTION

"We have shared the incommunicable experience of war,

we have felt, we still feel, the passion of life to its top.

In our youth our hearts were touched with fire."

—Oliver Wendell Holmes Jr.

apturing *Skunk Alpha* is the true story of a five-man crew of Navy combat boat sailors selected at random to serve under the command of a young naval officer. Ours was a dangerous undertaking along the coastal waters of the Republic of Vietnam—Swift Boats in Operation Market Time, the longest continuous US military operation in Vietnam War history.

I served for three years on destroyers and had many nautical miles of salt water under my keel. I experienced the winter storms of the North Atlantic, circumnavigated South America, and operated with all the South American navies. On several occasions I spent many weeks in the Caribbean on Operation Springboard. Aboard the USS *Van Voorhis* (DE-1028), I was First Lieutenant, Anti-Submarine Warfare (ASW) officer and was in line to become Weapons Officer (Gun Boss) when I volunteered for Swift Boats.

I was a Lieutenant Junior Grade when I was assigned Crew 74A upon my arrival at the Naval Amphibious Base in Coronado, California. I sensed my lead petty officer was an old-Navy boatswain's mate. I greeted him with relief and trepidation. Second Class Boatswain's Mate Bobby Don Carver's handlebar mustache and tattoos were a witness to his sea-tested experience. I was confident he would know his business, but I suspected he would not fancy serving under a skipper five years his junior. We would have to establish who was boss. A similar situation arose with an ASW Chief Petty Officer while on the destroyer. Our head-butting culminated in his being relieved. I didn't want to go through a similar occurrence again. In Vietnam, I believe my challenge to duke it out or arm wrestle with him cemented our relationship. I won and conceded it was his boat—when we were in port. It became mine when I stepped aboard and we were underway. To his credit, my boat was always fueled and armed and the crew ready for patrol.

Handling our propulsion system was a second-class engineman. He stepped up and told me his name was Ronald M. Rinehart, but everyone called him Porky. He was not overweight, and to this day I never found out how he got the nickname. Maybe I would have regretted learning the answer. He was more than an engineman; he was an elite diesel motor specialist. My boat, PCF-79, always met her seaborne commitments while I was officer in charge.

Bob Middleton, a third-class torpedoman and my gunner, was not schooled in machine guns and mortars. He didn't like the chores of a gunner—rearming, cleaning all the small arms weapons, setting head space and timing on the machine guns, and all the associated duties of preparing the weapons for patrol. Regardless, he proved his worth behind the twin M2 Brownings (side-by-side .50 caliber machine guns). He was deadly accurate in suppressing enemy fire as well as deforestation of dense jungle. The enemy could not survive five seconds in front of the twins with Middleton tapping the butterflies.

Seaman Timothy McNamara became our deckhand when we arrived in Da Nang, South Vietnam. We lost him to the psychological stress of war. He was on his second Swift Boat tour. Tim served valiantly and was with us when we engaged Skunk Alpha, the North Vietnamese ammo-laden trawler. He, along with the rest of the crew, was decorated and personally congratulated by Premier Nguyễn Cao Kỳ and Chief of State Nguyễn Văn Thiệu for the capture of an enemy ship twice the size of our craft.

I also had a designated draftsman on my combat boat, Seaman Raúl Herrera, the author of this book. We made him our communications expert, Ops Boss, and assigned him as our radio and radarman. He relates his on-the-job training story well in this book. He went screaming and fighting into his new designator, all the while reminding us that he was a draftsman striker. He, like all the others, excelled at his work. His mother made sure her monthly care packages contained good Mexican food for his adopted brothers.

My crewmen weren't all trained in their key positions, but I had the mainstay of the Navy I could depend on to make certain my orders were obeyed and carried out. Carver and Rinehart took their jobs seriously and helped weld our crew into a lethal Navy Swift Boat designed to take out our enemy. All "our hearts were touched with fire," and the passion of being in a volunteer elite unit kept us sharp and willing to go the extra mile to succeed in our mission.

The Sa Kỳ River Victory, as history records the capture of Skunk Alpha, is exemplary of the many heroic actions that placed these brave Swift Boat sailors in a patriotic and positive light. Swift Boats must be remembered for what they were. This book disproves many of the negative opinions directed against Vietnam veterans. Swifties are a group of valiant men, a brotherhood, who fought and died for their country and who today continue to correct the lies and disdain that greeted them upon their return home.

This is a true story of what Swift Boats and their gallant crews accomplished during that underappreciated war in South Vietnam. *Capturing Skunk Alpha* will secure our honorable place in US military history.

CAPTAIN EDWARD J. BERGIN (USNR, RET.)

CAPTURING SKUNK ALPHA

CHAPTER 1

SPIRIT

A cold, heavy pressure pulsated on my chest. Fearing its origin, I lay motionless on my bunk, waiting. Anguished moans echoed from a distance through the still night air, mimicking the hideous yowls of prowling cats in the middle of a stormy night. The kind that makes you envision zombie children wailing outside, beneath your bedroom window.

The pressure intensified. I sank deeper into my rack as the muffled moans drew closer. Sweat trickled from my fevered flesh, only to be overwhelmed by a morbid chill that made me jerk and twitch to near convulsion.

It was a force too powerful to challenge. I couldn't break free. The circumstances pointed to demonic possession. My mind raced with possible explanations. *Am I dreaming? Is it a nightmare? Yes, a nightmare, the only logical answer. But why can't I awake and regain control?* I struggled to move, but my mental commands drew no physical response. I lost control over my body. *I'm doomed, but to what? Horror? Hell? Death? What?*

My pounding heart seemed to be galloping up my throat in a desperate attempt to escape the terror. Piercing puffs of frosty air jabbed me at random, causing isolated areas of goose bumps to surface and fade almost at once. They evolved into a concentrated bone-chilling wave that slid along the length of my scrawny frame, beginning at the bottom of my feet and raising every hair on end as it inched its way to the top of my head for what seemed an eternity.

Suddenly, like the horrified passengers on the Titanic must have felt after jumping off the sinking ship and crashing into the icy waters of the North Atlantic, I turned stone rigid. Faster and faster the haunting waves sped freely back and forth from head to toe, leaving in the wake a statically charged body. Still trapped by the invisible force, I struggled again to break free but was unsuccessful. I yelled out to Gunner, lying in his rack just four feet away, but heard only the agonizing moans, now terrifyingly louder. In desperation, I called upon divine intervention: *"¡Dios mío, por favor, ayú-dame!"* I pleaded to all the saints Mamá often listed in her favorite religious litany to intercede for me. They, like Gunner, did not hear my cries.

Then, the image of Boats—Bobby Don Carver, our crew's boatswain's mate—flashed into my mind. His spirit had to be the unnatural force weighing heavy on my chest. An eerie fright came over me. Discovering I had been making the morbid sounds all along left me disoriented. I still lay pinned to my sweat-soaked bunk, helpless, exhausted, and petrified to the point of surrender.

The more I denied his presence, the harder his frigid spirit pushed down on my trembling torso. Gathering all my strength, I finally thrashed my way from his hold and found myself standing next to my bunk, shuddering uncontrollably, and scream-ing wildly. This time Gunner heard me and jumped out of his sack, confused. He shook me vigorously, while attempting to shout me back to reality.

"He was here, Gunner! Boats was here," I screamed, still quivering in his grasp. "I felt his cold body on top of me, Gunner. It wasn't a nightmare. Fuck! What does he want? It was hideous. Didn't you hear me yell for help?"

Gunner stood silently before me, his ashen face indicating he too sensed our bosun's spiritual presence. Neither uttered a sound as we shared the gray pain of grief.

I bolted from Gunner's grip and raced from the long wooden barracks. A full moon shone on the red dirt trail leading down to the Swift Boat pier. I stumbled along the floating dock and climbed aboard our Swift Boat, PCF-79. The guard on watch found me sitting atop the ammo locker on the fantail, in my skivvies, staring aimlessly into the glistening water of Trường Giang River,[1] oblivious to the cold December air.

"Come on, let's get you inside." He led me into the boat's cabin. "Lie down on this rack," he ordered, covering me with an itchy Navy-issue gray wool blanket. "Get some rest. I'll keep an eye on you 'til morning." He went back out onto the fantail to resume his watch.

My mind's eye kept taking me back to the day before, December 6, 1967, when our crew witnessed Carver's death. I saw his lifeless body lying in a pool of blood amidst a scattered mass of expended brass casings from the fantail .50 caliber machine gun he had been firing at the enemy positions on the beach.

The star-studded darkness peered through the open rear cabin door. Staring into the beyond, I silently questioned my fallen mentor. *Boats, are you trying to warn me that I'm next?* Several shots from a stashed bottle of I. W. Harper bourbon and the constant hum of the Onan generator lulled me into a deep sleep.

That night, the odds of surviving the remaining four months of my Swift Boat combat tour in that hellhole called Vietnam were cut to almost nil with Bobby Don's untimely death. All I wanted was to fulfill the promise I made to my parents, to get home safely. So much had happened since leaving behind the barrio: childhood and adolescence, a high school sweetheart, and the comfort and safety of home life in San Antonio, Texas.

My time as a Swift Boat sailor in Vietnam had changed me forever.

CHAPTER 2

BARRIO YEARS

I was born to Frank and Sara Herrera on November 11, 1946. Mom said the entire city celebrated my arrival. Marching bands, troops, and decorated floats from Fort Sam Houston Army Base, Randolph Air Force Base, Lackland Air Force Base, Brooks Air Force Base, and Kelly Air Force Base wound in a parade through the downtown streets in celebration of Armistice Day. She could hear the marching bands play as they passed in front of Santa Rosa Hospital.

The military is in my blood. I was named in honor of my mother's brother, PFC Roy C. Berrones.[1] He was attached to the 318th Infantry Regiment in World War II when he died on October 8, 1944, nine days shy of his twenty-second birthday. The only difference in our names was that I was given the Spanish version—Raúl. The family always called me Roy, probably in my uncle's memory. Although I was my parents' only child, I was brought home to two half-sisters, Martha and Regina. Their mother, Romana Barrón, passed away shortly after Regina was born.

In the old sector of San Antonio where I was raised, on the west side, we called the neighborhoods barrios. The majority of its inhabitants were Mexican American. When I was bad, my mother would say, "*Hijito*, you better behave, *si no, El Viejito* will come and take you away!" (Son, if you don't behave, the Boogeyman is going to come get you!) Grabbing me by the ear, she'd take me to the front windows and let me see for myself. In the late afternoons, just as the sun started casting long, eerie shadows toward the Alazán Creek, a gray-haired bearded old Mexican man in tattered clothes shuffled slowly down the gravel alley in front of our house and mysteriously disappeared into the creek underbrush.

"No, no, Mamá, don't make me look. *¡Tengo miedo!*" I was afraid that if I dared to look at him, *El Viejito* somehow would sense I was staring at him and come after me.

He carried a lumpy burlap sack on his back that made him hunch forward as he trudged onward. My mother, God bless her, continued her scare tactic by making me look at the sack. *"¿Ves el saco?"* she asked. "Bad *muchachitos* are in that sack," she insisted. "*Los lleva* down to the arroyo and he will throw them in to drown!"

I was certain *El Viejito* was looking for me for having shot a mourning dove with my Daisy BB gun the week before. I promised God I would never kill anything ever again if I wasn't found out. No one ever discovered my horrible deed.

We shared a backyard with my father's older half-sister, Tía Panchita. This was convenient for us to go to her house to use the bathroom. Until a toilet and tub were finally installed in our house, I was bathed in a fifteen-gallon galvanized washtub. I can't remember my age, but I slept in my crib way past the time that I should have been out of it. At night, Dad would bring out a rolled-up mattress from the back room and place it on the living room floor, where he and Mom slept, next to my crib. My sisters slept in a separate room in twin beds.

I attended pre-kindergarten at La Escuelita, the nearby Catholic neighborhood daycare center, run by the Sisters of Perpetual Adoration of Guadalupe. I knew them simply by their Spanish translation las Adoratrices. The nuns dedicated their lives to silence, solitude, prayer, adoration of la Virgen de Guadalupe, and to serving the needs of the church.

My formal education was under the tutelage of the Benedictine nuns at Sacred Heart Elementary School. I would later have no problem taking orders because at Sacred Heart, discipline was the order of the day . . . every day. Pulled ears, pinched arms, and ruler-slapped knuckles were their methods of instilling respect for a strict disciplinary code of conduct. Sister Henrietta Marie, Sister Benedicta, and Sister Scholastica were experts at administering the "hand of knowledge to the seat of wisdom."

Mom and Dad argued about what high school I should attend. Dad wanted me to go to Fox Tech High School downtown because he knew they had an excellent architectural drafting department. I don't know if he gave any consideration to my going to college. He felt that I needed to study a trade, and Catholic high schools didn't offer that opportunity. Besides, my sisters were already attending Saint Teresa's Academy, and their tuition payments were often in arrears.

Mom, on the other hand, was determined to send me to four more years of Catholic education. Dad lost the battle and instead of becoming a Fox Tech Buffalo, I was on my way to become a Holy Cross Knight. It was a new all-male school, located in one of the poorest neighborhoods in the far westside of town. It didn't take me long to realize the Brothers of Holy Cross accepted nothing less than 100 percent respect and obedience. Detention was available for those of us who didn't succeed in that area. I became a persistent figure there.

The school permitted me to work my way through my freshman and sophomore school years at Holy Cross by doing custodial work after school and on weekends. Tuition was around $100 per year. At a minimum hourly wage of $1.15, I paid off my tuition in eighty-seven hours of work. My job consisted of cleaning classrooms, stripping, waxing, and buffing floors. I also helped the school's custodian, Mr. Rosas, with yard work on weekends. During my junior and senior years, I worked downtown at Burt's Shoes on Saturdays.

Mom never cared for me to play football in high school. I lived for it. To me, the cracking sound of helmets and shoulder pads colliding was euphoric. Short quarterbacks were the norm and worked well with a T-formation since the defense couldn't see who I was handing the ball off to. On the occasions that my mother attended any of my games with Tía Toñia, her sister-in-law, she'd spend the entire game praying the Rosary, losing track of where I was on the field. Tía Toñia would wait until I was at the bottom of a pile and point, causing my mother to start her prayers all over again.

I grew up understanding that my people were often racially categorized in various forms. To the establishment, we were called Mexicans, as well as the derogatory wetbacks or greasers. In the barrio, we were happy calling ourselves Chicanos. It's been said that the term goes back to the turn of the century when the Spanish word for little boy, *chico*, was merged with the Spanish word for Mexican, *Mexicano*. Adding to the uniqueness of the barrio was its Tex-Mex dialect. At home, we spoke both English and Spanish, but almost always Tex-Mex kicked in. If we started a conversation in Spanish, we interjected an English word if the Spanish equivalent did not automatically come to mind. We did this without hesitation, employing both languages in our conversations. The term Tex-Mex also found its way into a genre of music and a unique Mexican culinary style called Tex-Mex cuisine that emerged out of the barrios in Texas.

The barrio was also the place where I learned the fear of death.

My skirt-chasing days were well underway by the time I went to high school. Weekend dances took place at outdoor venues like the Patio Andaluz, La Villita, and the Villa

Fontana Ballroom. In the early 1960s, local rock 'n' roll bands abounded in San Antonio. Sunny & the Sunliners and the Royal Jesters were the top bands of the day. There was always a weekend dance being sponsored by one of the many car clubs around town, like the Piston Knockers, Gear Grinders, King Cobras, Road Griffins, Slow Pokes, or the Slicks Car Club. Oddly enough, I never saw any hot rods outside these venues!

My parents reluctantly allowed me to attend these dances. They were aware of the trouble local gangs could cause. In my barrio, a gang called La India controlled the streets. Other notorious teenage gangs at the time included La Tripa, Riverside, La Loma, Los Courts, Lake Gang, and La Dot, to name a few. The gang with a reputation that surpassed all gangs in SanAnto was the Ghost Town Gang. Their name alone was an intimidating feature.

Gang members were known as *pachucos*, or *chucos*. They fought primarily with neighboring rival gangs to defend and maintain their own territory. La India took on the name of the Mexican bakery located at Colorado and Martin Streets, where they hung out. Some were junior high or high school dropouts. Their preferred style of dress included khaki pants and tangerine shoes such as Plymouths or Stacy Adams. Most of the time the only kind of shirt they wore was a white, neck-high T-shirt, and always . . . always, they sported either a thin silver or gold belt. *Chucos* normally kept to themselves. Like with a hive of bees, if you didn't poke the nest, they wouldn't attack.

My first near-death experience occurred when I was a freshman in high school at the hands of the notorious Ghost Town Gang. A girl named Carmen lived down the street from my cousin Lupe's house. We started going together soon after I was her escort at a *quinceañera*, which is the equivalent to a blonde, blue-eyed girl's sweet sixteen party. As the name in Spanish implies, the event celebrated a young lady's fifteenth birthday, her coming of age. Carmen was one of the fifteen debutantes, and I had been invited to her birthday party. She asked me to bring some friends from Holy Cross.

I often rode my bike to her house, but only during the day. I wouldn't dare consider a bike ride to her house through certain barrios at night. So, one afternoon after my father got home from work, I waited to ensure that he was in a good mood and popped the question.

"Dad, Carmen invited me to her birthday party." Before he lifted his eyes from the newspaper, I blurted out, "Can I take the car?" Brazenly I bypassed the permission request. *One thousand one, one thousand two,* I thought to myself. *Oh, please say yes!*

"You know I don't let you drive by yourself, *¡y menos por la noche!*" Dad responded. *Now, was that a trick answer? Was it a Yes or a No?* My subconscious brain kicked in—even though I had been driving for four years, Dad never let me drive by myself, not until I passed my driving test and got my license. I said, "Raúl Hernández can drive the car."

"*Muy bien*, but only if Raúl drives," Dad demanded. "And I want you home by midnight. *¿Entendido?*" he added. He didn't even know if Raúl had a license, but he was tall and looked the age.

"*Sí, señor*, by midnight," I assured him. "*Gracias*, Dad. *¡Muchas gracias!*"

I was excited and first dialed up Raúl. His parents gave him permission as well. One after another we picked up George "Pee Wee" Galván, Tony "La Pera" Pérez, and finally, Alfonso "Al" Cano. They were my *camaradas*—my best buds. We'd been best friends since first grade at Sacred Heart. To ensure that *la carrucha* had enough petrol, we stopped off at an Indian gas station on West Poplar Street to take advantage of the gas price wars going on at the time. Filling up at nine cents a gallon left us with plenty of spare change for a stop at the Malt House on Zarzamora Street after the party.

Carmen's mother met us at the door. "*Pásenle, muchachos*, come in. The party is in the backyard," she said, motioning the way.

I found Carmen in the kitchen. She was wearing a pastel yellow summer dress with spaghetti straps. Her black hair framed her fair complexion, and a small matching yellow bow was pinned to her hair.

"You look pretty, Carmen. Happy birthday!"

"Thanks," she said, grabbing my hand and pulling me toward the door. "Come and meet my friends."

Her mother had done her best to make her daughter's party festive. She strung up colored light bulbs and nailed party decorations to the back of the house. There were only a couple of *rucas* and a few *vatos*—girls and guys—already there. I hoped it was because the night was still young, and the rest of the crowd would soon be arriving. After some awkward introductions, Carmen went to the table where stacks of 45s and LP *rolas* were laid out on a table next to the record player. She picked one out and placed it on the flat spinning disk.

More of Carmen's friends arrived and the party atmosphere improved. Regardless, I sensed that my friends found the party to be a drag.

"*Órale, vatos*, take the *rucas* out to dance," I pleaded.

"You're here for your squeeze, *ese*," Pee Wee noted. "So, you're happy, but we want to split."

"*Órale*, come on, *ese*, stay a while longer, an hour maybe, and after Carmen cuts her cake, we'll split," I insisted.

"Pee Wee's right, Roy," La Pera interjected. *"Va a haber mejores rucas* at La Villita."
I gave them that one—there would be a better girl selection at La Villita.

Al agreed and said, "You stay with Carmen and let us take a quick ride down
there, check it out, and come right back."

I had no interest in going downtown and didn't want to leave Carmen, especially
on her birthday, even though Sunny & the Sunliners were playing. "Okay, you guys
can go, but be back in an hour," I demanded.

They were off. I kept dancing with Carmen, and everyone was having a great
time. One of Carmen's friends untwisted light bulbs every now and again, and
soon only a couple of red and green bulbs stayed lit, improving the mood. An
hour and a half had passed, and I hadn't realized it. We were all startled by the
sudden sound of squealing tires and the crashing clatter of loose gravel hitting
garbage cans in front of the houses at the corner. Another short screeching of
tires seemed to come from the front of Carmen's house. Raúl burst into the
backyard, followed by La Pera and Al. Pee Wee was missing. They all had the
look of death on their faces.

Raúl snapped his head to one side, calling me to where the three of them had gathered. Pera was pacing back and forth, and Al just hung his head and kept punching
the palm of his left hand with a balled right fist.

"I got some bad news for you, *ese*," Raúl confessed.

"Bad news? What the hell are you talking about, and *dónde está* Pee Wee?" I asked.

Teeth clenched, Al blurted, *"¡Chingao!* I loved him like a brother, *ese!"* His voice
was filled with anger.

I pushed on his chest hard, bouncing him up against the chain link fence and
cried out, "What do you mean, 'loved him'? Is he in the car? Where is he?" No one
said a word. "Shit, this ain't no fuckin' good, *pendejos*! Somebody tell me what's
going on," I demanded.

In a low tone, one of them said, "He's dead!"

"You're really pissing me off, *cabrones*! DEAD?" I shouted. The music stopped.
Carmen approached and grabbed my arm tight, her face aghast in fear. The rest of
Carmen's friends whispered to each other, shocked looks on their faces.

Pera stepped in and said, "We pulled up to the front of La Villita. Pee Wee got out
of the car to go see if there was a good crowd at the dance and . . ."

"And that's when they shot him!" Raúl exclaimed.

"¿Lo plomiaron?" (They filled him full of lead?) "You went to check out the place,
not to get Pee Wee shot. *¡Pendejos!"*

The news took my breath away. Something didn't add up. "No, no! *¡NO*

11

CHINGES!" I shouted. "So, why are you here and not with the police or at the hospital with Pee Wee?"

"It all happened too fast," Pera explained. "We didn't know he was dead! Al and I pulled him back into *la carrucha* and we took off."

"So, is he at the Santa Rosa emergency room?" I asked.

Raúl declared, "No, we were too scared to go there and didn't want to get involved."

"*¡Pues que pendejos!*" I exclaimed, starting to grow a bit skeptical of the story. "So, just what the hell did you do with his body?"

"We drove by his *chante* (house) on Houston Street and dumped his body on their front yard and split," Al informed.

Then it hit me. "Shit! *¡A la chingada!* Oh fuck! What about my *jefito's carrucha*? Are there any bullet holes in it? What about the blood?" I'd be the next one to die once my father found out about what happened.

A possible answer was interrupted by the sudden commotion coming from the alley behind the house. Two by two, *chucos* started jumping the chain-link fence and into Carmen's backyard. Making matters worse, they were all carrying zip guns and switchblades. In less than a minute, the *chucos* were in our faces, gun barrels pushed in all parts of our bodies and shiny stiletto push-button blades waving threateningly. The *chucos* numbered a dozen or more, all eager to pull their triggers or punch slits into our bodies. Pera always carried a small—no, tiny—pocketknife, about as much use to us then as a Steinway grand piano is to a mariachi band. It wasn't difficult to surmise that these *vatos* were members of the Ghost Town Gang. Their turf hangout was the Good Samaritan Center, located at Saltillo and 19th Streets, just five short blocks north of Bronte Street. Basically, we were dead meat: Ghost Town Gang FOUR, Knights of Holy Cross ZERO!

A skinny *vato loco* walked up to my friend Raúl, probably thinking that he headed up our *clika*. "*¿De dónde son, cabrón?*" he asked. Thinking that we were from a gang, he wanted to know where we were from.

"Lighten up, *ese*," Raúl said. "We're not part of a *clika*. We go to Holy Cross." *Oh, like that's supposed to make all things better*, I thought to myself. Right then we needed a miracle. We were about to become front page news in tomorrow's *San Antonio Light*.

"*Pasaron por el* Good Samaritan *y nos echararon madres*, and *you* shot the finger at us *también, ese*," the *chuco* fumed, pointing at Raúl. That explained the screeching tires. Looking for a little harmless fun, my brilliant *camaradas* thought that it would be a good idea to swat the Ghost Town Gang hive by yelling a foul language litany at them as well as waving bye to them with their middle fingers. Brilliant! "*Carnal*,"

La Pera said. "That wasn't us, *ese*. Really, we've been here all the time." One touch of the car's hood would have sealed the case against us.

Out of nowhere, Carmen's mother appeared and stepped in between us and said, "*Sí, mijito,* I invited them to *mija's* birthday party, and they've been here *todo el tiempo. Ellos son* good boys. *Cálmense* todos, *por favor. Guarden sus armas* and calm down. *Coman* cake *y* drink some punch. You are welcome to stay all you want, *pero* behave yourselves, okay?" Like the biblical parting of the Red Sea, the *chucos* backed off a distance, maintaining their death wish looks on us.

So here we were, having cake and punch with the Ghost Town Gang. Just like Carmen's mother asked, *los chucos* stayed and miraculously behaved themselves! They even asked some of the *rucas* to dance. I was so busy dancing with Carmen that I didn't notice that Raúl, Al, and La Pera were suddenly gone. I feared that *los chucos* had taken them out one by one and I was going to be next. A morbid fear overwhelmed me.

A "psst... psst" caught my attention. I turned toward the back door of the house and saw Al peeking through a slightly open door. He motioned at me to come. I walked toward the door with Carmen at my side so as not to cause suspicion.

"*¡Órale, vámonos!*" Al said, in an anxious tone. "The *vatos* are in the car waiting for you!"

"I'm sorry, but I've got to get out of here," I told Carmen and kissed her goodbye. The corner streetlight shown on Dad's car, but I couldn't see anyone in it. As I got closer, I saw that they were all slouched down in the seats. All I could see was the tops of their heads. I jumped in and Raúl stepped on the clutch, making the car roll down the driveway. Once in the street, he popped the clutch, slammed the gas pedal, and peeled out. We were gone!

Still in shock from our one-on-one encounter with San Anto's number one gang, we sat speechless. Raúl drove towards town. We cruised downtown once or twice before he stopped in front of the Majestic Theatre. People were coming out the exit doors.

"Get going, Raúl, the cops are going to write you a ticket, *ese*," I casually informed him.

"We won't be here long," he replied.

I didn't need more excitement tonight. Before I could make another remark, Al hollered from the back seat, "Pee Wee, over here, *vato!*"

"*Pee Wee*?" I asked as I turned my head back. Sure enough, here came Pee Wee, arms around his *ruca* as they left the theater.

"*Pinches vatos culeros,* all of you!" I cursed. Raúl, Al, and La Pera broke into uncontrollable laughter. "You assholes almost got us killed back there," I said. The knots in my stomach suddenly disappeared and I too burst into laughter. We drove around town once more then headed back to the Westside to drop off the fine group of misfits I called *mis carnales*—brothers through thick and thin. Be it Mom's prayers, a Catholic education, or the horseshoe up my butt, regardless, I survived growing up in a barrio on the west side of SanAnto. I prayed I'd never have to experience that morbid fear of death ever again.

After graduating from Holy Cross, I picked up a summer job with the San Antonio Neighborhood Youth Organization as an activities coordinator at one of their youth centers. Not long after I began working at the center, one of the girls working for the program caught my attention. It was more of a mutual attraction from the instant we locked eyes. Her name was Norma Villanueva. She was going to be a senior in the fall at a high school in the downtown area.

Since I was the center's activities coordinator, I could ensure that Norma's daily group assignments always remained close to the center. Our spare time was spent goggling at each other. Mr. Durham, our center supervisor, discouraged sweetheart relationships between staff members. That made it difficult, but not impossible, to steal moments of closeness every now and again.

One day, while closing the facility, I noticed that Norma was all alone and sitting in the shade of a mesquite tree in front of the center. I thought of offering her a ride, but my bicycle did not have a passenger seat as many bikes did back then. Even if it had, I would have been too embarrassed to ask her to hop on a kid's bike for a ride home. How could I even think of such a thing? Some of my friends already had their own cars, even if they were old jalopies. I only had a bike.

"Hi, Norma! Is your ride late?" I asked, hoping that would be the case so I could volunteer to stay with her until they arrived.

"I think my brother forgot he was supposed to pick me up today," she replied, her voice filled with frustration. My heart fluttered with delight that we might have some alone time, even if it was to be spent simply sitting on the curb next to each other under a tree. We passed the time in idle talk for a while, mostly about school and weekend dances. I was glad to learn that she often went to dances held at La Villita. Captivated by her natural charm, I stared at her soft lips and tuned out the words coming out of her mouth. Her eyes seemed to express a desire for us to be in each other's arms.

A half hour passed, and I saw that she was getting agitated with impatience.

"Why don't we go inside? You can call your brother from the pay phone," I suggested.

She hit my shoulder with a clenched fist. "Hey, that's a great idea, Raúl! Why didn't I think of it?" She said this in a manner that made me wonder if in fact she was glad that I *finally* thought of the idea.

The facility was eerily silent for a change, in sharp contrast to the often unbearable shrieks the children made all day long while at play. The whiff of their heat-produced perspiration hung over us like a typical brown-yellow Los Angeles smog blanket. Norma led the way down the dark hall towards the pay phone. My heart raced with excitement as I followed behind her, my eyes locked on every move that her slender body made. Her white short-sleeved blouse was neatly tucked inside her baby blue culottes. White bobby socks and black penny loafers completed her uniform. I wanted to race up to her, run my fingers through her soft, dark-brown, wavy hair and embrace her.

Until that moment, all we had done was hold hands and then for just seconds at a time. Norma gently picked up the black plastic receiver, dropped in a dime, and dialed her home phone number. She turned facing me and then leaned her back against the gray cinder block wall. She waited impatiently. "It's about time you answered!" she screamed. "Why didn't you pick me up, Jesse?" Our eyes were locked on each other all the while.

Norma spun around and slammed the receiver as if the pay phone was her brother's head. "Oooh, I could kill him," she said with rancor in her voice. Her arms crossed in frustration. She leaned up against the wall and took a deep breath, making her bosom expand. The buttons on her white blouse stretched to their limit.

My young brainless hormones took over as I drew her near, reaching my arms behind her thin waist and pulled her body against mine. I felt her tremble as we stood facing each other. Our hearts raced with excitement. Norma seemed a little hesitant, perhaps due to the element of surprise, but instinctively wrapped her arms around my neck and kissed me with equal teenage want.

Our feet seemed to never touch the black-and-white tile as we slowly made our way out of the building to wait for her brother and cool off in the late afternoon. We sat near, yet apart, from each other at her suggestion. Norma was afraid that her brother might get mad at me, should he arrive and see me too close to his little sister. That's the way it was in the barrio. Older brothers always watched out for their sisters, regardless of age. In time, he arrived. She stood up suddenly when she saw a powder-blue '59 Chevy approach. I trailed behind her as she walked up to the car.

"Jesse, this is Raúl," Norma said. "He's our center coordinator. He offered to wait with me until you finally decided to show up!" Although Jesse and I made glancing eye contact, no verbal exchange was made. However, in typical barrio form, we simultaneously cocked our heads back ever so slightly, acknowledging each other's existence.

"See you tomorrow, Norma," I said as I closed the passenger side door. I climbed on my bike and started to pull away.

"Wait!" Norma exclaimed, as she turned to her brother. "Can't we put his bike in the trunk?" she pleaded to Jesse. "After all, he did sit and wait with me. The least you could do is offer him a ride home."

Jesse was no more than a year older than I was, but I felt like a little kid just the same, having my new girlfriend's older brother put *my* bike in the trunk of *his* car. My embarrassment was short-lived once I got into the car and sat next to Norma. The bench seat of the '59 Chevy Bel Air made it possible for Norma to slide over next to her brother and make space for me to sit snugly next to her. The trip home was too short, but we enjoyed every minute of it. As was typical in 1965, Norma and I became "steadies" and enjoyed our summer job much more from that day forward.

Toward summer's end, I realized I had a major decision to make: what to do with the rest of my life. I had graduated from Holy Cross a few months earlier, so naturally my thoughts turned to college. The unfortunate reality was that higher education was simply out of the question. My parents could not afford it.

Unsubtle messages from Uncle Sam guided me to consider the military. It was common in those days to see posters showing the distinguished Uncle Sam, decked out in his white shirt, blue coat, and white top hat with a wide blue band and white stars all around, and pointing his index finger right at you. The tall red letters read, "I WANT YOU." I'd look straight back at him and think, *No, no, no, Tío Samuel! On the contrary, I need YOU!"*

I was anxious to leave the nest. Over time, my father's bad days gradually outnumbered the good. Alcoholic demons were winning the battle in his head. My mother struggled to keep the family together, and I've got to tell you she did an outstanding job. The way Mom kept us dressed, folks never knew what really was happening in the Herrera household, except of course for the neighbors. Often, my father would come home drunk and start cursing the relatives and even the parish priests at the top of his lungs. This was accompanied by the tossing of pots and pans out the back door and into the backyard. I wanted out.

One day, I left work early and took the Guadalupe bus into town. I toured the various recruiting stations at the post office building. Each recruiter walked the fine line between encouragement and direct insistence that I sign on their dotted line. I finally settled on the Navy. My decision was made easy after the recruiter promised me Draftsman A School in exchange for four years of my service. I bought it hook, line, and bell-bottoms! Soon after I signed my letter of intent, I learned that Joey Sifuentes, a fellow Holy Cross Knight who graduated one year ahead of me, had also committed to the Navy. He had received his draft notice and decided he wanted nothing to do with the Army. It pleased me that I wouldn't be going on this adventure with total strangers.

Some of the recruit candidates' parents were present to witness their sons' swearing-in ceremony. I wanted the ink to be dry on my enlistment documents so that my parents couldn't try to convince me otherwise. Our group was moved to a small room and positioned in rows, facing the US flag. The amendment to the oath of enlistment[2] that we were about to take had become law on October 5, 1962. I stood at attention, raised my right hand, and took the oath. Joey and I were officially seaman recruits. Our civilian lives were now on hold for the next four years.

I shocked my parents with news of my enlistment. My quest for the Navy severed the cord of childhood dependency. I think I broke their hearts that day, but they never said a word. It was time.

"Anchors aweigh" took place on September 16, 1965. I was eighteen years old. Most Mexican Americans celebrate that day with deep pride and emotion. On that day, in 1810, Father Miguel Hidalgo y Costilla, from the church pulpit of the small village of Dolores in the state of Guanajuato, Mexico, issued a call to arms for independence from Spain to the crowd of peasants and mestizos gathered there. Independence would at long last be attained on August 24, 1821.[3]

One hundred fifty-five years later, I was answering a similar call, ironically from a land that was once part of Mexico. As far as I understood, I wasn't going off to war. When I volunteered, I hadn't the slightest idea that the United States had been militarily involved in the Republic of Vietnam since September 1950. All I wanted was an education and a chance at a respectable future.

California, here I come!

CHAPTER 3

ORDERS

Our flight full of Texas Navy recruits arrived in San Diego early Friday morning, September 17, 1965. Several gray Navy buses transported us to the Naval Training Center (NTC). The Navy base was located adjacent to Lindbergh Field. A guy sitting next to Joey said that the Beatles had landed there just three weeks earlier, en route to a performance at Balboa Stadium.[1]

On the short drive to NTC, Joey and I looked out both sides of the bus like grade school children on a field trip. Inside the base, the buildings had a sandy-brown stucco façade and were surrounded by well-manicured lush green lawns. The buses stopped near a two-story Mission Revival building. I was startled by loud crashing sounds on the sides of the bus. A sailor in a white uniform stepped onto the bus screaming, "Off the bus NOW, you puke recruits!"

"I want three rows facing the building, on the double," barked another instructor. Joey and I hustled out of our seats and took positions in one of the lines being formed. Anxiety was running high. The last person that yelled at me in such a manner was coach Jim Amicone during football spring training at Holy Cross. But this wasn't practice. I was in the Navy now.

A man wearing a khaki uniform and a matching-color hat with a glossy black brim approached. A small gold-plated anchor was pinned to each side of his shirt collar, and a larger one on his hat. He was followed by an officer and other men in khakis.

The first sailor wore a single red braided aiguillette over his left shoulder. He had a two-striped chevron on his left upper arm, and a long black hash mark across his left forearm sleeve. I presumed these insignia to be his Navy rank. Later I learned the long

hash mark indicated he already had at least four years of service behind him. In the
Navy, officers hold ranks such as captain with a paygrade of O-6, and enlisted men
are designated by occupational rates and grade level. An E-6 engineman is classified
as an EN1, Engineman First Class Petty Officer.

"The first two things you will learn as Navy recruits is how to stand at attention and shut up!" he told us. "RECRUITS, drop your gym bags," he ordered.
"ATTEN-HUT," he commanded and concluded with, "Now, SHUT UP!" We
snapped to and stood rigid. Braced to a small building's roof to our right and a
carport awning on the left was a large navy blue wood sign. It was outlined with an
ornate gold-painted rope border, anchors on two diagonal corners, and square knots
on the others. In big bold gold letters read the following:

WELCOME ABOARD
YOU ARE NOW MEN OF THE
UNITED STATES NAVY
THE TRADITION OF THE SERVICE
DEMANDS YOUR UTMOST EFFORT
GIVE IT CHEERFULLY AND WILLINGLY

"Welcome to the Naval Training Center. I am Chief Boatswain's Mate Merrit,"
said the man in the khaki uniform. "Lieutenant Williams has a few words for you."

"Gentlemen," the officer sounded off. "On behalf of Captain Ralph H. Lockwood,
United States Navy, Commanding Officer Recruit Training Command, San Diego,
I welcome you aboard. It is our intent to shape you into worthy seamen. You will
achieve that status through your own initiative and dedication. Make the Navy
proud, sailors." He glanced over his right shoulder and concluded, "Carry on, Chief."
Another man in khakis, well into his forties, approached the group.

"I'm Engineman Chief D. W. Moore, your drill instructor," the soft-spoken man
informed us. "Here forward, you will be known as Recruit Company Number 498.[2] We'll
be boarding the buses in a moment." He then turned and walked back into the building.

The barking sailor ordered, "At ease, recruits. You can break ranks, but stay by
your bus."

A group was congregating beneath the carport awning. I walked over and saw that
they were busy jotting down information off the board. The sign read:

YOUR MAIL ADDRESS IS:
YOUR NAME
COMPANY NUMBER
U.S.N.T.C.
SAN DIEGO 33, CALIFORNIA

I was anxious to send a letter to Norma, as well as one to my parents. I wondered if we would be allowed to do this often—that is, communicate with loved ones. It would be a week or two before mail from home arrived.

Our nine-and-one-half-week training program got underway. We were herded back onto the buses once again. Next stop was the base barbershop, where the transition from civilian to military life began. A long line formed outside the small building but moved at a fast pace. We were all still in our "civvies," as Navy uniforms hadn't been issued yet.

Reluctantly, I climbed into the barber's chair. The man threw a white barber's cape over me and secured it behind my neck, tight. And then it began. Clumps of wavy black hair fell off all around my head. It pained me to see my Sal Mineo doo-wop coif fall onto the floor. The barber's electric shears cut swaths along my scalp. The thought of huge green John Deere wheat harvesting machinery rolling over my head crossed my mind.

"You look like a prisoner now, Roy," Joey joked.

The dreadful ordeal took twenty seconds. Although I hated to lose all my hair, I laughed, along with Joey and the other recruits. We all resembled the Wooly Willy magnetic hair toy.

Another bus ride took us to Receiving and Outfitting. Entering the building was like stepping into Buelita's closet—it reeked of mothballs. I recalled that my cousin Lupe's father had once told me that Air Force recruits were called Rainbows for the colorful array of clothing they displayed upon their arrival on base. For obvious reasons, Navy recruits were called Mothballs.

The first item we were issued was a 26″ x 36″ heavy-duty green canvas seabag. The clothing we were about to receive was supposed to fit in it. Each recruit received a last name and service number stencil and a permanent marker for our clothing. Prior to moving on to the next phase, they showed us how and exactly where to stencil our surname and service number on the seabag. I carefully stenciled HERRERA, and below that, 997 03 36.

The issue room was a long, gutted building. It had two continuous rows of waist-high narrow wood tables and a bench on one side. Wood clothing bins lined an outer wall. Issue personnel took necessary measurements—chest, sleeve length, neck, pants inseam, waist, and shoe and hat sizes. And so it began. I received and tried on my wool dress-blue thirteen-button flapped-fly bell-bottom pants and pull-over jumper. I could hardly wait to get home and walk down Houston Street in my dress blues. I also tried on the white uniform jumper, the traditional enlisted man's iconic "Dixie Cup" style white hat, a black knit watch cap, and blue working jacket, peacoat, and shoes. I looked like I was in the Navy now.

During our General Classification Test lecture held in a large auditorium, I was shocked to find out that the Draftsman Class A School was closed. The recruits around me heard my "but my recruiter promised me" remark, and they all broke into laughter. The Navy chief onstage just shook his head.

Adding insult to injury, as we exited the side doors to the auditorium, upperclassmen sitting on lecture bleachers sang in unison, "Mothball, Mothball, don't feel blue, our recruiters screwed us too."

Chief Moore authorized me to walk from Recruit Camp Decatur, across the parade field, and on to the Classification Building. In hand, I carried what my parents sent via airmail special delivery: my first-place drawing of a lakeside resort from my senior year drafting class at Holy Cross plus three letters of recommendation.

To my surprise, the doors to Class A Drafting School were open to at least one stubborn Mexican American Navy recruit. However, the offer came with an option. I was given the choice between schooling or two years of on-the-job training at the base public works engineering office. Destiny was in my hands. I chose door number two. I couldn't pass up twenty-four months of sunny California fun.

Recruit Brigade graduation took place on Saturday, November 20, 1965. I had just turned nineteen. Uncle Dan Berrones, Mom's brother, took the bus down from Los Angeles to attend my graduation. We had dinner together at our mess hall after the ceremony was over. I was glad that I had family attend my graduation. I was now a Seaman with an E-3 pay grade.

After a short two-week leave in San Antonio, I reported back for duty at the Naval Training Center in San Diego on Wednesday, December 8, 1965. My first impression of Navy life was excellent. I had clothes on my back, a roof over my head, three squares a day, and a guaranteed check that put money in my pocket, albeit only $117.90 per month. I learned to deal with the aggravation of standing watch (security detail). I would either stand watch in the barracks or pace the dreaded public works complex perimeter. You could expect to stand more watches than you cared for if you were on the lower rungs of the enlisted men's rate ladder.

Petty Officers Company 498: Naval Training Command, San Diego, California, 2 November 1965. Raúl Herrera, flag bearer, right side. (Photo credit: Raúl Herrera)

On a weekend off from Chief Open Mess duty, I happened to be at the chow hall, waiting in the serving line. The guy ahead of me grabbed his food tray and placed it on the metal shelf in front of the food pans. I noticed something peculiar about the gold ring on his right hand.

"Hey, man, did you graduate from Fox Tech?" I asked.

"Yeah," he replied. "How did you know?"

"The buffalo on the side of your graduation ring gave it away."

We got to the end of the chow line and found us a table and continued the introductions. His name was Eddie Rodríguez. I told him who I was and that I was assigned temporary duty to the Chiefs' Open Mess and would be transferring soon to the base Public Works Department. It was great finding a Chicano from SanAnto.

Eddie was a Seaman attending Radioman Class A School. Everywhere we walked together on base he was busy rattling off Dit, Dah Dit-dit, Dah Dit-dit, Dit-dit, Dit, over and over. He never stopped.

"Shut up with that Dah Dit-dit shit, *vato*," I demanded. "What the hell is it anyway, *ese*?"

"We're learning Morse code in school right now and I'm practicing by sounding out the letters of my name, Dah Dit-dit . . ."

"Okay, *pendejo*. *¡Ya!* I got it already."

One night the group from Up With People was performing at the base theater, and Eddie and I decided to attend. They were a feel-good youth group made up of teenagers and young adults from around the world. Their performances focused on love, honesty, purity, and unselfishness. I was touched by one of their songs, "What Color Is God's Skin?" The verse that I remember most was "... It's black, brown, it's yellow, it is red, it is white. Everyone's the same, in the good Lord's sight."[3]

Prior to entering the theater, Eddie suggested we stop by the "geedunk" machines across the street to pick up some snacks. Halfway through the performance, I popped open a can of sardines. It didn't take long for people all around, front, back, and to the sides, to begin casting looks of repulsion at me. For a moment, I wondered if they regretted not having bought some themselves before coming inside. I was just about to take my first bite when an usher ordered me to leave. Even after they explained why I was escorted outside, it still didn't make sense to me. Unfortunately, maturity hadn't set in yet. You can take the Chicano out of the barrio, but you can't take the barrio out of the Chicano.

On Christmas Eve, I decided to attend the big fling at the enlisted men's club. The place was buzzing with activity. There was a good mixture of service men and women, some wearing uniforms and others opting for civvies. The loud lyrics of "G-L-O-R-I-A" brought an immediate response from the lively crowd, and the dance floor filled up quickly. I looked around for a dance partner but discovered I was too slow.

Then I spotted a cute brunette across the floor. I swore she was Mexican. How I managed to take the last few steps toward her and then ask her to dance, I'll never know. She was beyond cute, more on the order of gorgeous.

"Care to dance?" I asked.

"Sure," she said, without even looking up at me.

Her hair was reddish-brown and *oh*, the smile ... simply alluring. As I followed her to the crowded dance floor, I was relieved she was a bit shorter. We shouted questions at each other as we danced.

"Where ya from?" I asked.

I was expecting something like California, Arizona, or New Mexico. I nearly flipped when she said, "I'm from Texas ... San Antonio."

"No way. You're joking, right?"

With a wondering look she asked, "You too?"

Suddenly, she stopped dancing and surprised me with a hug and soft kiss on my cheek and said, "Merry Christmas!"

Her name was Gloria Martínez, and she had graduated from Brackenridge High School. We laughed and joked about the unbelievable coincidence, discovering more about each other's background as we danced. I also learned she was a Marine—a Marine sergeant. My heart sank: game over. I was only a pollywog sailor—two grades up from a slug-recruit, a Seaman.

We got into a conversation about our Christmas traditions. We were both Catholic, and we decided to attend Midnight Mass. St. Charles Borromeo Catholic Church was just across Barnett Avenue from the North Gate. The large choir sang many of the traditional Christmas songs during the service. Arm in arm, Gloria and I strolled back the half-mile to the Marine Corps Depot. Taking advantage of the moment, I spun her around, pulled her into my arms, and gave her a big Christmas kiss.

At the steps in front of her quarters, we agreed to stay in touch, perhaps see a movie, go bowling, or spend some time at the club.

Gloria lunged toward me once more and gave me a quick sweet kiss.

"Buenas noches," she said softly and darted into her barracks.

The crisp night air seemed to lighten my step all the way back to NTC. I hadn't considered pursuing a relationship. After all, Norma was waiting for me back home. Gloria and I stayed good friends all through the following year, going to the movies, bowling, and just enjoying each other's company.

On November 7, 1966, my mother's fifty-second birthday, I was on the barracks' midnight-to-four watch. To pass the time and help me stay awake, I was silently singing "Las Mañanitas" to her, our traditional Mexican birthday tune.

A tall, slender man wearing a dark civilian suit walked into the building. I noticed he had a Red Cross pin on his lapel.

"Good morning, sir. Can I help you?" I asked, standing up to greet him.

"I need to speak to Seaman Raúl Herrera. I understand he's assigned to this building," he informed me.

His query took my breath away. Immediately, my stomach twisted into a tight knot. I replied, "I'm Seaman Herrera. Why are you looking for me?"

He handed me an envelope, saying, "Son, you need to fly back home immediately. Your father has been in a near fatal automobile accident. He's alive, I've been told, but in critical condition. Your airline tickets are in the envelope, and you're preapproved for a two-week emergency leave. Get to the airport right away."

I literally collapsed into the chair. I woke up the sailor who was supposed to relieve me in a half hour, quickly explaining the situation. I went to my locker, grabbed some spare change, and ran outside to the nearest pay phone. It was nearly 6 a.m. in Texas, and I knew that Mom would be awake.

"Mamá, are you okay?" I painfully asked.

"*Sí, mijo*, just afraid your father might die. Can you come home, *mijo*?"

"*Sí*, Mamá. The Red Cross told me that Dad is in critical condition in a hospital in Eagle Pass. What was he doing over there?"

"*Pues, hijo*, he must have been over there with his cantina friends," she explained, her voice filled with anger.

"It will be okay, Mom. I'll be there by early afternoon," I said. "The Red Cross paid for my plane fare, and I have two weeks of emergency leave."

My father, the owner of the watering hole he patronized, and a couple of other *borrachos* had decided to make a midnight run 146 miles west of San Antonio to Piedras Negras, Mexico, across the border from Eagle Pass, Texas. They were on a hard liquor resupply mission of tequila for the cantina. Dad fell asleep at the wheel and missed a curve in the road. The car rolled, throwing him out onto the pavement, and partially crushed his skull.

I feared for my father's life, but at the same time I was furious he had put my mother through this, and on her birthday no less. I wondered what she had endured in the past year. My decision to leave home and join the Navy was the best thing for me, but not for my family. I thought that I'd failed them by leaving them to deal with my father and his erratic alcoholic behavior.

Dad was a short man, an easy target for ridicule. Growing up in León, Guanajuato, Mexico, the neighborhood hooligans refused to let him into their band of bullies. They made Panchito an offer they were just sure he would never accept—kill Doña Hortencia's chickens, and they would let him in. He did. He was "Pancho Mata Gallinas" from that day forward. The moniker fit him well, as it attested to his hot temper.

Mom and I were present when a priest administered his last rites late on the evening we arrived at the hospital. The doctors in the small Eagle Pass hospital didn't give us much hope for his survival. A fist-size area of skull was broken into so many pieces, they had to remove them. Due to the doctor's excellent care or divine intervention, my father survived. I asked for and received an extension to my leave.

It pained me to leave my mother tasked with caring for my father alone and, worst of all, with no financial resources. Back in San Diego, I visited the Red Cross office to thank them for making the necessary arrangements enabling me to fly home on emergency leave. They helped me further by saying that I could probably have my parents become my dependents, given their current circumstances.

God was watching out for us. Because of my service, my parents became my dependents and were both able to get medical attention at Fort Sam Houston, as well as benefit from shopping at the post commissary. My hopes were that my father had finally hit bottom and that he'd turn over a new leaf, mainly for my mother's sake.

Regrettably, the sun set too soon on my ideal California vacation when, after only one year out of boot camp, I received unexpected orders. I was headed across the bay to the US Naval Amphibious Base at Coronado for PCF Crew Training. No one seemed to know what a PCF was, not even the old salts. Eventually, after several phone calls, I learned that PCF stood for Patrol Craft Fast—a combat boat!

"You're going to Vietnam, son," the Navy chief announced.

I stood frozen in disbelief. Vietnam had only been a word I heard from time to time in radio and TV newscasts. I had joined the Navy with no consideration for what was developing over there. Hell, I didn't even know where it was. Perhaps I would have felt more trepidation had I become aware the US had already lost 2,344 servicemen in the conflict through the end of 1965. That number would dramatically increase to 8,694 by the end of 1966.[4]

I checked out of the Naval Training Center on December 1, 1966. While waiting at the airport in San Diego, I struggled with the approach I should take in telling my parents about my new duty station. I was certain that disclosing my true destination would destroy them, since I was their only son. I decided to never let my family know.

During my month-long leave in San Antonio, I found myself preoccupied by what lay ahead of me. The days went by too fast. It felt like I was in Huntsville State Penitentiary on death row, and my checkout date was fast approaching.

My resolve almost cracked one night while I was at home. Mom had set up the *nacimiento* midway through December. She always made sure the manger was the focal point of all our Christmas decorations. In keeping with our Mexican Catholic tradition, we knelt in front of the *nacimiento*.

As I listened to Mom recite the appropriate prayers in Spanish, I began to admire the beauty and serenity of the occasion. Everything looked so perfect, and the scent of incense helped my mind wander as I glanced at my family. *Will I ever be able to share another Christmas season with them?* It pained me to think I wouldn't. I looked intently at Dad, Mom, and then Regina, praying to God that I'd always remember that moment. My mind could no longer suppress my emotions. Like Mount Vesuvius, I erupted into an uncontrollable outburst of tears.

"¡*Mijito!*" cried out my mother. "What's wrong?"

Regina helped Mom rise from the blue flowered linoleum floor. They all circled around me, puzzled by my display.

I managed to regain partial control over myself. "Oh, I'm just overjoyed by the moment. This is the best Christmas present anyone could ever ask for."

Over time, Norma and I grew closer, romantically speaking, that is. Our late-night steal-away moments at Brackenridge Park began pushing the envelope of carelessness. One night, after I gave her a gold, diamond-studded dome ring, we finally agreed that it was time for indoor sports. Word on the street pegged the Elmira Motel as the go-to place. I was inexperienced in such matters, making the planning difficult. I drove by the place one afternoon to case the joint. I was glad to see that there was no check-in office, just a window on an outside wall with a blinking red neon OPEN sign to one corner. In my mind, I practiced how I'd approach to ask for a room. I hadn't the foggiest idea how much I'd have to pay. I pictured the guy behind the window laughing at me and saying, "Get outta here, kid, or I'll tell your mommy!"

When the night finally came to take the plunge, I was a nervous wreck, heart pounding, sweaty palms, and an up-to-no-good look on my face. Just for grins, I looked around to make certain *El Viejito* wasn't anywhere around. The check-in went down with only one hitch.

"How long?" the man behind the window asked.

Like a deer caught in headlights, I froze, not fully understanding his question. I fumbled for an answer as I felt my forehead break out into a cold sweat, but nothing came to mind. I had no idea what the hell he was talking about. It had to be the loneliest feeling on earth anyone could experience. He guessed that had to be the case and piped back, "An hour, two hours, half an hour, fifteen minutes? You call it, Junior!"

Not wanting to embarrass myself further by possibly not having enough money, I said, "Fifteen minutes, please."

"Sure," he said with a grin. "Take room three around the corner. The door isn't locked."

I couldn't get away from that window fast enough.

"How did it go?" Norma asked sheepishly.

27

"Okay," I softly replied as I pushed open the door. Once inside, I closed and locked the door. Both of us started checking out the room, turning the lamp on the nightstand on and off, opening drawers, peeking into the bathroom, and checking how soft the bed was. The room was just big enough to fit a small bed, the nightstand, and a small chair to one corner . . . and cold, cold, cold! We turned our attention to each other and managed to make some initial warm-up moves when there was a sudden loud bang at the door and we heard a lady's voice in broken English say, "Time up. You leave. Now."

We looked at one another, mouths agape, eyebrows stretched up high, and began to laugh uncontrollably. We had yet to pull the bedspread back, much less take our coats off, and already we had to leave!

It was a quiet ride all the way back to her house. I'm almost certain that Norma was just as glad as I was that the lady had knocked on the door telling us to leave. We were a novice pair in the game of intimacy. It was obvious we hadn't a clue as to what to do when we got onto the playing field! I longed for the occasion when our desires would finally come to fruition.

My report date at Coronado was December 31. New Year's Eve is traditionally a day for hoopla—a day to create good memories, not to commemorate the day you went off to war.

One of my relatives drove Dad's old '51 Chevy to the airport, as my father was still recovering from his near fatal accident. The car was loaded with passengers that Saturday afternoon. The thought of going to Vietnam right after training left a tightening knot in the deepest part of my stomach. This was it for a year. There was no guarantee of my safe return. It was all in the hands of the Lord now.

At the airport, boarding time came too soon. Having said my goodbyes to all, including Norma and my father, I stepped up to my mother. In her eyes, I saw her heart breaking. I kissed and hugged her goodbye, hopefully not for the last time. Sensing that I wouldn't be able to handle seeing her collapse, I headed quickly toward the gate, waving to the family as I went along. The plane taxied away from the boarding gate onto the runway, and soon we were airborne. I was on my way to whatever destiny had in store for me.

CHAPTER 4

CORONADO

I checked into the Naval Amphibious (NAVPHIB) Base, Coronado, California, on Saturday, December 31, 1966. Toward the end of the month, I received official notice that PCF crew training was to begin the first week in February. I was ready. My anticipation, based on curiosity, was mounting. All during the month, however, I kept hearing how difficult Swift Boat training was going to be.

The NAVPHIB Base at Coronado was also the West Coast training center for the elite Navy SEALs. Their creation evolved out of the special combat units of World War II and the Korean War. A joint session of Congress, on May 25, 1961, heard President John F. Kennedy say, "I am directing the Secretary of Defense to expand rapidly and substantially . . . the orientation of forces for the conduct of . . . unconventional wars. In addition, our special forces and unconventional warfare units will be increased and reoriented."[1]

On June 5, 1961, Vice Admiral Wallace M. Beakley stated, "To augment present naval capabilities in restricted waters and rivers with particular reference to the conduct and support of paramilitary operations, it is desirable to establish Special Operations teams as a separate component within Underwater Demolition Units One and Two. An appropriate cover name for such units is 'SEAL' being a contraction of SEA, AIR, LAND."[2] The first two SEAL teams were formed in January 1962— SEAL Team ONE in Coronado and SEAL Team TWO at the NAVPHIB Base Little Creek in Virginia Beach, Virginia.

At Coronado, their reputation preceded them. It was understood that you don't get in their way—ever! They never walked. Wherever they went as a team, it was always double-time accompanied by loud grunting or chanting. New SEAL candidates ran a two-week indoctrination program that focused primarily on physical endurance in preparation for the BUD/S (Basic Underwater Demolition / SEALs) phase of their training—corporal stamina to the highest level.

PCF training began on February 3, 1967. Early that Friday morning, we mustered outside Swift headquarters. The chief hollered roll call, assigning a boat crew number to each person as they responded to their name. I heard mine a few minutes into roll.

"Seaman Herrera, Raúl," called out the chief.

I raised my hand. "Here, sir!"

"Crew 74-A [Alpha], son," he informed, pointing toward a tall lieutenant junior grade. As a matter of fact, from my perspective mostly everyone around me was tall. Built closer to the ground than most, I managed to stretch, when necessary, to maybe five-foot-five. It ran in the family. My cousin, Lupe V. Reyes Jr., Sidney Lanier High School's drill team cadet colonel, was so short that he was known as the Walking Helmet.

I weaved my way around the officers and sailors toward the general direction the chief had pointed. Some of the men double-timed in place, attempting to stay warm in the brisk February morning air.

"Herrera?" asked the officer, returning my salute. He was tall—six feet two and a solid one hundred ninety-five.

"Yes, sir," I replied.

"Ed Bergin, Lieutenant Junior Grade. This is 'Boats,' Bobby Don Carver, our crew's lead petty officer."

I extended my right hand to greet him, but Bluto just stood there looking down on me, pursing his lips, making his reddish-brown handlebar mustache dance on his stern face. After the chunky five-foot-nine second-class bosun scanned me from top to bottom, he gruffly bellowed, "Whaz' goin' on, 'Bean'?" I expected at any second he'd turn his head to one side and spew out a wad of chew-juice.

I was stunned. I kept my Mexican pride in check but maintained my piercing eyes on his all the while. I was certain that one day my inherited Pancho Mata Gallinas stubbornness would catch up to me. But for now, I cast a disdainful look on him.

"You don't mind, do you? That's better than 'Taco,' isn't it?" he added. Reacting to my scowl, he quickly interjected in a softer tone, "No harm, is there? I mean, none was intended. It's just a nickname—hell, all *you* guys answer to the same name aboard ship." He obviously was implying the moniker was given all Hispanic sailors, be they Mexican, Puerto Rican, or from any Spanish-speaking country.

"You just took me by surprise," I answered, not sure how I should have taken it.

It was the first time I had ever been insulted in such manner. Coming from San Antonio's barrio, I grew up within an ethnic environment and, as a result, never had been exposed to racism. I wasn't hurt or angry because he didn't say it in a harsh tone. Yet somehow the term sounded different from the *choteos* that the *vatos* freely threw at each other every chance we could.

Until joining the Navy, I hadn't given much thought to the flag I proudly flew— my ethnicity. Unexpectedly, I was now faced with having to explore who I was and what it meant. It made me think of an episode when I was registering with the Selective Service board while I was a senior at Holy Cross. The group being processed heard instructions on how to fill out the numerous forms. Right out of the chute, I had a dilemma and raised my hand. A stout, cigar-toting Black sergeant approached my table.

"What's the question, son?" he asked.

"Well, sir," I tried whispering. "I don't see a box to check for Mexican, sir."

He leaned back, removed his drill instructor hat, and exclaimed, "Just check Caucasian, *boy*!" All around, guys laughed at his remark, understanding what my question must have been. He walked away, shaking his head, and belly-laughing all the way back to his desk. I felt the warm glow of embarrassment on my face.

I pondered my newly acquired moniker. *Bean. Bean. Guess it's too difficult for Bluto to roll the R in Rrrraúl.* "Bean" was fine, I decided.

"Boats, here comes our gunner," noted Mr. Bergin.

A tall, dark, brawny-shouldered sailor approached our group.

"Torpedoman Third Class Robert J. Middleton reporting, sir," he announced, saluting Mr. Bergin.

"Swifts aren't like PT boats, Middleton. We don't carry torpedoes," Mr. Bergin pointed out.

"A mortar and machine guns will have to keep me happy, I suppose," replied Middleton.

Last to join the crew was our snipe, EN1 Ronald M. Rinehart. He would be our boat's engineman. Mr. Bergin and Boats introduced themselves. Rinehart and I were both about the same height, but he was of average weight, where I, on the other hand, hadn't gained more than ten pounds since becoming the Holy Cross Knights' first freshman quarterback, tipping the scales at a menacing ninety-nine pounds, in full pads and helmet.

Boats turned to Rinehart. "This is Gunner and Bean."

"Just call me Porky," he insisted, shaking hands.

Crew 74-A was formed. Except for our boat officer, Mr. Bergin, the crew had lost their identities to "Boats," "Porky," "Gunner," and "Bean." Only "Bugeye" seemed to be missing from our motley crew. In fact, a sixth man, our deckhand, would be picked up from broken crews once we arrived in Vietnam.

PCF crews were housed in Butler huts on base. One late Friday afternoon, Boats and Porky were on their way out to wet their whistles and stopped by Jim Schneider's bunk. Jim was a lanky nineteen-year-old FN (engineman striker), born and raised in the Black Hills of South Dakota.

Porky invited Jim to go out drinking with them. They were headed up to a watering hole in National City. Harold's Club, known to sailors as the WESTPAC Widow's Club, was *the* go-to place.

"Get moving, sailor. Let's go get some," Porky commanded.

"Can't go with you fellas," Jim replied. "I ain't old 'nuf to drink, mates."

Boats jumped in. "Get your skinny white ass out of that rack and let's head out, sailor."

"Really, Boats, I ain't legal yet," Jim insisted.

Boats yanked Jim out of his rack by his curly blond hair, put a Wahoo McDaniel head lock on him, and said, "Porky didn't ask how old you were, sumbitch. Get your dress blues on now, you sawed-off, hog-jawed motherfucker! Let's go get shit-faced!"

That night, Porky and Boats baptized Jim in the sacred waters at Harold's Club. As a result, Jim Schneider joined the celebrated ranks of one-name wonders like Elvis, Ringo, Groucho, Dion, Sonny, and Fabian. We now had "Hogjaws." The trio became inseparable Swift mates from that point on.

Enemy Seaborne Infiltration Missions

What was the reason for Swift Boats in the first place? During the early years of the war, the United States had been getting more involved in assisting the Republic of Vietnam (RVN) in their fight against communism. In one vital area of concern, the Democratic Republic of Vietnam (DRV) carried out approximately 122 successful secret resupply missions into South Vietnam between October 1962 and October 1965.

In North Vietnam, Group 759 had been formed on October 23, 1961, partly in response to the call for desperately needed arms and supplies from the communist element in the south. They had been feeling the heat of Ngô Đình Diệm's government anti-communist crackdown. Group 759's secret mission was to "create a functional and secret 'strategic maritime route' running along the Vietnamese coast between Haiphong and the southern tip of Vietnam." Even the initial wooden and steel-hulled vessels in Hanoi and Haiphong were made in secret.

Group 759's maiden voyage took to the sea from the Do Son Peninsula near Haiphong, "making their way through the Gulf of Tonkin, down the coast or hop-scotching across Hainan and the small islands of the Paracels before darting towards the coast in search of inlets and reception points, linked to the interior of Vietnam by a myriad of rivers and canals."

In North Vietnam's first four resupply missions to Cà Mau from October to November 1962, 111 tons of arms and supplies were delivered. By the end of 1963, twenty-three missions had dropped off 1,318 tons; in 1964, forty-nine vessels delivered 2,971 tons; and from January 1964 to February 1965, Group 759, now reorganized into Brigade 125, an official naval command, successfully shipped approximately 4,000 tons over eighty-eight missions. The DRV had created an infiltration "cache cow," safely delivering more than 8,400 tons of war materiel to the Viet Cong in a twenty-six-month period. This maritime effort surpassed the overland campaign and was known as the Ho Chi Minh Trail by Sea.[3]

The Bucklew Report

By this time there was growing speculation by US officials that the enemy was being resupplied with weapons and ammunition via coastal infiltration—but there was no proof just yet. Then Navy captain Phil H. Bucklew, commander of the Pacific Fleet's Naval Operations Support Group, became head of an eight-man Vietnam Delta infiltration study group. The early 1964 fact-finding group was on orders from Admiral Harry D. Felt, Commander in Chief, Pacific. Their mission was to "observe, analyze, and provide recommendations pertaining to the improved control and prevention of infiltration of equipment, materials, and personnel into South Vietnam in support of military operations of the Communist Viet Cong."[4]

The findings of the study pointed to a higher degree of river infiltration in the Mekong Delta than from the sea. It also noted that, based on the capture of special Viet Cong agents, common fishing junks and coastal traffic boats were being used for that purpose in the northern part of South Vietnam. These infiltration attempts were opposed by only a limited—and in some cases nonexistent—action taken by the South Vietnamese Navy's River Force or the coastal Junk Force.

The lack of leadership was singled out as the root of that problem. To solve that issue, Bucklew's February 15, 1964, report recommended the creation of a Chief of Naval Operations. This was the only suggestion implemented by the South Vietnamese government. Up until this point its navy had operated under the control of the Republic of Vietnam Army (ARVN). Also included in the report was the recommendation for "air reconnaissance patrols and the creation of a coastal blockading force that included ships and aircraft from the US Navy's Seventh Fleet, already on station in the Gulf of Tonkin and in the South China Sea."[5] It was also suggested that US naval advisors be inserted into the coastal Junk Force and River Force operations.

The Vũng Rô Bay Incident

Located along the central coastline of South Vietnam, Coastal Zone II, approximately sixty miles north-northeast of Nha Trang in Khánh Hòa Province, is Vũng Rô Bay. It was a pirate's hideaway dream come true. It had deepwater access and was geographically hidden by Cap Varella, a three-mile mountainous peninsula that concealed the bay from the South China Sea. North Vietnam's Brigade 125 "sent its first iron-hulled vessel [number 41] to Vũng Rô in November 1964, successfully delivering forty-four tons of arms and munitions. Two more missions followed, yielding a combined total of 171 tons."[6] However, Brigade 125's lucky infiltration streak finally ran out on its fourth mission to Vũng Rô Bay, vessel number 143.

Army First Lieutenant James S. Bowers reported to the 117th Assault Helicopter Company, 52nd Aviation Battalion, on September 3, 1964. The 117th at Qui Nhơn, on Vietnam's northern central coastline, was not strictly a Dust Off unit. They also supported various ground elements with troop insertions, extractions, resupply, and gun support.

On February 16, 1965, five months after arriving in-country, Lieutenant Bowers was called away from an active mission to a medevac run. An Army Special Forces (SF) officer had been wounded and was requiring extraction. He and his copilot, Chief WO-2 Clifford Adkins, and two enlisted personnel, a crew chief and a door gunner, boarded a UH-1D helicopter, commonly known as a Huey, and headed southwest to a landing zone (LZ) about fifty miles away. Lieutenant Bowers was at the LZ within a half hour, where enemy resistance was limited to small arms fire. Men on the ground loaded the officer on board the chopper and it was quickly airborne once again.

Due to a decreasing cloud ceiling, Lieutenant Bowers headed due east. Once he reached the coastline, he turned his ship onto a south-southeasterly direction and stayed parallel to the coastline at a cruising altitude of 1,000 feet. He reported to the 117th at Qui Nhơn that he was on his way to the 8th Field Hospital in Nha Trang with a passenger (PAX) on board with noncritical injuries. Headquarters would be contacting the hospital via landline, providing them with an ETA and patient details.

Vũng Rô Bay lay ahead. From Bowers' vantage point, just below the cloud cover, something in the bay caught his attention. In open water near shore there appeared to be a tiny floating island.

"Cliff, is that an island moving down there?" Lieutenant Bowers questioned his copilot.

"What the hell?" remarked Adkins.

"Let's take a closer look. Crew Chief, shout in SF's ear if he's okay in taking a spin around the bay."

Adkins looked back. "Boss, our PAX is nodding in the affirmative."

Lieutenant Bowers took his ship on a wide 180-degree turn to the right. Heading in a northerly direction, Cap Varella peninsula was now on his right and the mystery floating island on his left.

"Crew Chief, you and Gunner man your .60s. Have a suspicious contact ahead to port."

"Copy. Locked and loaded, Lieutenant."

They were still too high to make out any significant detail. Lieutenant Bowers circled left for a second pass. He dropped to 500 feet. As they approached the contact, it suddenly became obvious the floating island was in fact a steel-hulled freighter. White muzzle flashes from beneath camouflaged netting on deck clearly classified it as an enemy resupply vessel.

"Fire, fire!" hollered Bowers at the crew chief.

Lieutenant Bowers pulled up hard and banked right, taking his ship into the low cloud ceiling and out of enemy firing range.

"You believe that shit, Cliff?"

"Goin' back in, boss?"

"Negative. Let the fast movers come in and take him out. Besides, we got a delivery to make. Any hits back there, Chief?"

"Negative, Lieutenant."

The odds of making a discovery of such magnitude, and by an Army helicopter crew on a noncritical hospital run no less, were close to zero at best. They had surprised North Vietnam Brigade 125, vessel number 143. Little did Lieutenant Bowers

Part of the 100 tons of contraband salvaged from the first North Vietnamese resupply trawler detected and destroyed at Vũng Rô Bay, Republic of Vietnam, 16 February 1965. (Photo credit: Army Lieutenant James S. Bowers)

and crew realize the importance of their find. This historic discovery was the catalyst leading to the creation of Task Force 115, Operation Market Time.

Lieutenant Bowers reported the incident to the Second Coastal Zone advisor, US Navy Lieutenant Commander Harvey P. Rodgers, in Nha Trang. He in turn advised his counterpart, Lieutenant Commander Hồ Văn Kỳ Thoại. An aircraft was sent in to investigate. The trawler was subsequently taken under fire by AD-1 Skyraiders from the South Vietnamese Air Force. After three air attacks, a fourth strike took the beach area under attack, where small arms fire had been received.

The next several days shed light on the unfortunate reluctance of the South Vietnam military, in many instances, to take the fight to the enemy. The mission evolved into a comedy of errors and omissions. Yet when the dust finally settled, large amounts of armaments as well as medical supplies had been gathered. "Area clearance and mop-up operations continued until February 24, plagued as before by continued foot dragging and intransigence."

Numerous caches were discovered in and around the area: "4,000 assorted rifles, submachine guns, BAR-type weapons, several thousand cases of ammunition, and very large quantities of medical supplies." In all, "the total quantity of arms and supplies recovered exceeded 100 tons, and documents removed from the trawler indicated the ship had made twenty-two other supply voyages to South Vietnam. A former member of 125 told American intelligence that the ships were regularly delivering 90 tons of arms, including AK-47s, ammunition, B40s, explosives and mines."[7] The Soviet- and Chinese-made contraband the trawler carried ended speculation that Russia and China were logistically supporting enemy forces in South Vietnam. This action heightened global political tension between the superpowers.

General William Westmoreland, Commander Military Assistance Command Vietnam, wasted no time when he was advised of the situation. On February 21, 1965, while the action at Vũng Rô Bay was still taking place, he asked Commander in Chief Pacific, Admiral Ulysses S. Grant Sharp Jr., and Commander in Chief Pacific Fleet, Admiral Thomas H. Moorer, to send representatives to Saigon to plan a joint US Navy–Vietnamese Navy offshore patrol. The conference took place ten days later, on Wednesday, March 3.

Operation Market Time was about to receive its marching orders.

CHAPTER 5

MARKET TIME

P rior to the Vũng Rô Bay incident, growing speculation about enemy sea-borne resupply infiltration led to a fact-finding initiative. Captain William P. Hardcastle, Chief Naval Advisory Group, published a staff study titled "Naval Craft Requirements in a Counter Insurgency Environment" on February 1, 1965.[1] It helped expedite the counter insurgency (COIN) effort. By March 11, two US destroyers, the USS *Higbee* (DD-806) and the USS *Black* (DD-666), were patrolling the coastal waters of South Vietnam.[2]

On March 14, Vice Admiral Paul P. Blackburn Jr., Commander Seventh Fleet, remarked, "Although there have been numerous unconfirmed reports of sea infiltration in the past, none of these have been verified. The event at Vũng Rô Bay, however, is proof positive that sea infiltration is occurring and raises the strong possibility that at least a portion of the unconfirmed reports of the past were, in fact, true."[3]

General William Westmoreland's plan for a joint sea patrol[4] was approved on March 16 by the US Joint Chiefs of Staff. Vice Admiral Blackburn took over operational control and activated the Vietnam Patrol Force, Task Force 71,[5] in the heavy cruiser USS *Canberra* (CAG-2). Navy Patrol Squadron One, already conducting anti-submarine warfare and shipping reconnaissance off the coast of Vietnam and operating out of Ton Son Nhut, Saigon, was added to the COIN equation.

The joint sea patrol operation was formally assigned the code name Market Time on March 24, 1965. The name was based on the planned inspection of thousands of sampans, cargo junks, and small trawlers transporting goods from villages and farms to markets along the 1,200-mile coast of South Vietnam.[6]

Coast Guard Answers the Call

Blue water Navy vessels, such as destroyers, were not capable of inshore patrol assignments due to their deep draft. High priority was ordered in the search for a suitable shallow draft vessel that was seaworthy and able to meet close-to-shore patrol requirements. Executive Assistant to Secretary of the Navy, Paul H. Nitze, Captain Elmo R. Zumwalt Jr., USN, traveled to South Vietnam on a fact-finding mission.[7]

On his return, Zumwalt met with Coast Guard Captain William F. Cass, a National War College classmate. Captain Cass was the assistant chief of operations for roles and missions at Coast Guard headquarters. Zumwalt unofficially queried Cass on the possible use of cutters for patrol in the coastal waters of South Vietnam, unaware that his boss had questioned the Treasury Secretary, Henry Fowler, about the availability of inshore patrol boats. The Coast Guard had been under the control of the Treasury Department.

The Coast Guard was quick to answer the call. They recommended the Point Class eighty-two-foot cutters. Named after coastal geographic points in the United States, they were commonly called WPBs. The PB stood for Patrol Boat. The W designation came about from a decision between the Navy and the Coast Guard: because the W was an unused letter in ship designation, the W prefix would always classify the vessel as a Coast Guard asset.

On April 29, 1965, President Lyndon Johnson committed the Coast Guard to service in Vietnam to assist with Market Time operations. They were placed under the operational control of the Navy Department.

Plans for a Coast Guard deployment to Vietnam moved rapidly. The USCGC *Point Banks* (WPB-82327) came in off its last day on patrol on April 29, 1965. The following morning it was hauled out of the water at the Bromfield Shipyard in East Boston for pre-deployment maintenance and modifications. A new Coast Guard piggyback gun mount design was implemented. The combination included a .50 caliber machine gun mounted atop a trigger-fire capable 81 mm mortar. This over-under gun mount was located on the cutter's bow.

A total of seventeen eighty-two-foot WPBs were signaled for duty in Vietnam by the Coast Guard on May 6, 1965. The freighter SS *Pioneer Mist*, docked at the Navy Supply Center Bayonne, New Jersey, loaded the *Point Banks* and three other New York area WPBs on May 21, 1965, for sealift to Subic Bay, Philippines. A similar operation took place in New Orleans. The freighter SS *Aloha State* loaded four cutters: *Point Orient*, *Point Lomas*, *Point Young*, and *Point Caution*.

Coast Guard Squadron One was commissioned on May 27 at a ceremony that took place at Coast Guard Base Alameda, California. Within two months, the seventeen

WPBs were loaded on merchant vessels from various ports across the United States and departed for Subic Bay, Philippine Islands. Next stop . . . Vietnam.[8]

Coast Guard Division 12—Da Nang, Vietnam

Coast Guard Division 12 (Cos Div 12) arrived in Da Nang on July 20, 1965, with eight WPBs, in company with the USS *Snohomish County* (LST 1126). Lieutenant Commander Richard J. Knapp, Coast Guard Division 12 Commander, oversaw the Operation Market Time activities for his eight WPBs: *Point Arden*, *Point Caution*, *Point Dume*, *Point Ellis*, *Point Gammon*, *Point Lomis*, *Point Orient*, and *Point Welcome*. The next day, five WPBs were deployed along the DMZ to begin their Market Time patrolling duties.

On July 24, at 0610 hours, Lieutenant John M. Cece, skipper of the USCGC *Point Orient* (WPB-82319), closed the beach to investigate a suspicious junk south of the Cửa Việt River and came under heavy machine gun and mortar fire. The *Point Orient* exchanged fire with Viet Cong elements ashore, making it the first Coast Guard cutter in combat since World War II.

Coast Guard Division 11—An Thới, Vietnam

Division 11, in company with the USS *Floyd County* (LST 762), arrived at An Thới, Phú Quốc Island, on August 1. On August 2, 1965, Coast Guard Commander James A. Hodgman officially assumed command of Task Unit 115.1.9. In addition, he oversaw the Market Time activities of nine WPBs: *Point Banks*, *Point Clear*, *Point Comfort*, *Point Garnet*, *Point Glover*, *Point Grey*, *Point Marone*, *Point Mist*, and *Point Young*.

Commander Hodgman's position was demanding. He was in charge of the Gulf of Thailand Surveillance Group, Coast Guard Division 11, and also served as the senior naval advisor to the Vietnamese Fourth Coastal Zone commander.

Trawler Infiltration Status

The capture of the Democratic Republic of Vietnam (DRV) vessel 143 at Vũng Rô Bay didn't stop Brigade 125's commitment to run seaborne resupply missions. "DRV strategists understood very well that the game had changed by 1965, following the Vũng Rô Bay incident. As the US stepped up its surveillance networks, Brigade 125 scored its last successes. Vessel 42, for example, delivered sixty tons of arms to Cà Mau Peninsula on October 24, 1965. Vessels 68 and 69 followed with similar quantities of arms."[9]

Task Force 115

Robert McNamara, Secretary of Defense, announced on April 30, 1965, the shift of Market Time Seventh Fleet operations from CTF 71 to Chief Naval Advisory Group, Captain William H. Hardcastle. Greater involvement by US naval assets in Vietnam called for major restructuring in the chain of command. In less than two weeks, Rear Admiral Norvell G. Ward relieved Captain Hardcastle as Chief Naval Advisory Group and as Commander Task Force 115 on May 10.[10] The official transfer took place on July 31. Captain Hardcastle remained as Ward's deputy and chief of staff.

General Westmoreland's joint sea patrol plan had included a request to have the Republic of Vietnam authorize US Navy vessels to "stop, board, search and, if necessary, capture and/or destroy any hostile suspicious craft or vessel found within South Vietnam's territorial and contiguous zone waters."[11] This recommendation was formally approved by the South Vietnamese government on May 11, 1965. On April 1, 1966, Rear Admiral Norvell G. Ward became Commander Naval Forces Vietnam (COMNAVFORV).[12]

Boat Squadron ONE (Boat Ron ONE)

To augment the patrolling Coast Guard cutters, the search was well underway to find a smaller combat craft to fit the bill. In June 1965, word of a fifty-foot crew boat servicing oil rigs in the Gulf of Mexico worked its way up the channels at the Navy's Bureau of Ships (BuShips). In 1959, two forty-five-foot crew boats survived Hurricane Beulah's devastating winds and cresting forty-foot waves during a delivery journey to Venezuela. Neither craft suffered any structural damage.

RADM Nathan Sonenshein led a BuShips visit to the Berwick, Louisiana shipbuilder, Sewart Seacraft, Inc. A contract specialist and a government lawyer wrote up the legal document and the design drawings were purchased by the Navy. The more than fifty design modifications requested were ready in one week. Bids went out and Sewart Seacraft was selected.

In the third week of August, Sewart Seacraft received a $4.6 million contract from the Navy to build the first thirty-eight of 104 Mark I Patrol Craft Fast (PCF), commonly known as Swift Boats.[13]

Thirty-eight-year-old Lieutenant Commander Arthur P. Ismay arrived in Vietnam in June 1965 to serve as flag secretary to Admiral Ward. He was "on the bow wave of a massive build-up of American naval forces in Vietnam." It didn't take long before he learned of a small craft shoreline defense unit being formed. The boats were already under construction. Ismay found himself at the right place and at the right time. Captain Phil Bucklew happened to be working for the chief of staff of Carrier Division 4, who was spearheading the program. Now a full commander, Ismay contacted the chief of staff and told him that if he really wanted the job—it was his.

The PCFs, as an off-the-shelf technology development, were pushed down the assembly line at a rapid pace. PCFs 1 & 2 had already been delivered to the Naval Amphibious Base, Coronado, California when Commander Ismay received official orders to establish the new combat boat squadron. Working mostly out of a briefcase, he immersed himself in learning as much as he could in a short period of time, about what the concept was, what the boats were, and how the training was being phased in.

The first crews to arrive were put through a two-week crash course. Everyone assigned to Swift Boats at the start-up of the squadron helped in developing operating procedures and protocols. The Navy had no recent coastal combat experience upon which to base this new inshore combat armada. The officers and enlisted men, mostly volunteers, took on the challenge in the truest form of naval tradition. On October 1, 1965, Commander Ismay sent out a message establishing Boat Squadron ONE. Soon after, Boat Squadron ONE staff, boats, and crews arrived in Subic Bay, Philippines to continue outfitting the Swifts, carrying out day and night exercises. This was followed by the establishment of Boat Squadron ONE Headquarters in Saigon.[14]

Swift Boat crews took on a huge task—bring the infiltration of arms by sea to a halt, all along the 1,200-mile coastline of South Vietnam. After Coast Guard units were on station along the coast, four North Vietnamese trawlers made attempts to infiltrate arms and supplies to awaiting enemy forces in South Vietnam. None succeeded; two were turned away, one was sunk or went down by self-destruct charges, and one was captured and towed to Vũng Tàu and then from there to Saigon.

USS *Hissem* (DER-400) Turns Back Two Trawlers

On separate occasions the USS *Hissem* (DER-400) intercepted trawlers, forcing them to return to open waters. On December 31, 1965, off the Cà Mau Peninsula, a trawler was intercepted and forced to return to communist-held waters.

A year later, on December 23, 1966, a Patrol Squadron 16 aircraft sighted a heavily laden steel-hulled trawler eighty miles northeast of Qui Nhơn. Detected by a second aircraft, the trawler headed back out to sea. Covert aerial surveillance was continued until noon on Christmas Day when the *Hissem* relieved the aircraft and tracked the trawler until it entered the Hainan Straits.[15]

May 9, 1966 Trawler

On May 9, 1966, off the western coast of the Cà Mau Peninsula, the Coast Guard Cutter *Point Grey* detected and intercepted a steel-hulled trawler.[16] Two hours before midnight, the WPB observed two large bonfires on the beach, south of the river mouth entrance to Rạch Giá, a provincial city. *Point Grey* suspected the fires to be visual landmark signals. A strong contact appeared on the WPB's radar screen at 0010 hours and on a westerly course parallel to the coastline.

The *Point Grey*'s skipper, Lieutenant Junior Grade Charles B. Mosher, gave orders to head on an intercept course at best speed to investigate. At a safe distance from the contact, the WPB issued a challenge at 0120 hours. The trawler did not respond to the flashing-light message, but it did change its course. It appeared to be heading toward the two bonfires. From a range of 400 yards, the WPB illuminated the contact by searchlight and confirmed it was a steel-hulled trawler. The cutter notified the Coastal Surveillance Center (CSC) at An Thới and continued shadowing the suspicious vessel.

At two in the morning, the ship went dead in the water. It began to drift toward the beach. At daybreak, the trawler appeared to be deserted, 400 yards from shore. *Point Grey* approached the ghost ship at 0700 hours, attempting to come alongside. They were met by fierce automatic weapons fire from shore. While returning fire, the cutter moved to seaward 1,500 yards.

The USS *Brister* and USS *Vireo* were already en route to the scene. The CSC at An Thới ordered the USCGC *Point Cypress* to the area as well. South Vietnamese Navy Coastal Group 41 immediately sent out five junks and requested assistance from the Fleet Command ship LSIL-328 and the gunboat PGM-614.

By early afternoon, the trawler was 100 yards from the beach. Commander Task Force 115 ordered the boarding of the trawler. As the *Point Grey* approached the ship a second time, two Coast Guardsmen and one Army soldier on the bow were wounded by enemy fire from shore. The WPB rendezvoused with the *Brister* for medical evacuation of the injured crewmen.

The trawler turned sideways to the beach at 1700 hours and ran aground fifty yards from shore, making it ideal for the Viet Cong to off-load the cargo. To prevent this, the order was given at 1726 hours to destroy the vessel. Surface units shelled it, and aircraft bombed and strafed the trawler with machine gun fire throughout the early evening hours. Numerous fires and secondary explosions were observed until 2030 hours, when an explosion ripped the trawler in two pieces. The massive blast extinguished the fires. Destructive action was halted, and aerial illumination continued throughout the night.

Material salvaged from the trawler included six crew-served weapons and approximately fifteen tons of ammunition, plus movie projectors, film, and other propaganda material. The explosion that split the trawler into two pieces also destroyed its communication equipment. There were no ship logs, charts, or other records found. Lieutenant Junior Grade Mosher received the Silver Star for his action in preventing the enemy gunrunner from delivering its cargo to the awaiting enemy.

June 20, 1966 Trawler

The Cà Mau Peninsula, in the southern tip of Vietnam, was under Viet Cong control. There were only a few South Vietnamese government operated population centers in the region. The west and east coastal regions, with numerous rivers and smaller inlets, made the Cà Mau a favorable enemy resupply trawler destination. Intelligence reports noted the creation of a well-developed enemy transportation group in the Mekong Delta. A trawler could count on uncontested movement of its resupply cargo throughout the area.

An SP-2H aircraft from the VP-2 Squadron detected a suspicious contact on June 19 at 1545 hours, eighty miles east of the Con Son Islands. Cà Mau Peninsula lay fifty-two miles to the west. The pilot ordered the crew to their rigging stations and took the plane down nearly to the surface. They reported a steel-hulled trawler with bow plate numbers 2135, on course 210 degrees and speed of ten knots. The trawler, reacting to the fly-over, altered its course slightly by ten degrees west.[17]

Market Time units in Patrol Areas six and seven were alerted to the possible trawler infiltration attempt. The Coast Guard Cutter *Point League* (WPB-82304) was in the vicinity of the mouth of Sông Co Chien. In command of the WPB was twenty-four-year-old Lieutenant Junior Grade Stephen T. Ulmer. He had been the executive officer (XO) of the *Point Gammon* in Da Nang and later served four months as Division Ops officer.

At 0245 hours Engineman Second Class Daniel R. Vaughan observed a contact on radar 7.8 miles away. Acting as the officer of the deck (OOD), BM1 Clyde Woodell was at the helm and directed Vaughan to alert the skipper. After checking the radar and getting a full report from Woodell, Lieutenant Ulmer sounded general quarters. His XO, Lieutenant Junior Grade Neil Markle, assumed his GQ station by the radar and Woodell remained at the helm.

The trawler was heading toward the river mouth. Closing the contact to within four miles, the *Point League* challenged the vessel with flashing light and drew no response, other than changing to a westerly course. Two miles offshore, the ship went dead in the water.

A second, smaller blip appeared on the WPB's radar, next to the larger one, making the disposition of the contact highly suspicious. The cutter raced at flank speed toward the target. Lieutenant Ulmer ordered the vessel illuminated at 0340 hours. The WPB was at a distance of 600 yards from the adversary. The flare exposed the two contacts like the center ring act at a Ringling Brothers circus under bright spotlights. A forty-foot green-hulled junk and a ninety-nine-foot steel-hulled trawler were revealed.

The junk cast off immediately, allowing the trawler to head for the beach at twelve knots. Responding to the trawler's evasion attempt, the *Point League*'s bow gun mount captain, Second Class Gunner's Mate Albert J. Wright Jr., fired warning shots across the trawler's bow. The evading ship ignored the WPB's order to stop. Two more warning bursts were ordered by Lieutenant Ulmer. This time the vessel's crew responded with their .50 caliber machine gun fire. Two rounds hit the pilothouse. An incendiary round exploded, momentarily blinding Ulmer. Lieutenant Markle was hit by shrapnel to his head, knocking him down. Realizing he had only a minor wound, he rose from the deck and resumed his battle station. The enemy guns were on target. A round grazed Wright's ankle. He kept pumping lead into the enemy ship from his machine gun mount on the bow of the WPB. The chase was on.

"Sepia, this is Elbow Golf 7, over."

"Go ahead, Elbow Golf 7."

"Sepia, this is Elbow Golf 7. Receiving fire from steel-hulled trawler. This unit engaging enemy ship. Pursuing contact at full speed in poorly charted waters. Out."

Sepia was CSC radio net control at Vũng Tàu. Sepia and other seaborne units kept attempting to raise comms with the WPB. They had their hands full and were in a fierce toe-to-toe battle with the evading ship.

Lieutenant Ulmer ordered his liaison officer, Ensign Tung, to respond to the interrogatives by giving them a lengthy official report. The nervous young Vietnamese officer grabbed the mic and said, "'Sorry, we are busy. Call back later." He hurriedly stuffed the mic into a coffee mug, inadvertently leaving the mic open. Everyone on the net got an earful of the *Point League*'s pilothouse chatter and gunfire for forty-five minutes. This allowed CSC to sense the WPB's urgent need for assistance and called in air support as well as naval vessels in the area.

At 0350 hours, the trawler ran hard aground. The cutter made several attack runs at the beached enemy vessel, the first at 1,000 yards and the next two at 1,400 yards. Each run commenced with two illumination rounds, followed by machine gun and mortar fire.

Before daybreak, an assault helicopter team from Can Tho arrived to provide additional fire support. A VP-2 aircraft also was in the area. At 0600 hours, the *Point League* closed on the trawler to investigate. It came under heavy automatic weapons fire from the beach and was forced to withdraw. Two US Air Force F-100 Super Sabres took the VC positions under attack. An explosion took place aboard the trawler at 0615 hours. Lieutenant Ulmer observed an intense fire in the vicinity of the cargo hold mid-ship and in the pilothouse area.

As assault helicopters attacked enemy positions, *Point Slocum* made several more passes at the beach. Each time they were met by a hail of bullets from heavy automatic weapons and recoilless rifle rounds. The WPB pulled offshore when aircraft assaulted the beach positions. The enemy was dug in well. They continued shooting sporadically until 0745 hours. The blaze intensified on the trawler, causing small arms rounds to cook off as well as additional explosions.

By 1000 hours, a small armada was on scene. Junks from Coastal Group 35 and River Assault Group 23 units converged on the area. The WPB *Point Hudson* arrived, as did the naval gunfire support ship, USS *John A. Bole* (DD-755). On board the USS *Haverfield* (DER-393) was Commander Escort Squadron FIVE, who took on the role of on-scene commander.

Volunteers began salvage operations by dowsing the flames using portable firefighting equipment and eventually boarded the vessel while small arms rounds were still cooking off.

Lieutenant Ulmer, following orders from CTF-115 in Saigon, came alongside the trawler and passed lines to the boarding crew to tow the ship to deep water. The *Point Slocum* was tied alongside the trawler's port side.

At 1020 hours, the USS *Tortuga* (LSD-26) arrived on station and assumed Officer Tactical Control of salvage operations. The ARVN 21st Division set up a beach perimeter at 1115 hours. Salvage crew members continued unloading cargo while others battled the flames. By 1315 hours, the fires were under control and completely extinguished by 1400 hours. As late evening approached, a heavily armed party took up guard of the ship during the night.

The tug MSTS *Winquat* took the trawler under tow up the coast to Vũng Tàu. It was accompanied by WPB *Point Jefferson* and LLC-1. The trawler later was moved to Saigon. In accordance with orders from the Vietnamese Joint General Staff, the Vietnamese Navy LSIL 328 transported more than 100 tons of cargo salvaged from the trawler to Can Tho.

The June 20, 1966, trawler had removable bow plates with the number 2135. In addition to fishnets, it carried fishing buoys and buoy marking poles for use as camouflage. Although most of the contraband was made in Communist China, along with some of Soviet origin, this was the first time that rifles manufactured in North Korea were discovered. Charts found on board indicated that the intended destination was possibly the Lang Nuoc River mouth in Vinh Binh Province. An alternate course was plotted to the mouth of the Con Chung River.

The loss of this trawler, combined with the loss of the May 20 trawler, represented a serious blow to the Viet Cong. For their brave action as part of the initial volunteer salvage operation, GMG2 Albert J. Wright and EN2 Daniel R. Vaughan received the Bronze Star. In a ceremony held at Can Tho, Lieutenant Junior Grade Stephen T. Ulmer was decorated with the Silver Star.

CHAPTER 6

SERE

February 5, 1967, was a cold and windy Sunday morning in the San Diego area. Forty-plus officers and enlisted men boarded gray Navy buses and departed the NAVPHIB Base in Coronado for the North Island Naval Air Station. They passed out box lunches prior to going on board an old prop job that looked like a relic from World War II. The flight was grueling, bouncing from one air pocket to the next. Eating was a fiasco.

I wondered what the next six days had in store for me. The special training I was about to undertake was designed in part to separate the men from the boys. That alone convinced me pain would be involved.

After the Korean War, military officials and surviving prisoners of war (POWs) concluded our military should be trained and prepared for both physical and psychological torture in the event of capture by the enemy in future conflicts. The Navy's Survival, Evasion, Resistance, and Escape (SERE) program was established in the early 1960s.

Our group's SERE training was set up at the Fleet Airborne Electronics Training Unit, Pacific Detachment Whidbey Island, in Oak Harbor, Washington.[1] The program was split into two parts. The classroom phase included moral aspects and code of conduct, survival psychology, area survival (tropics, desert), sea and seashore survival, edible foods, and survival medicine, among others.

I didn't understand why our survival training was taking place in a climate zone where freezing temperatures were part of the daily winter forecast, when we were ultimately headed for a land where 102 degrees in the shade was considered pleasant.

During that week the average low temperature was thirty degrees, and the average high was forty-eight degrees. The first four days were spent in classes learning how to survive off the land. No supplies were issued, aside from parachutes. We were shown how to convert them into a lean-to for sleeping.

We were taught to search the woods for nature's food, only to discover that those before us had stripped Mother Nature of all her goodies. We also learned how to make gill nets to place in the water near the beach. Unfortunately, none of our traps or gill nets produced critters or fish. At the end of the third day, Wednesday, having had only straight black coffee in the mornings and a few berries, wild potatoes, and several mussels to eat, we were allowed to kill a rabbit that was kept in a cage near one of the classrooms.

On Thursday morning, as the group's highest-ranking officer was calling us to muster at the center of our encampment, loud bursts of machine gun fire, diesel engine clatter, and screaming voices came from all directions around the camp site. Before we could evaluate the situation, we were surrounded by Jeeps and trucks. Men in foreign combat gear held us at bay with automatic rifles. My heart wouldn't stop pounding. I moved closer to Gunner in a futile attempt at safety. Exhausted and emotionally distressed from the lack of food, we reacted with total chaos.

Everyone looked about for orders, but no one moved. Instinctively, we backed ourselves into a tight group that resembled a herd of musk ox retreating into a defensive posture. A huge man—a sergeant major, as denoted by his stripes—stepped out from the lead Jeep and approached our group, accompanied by two heavily armed men. With a harsh German-style accent, he called for the highest-ranking officer present. Immediately, one of our boat officers stepped forward. Before he could identify himself, the sergeant major decked the young officer with one blow to the face. Another officer stepped forward to take charge, and he took a blow to the stomach and went down just as fast.

No one moved after that. The sergeant major brutally shoved his way through our petrified bunch. From the back, he dragged out the oldest man in the group. "Pappy," as we called him, was an ol' salt perhaps in his late thirties. He looked diminutive in the sergeant major's grasp.

"I hate American pigs!" the towering man shouted. "You don't belong in my country. No one invited you. We will teach you a lesson so that you will know who controls this land."

He pulled Pappy's knit watch cap over his face, flung him into the mud, and with his twenty-pound boot, the sergeant major stomped on Pappy's chest and then slid his foot up to his neck, pushing his head back.

"I especially hate old, useless men like this bag of bones. You American pigs are fools to think you can overpower our forces with helpless little men like this."

He grabbed a canteen from one of his comrades and poured its contents up his victim's nose. Pappy tossed about violently under the sergeant major's boot. He was literally choking to death right before our eyes, but we dared not move for fear that it wasn't a game, and we were all about to die.

The sergeant major ended the confusion by suddenly changing his voice to a more familiar and quite welcome American accent. Two goons picked up Pappy and pushed him back into the crowd.

"You men are here for a purpose," he said. "Our job the next two days is to instill fear into your hearts and minds, and then break you into submission. We will meet again very soon, so prepare yourselves," he ended, making his way toward his Jeep.

All around, the group was buzzing with chatter as we made our way to the next phase of our training—the navigation exercise. We were split into teams, and each group was given a map and a compass. Our job was to get from Point A to Point B in a specified amount of time. This required a careful study of the map, seeking out and eliminating difficult routes. We took turns navigating. I suspect that we didn't make Point B in the required time because we heard loud horn blasts from the general direction that we were headed. The horn blast continued every ten minutes. The remaining teams used this sound blast to guide them to the Point B location.

On Friday morning, after a much-needed cup of hot coffee, we made our way toward Navigation Point B once again. We climbed a small ridge. The evasion course was about to begin. The goal was to avoid being captured by enemy soldiers as we trekked a mile through the dense underbrush on the way to Freedom Road. The instructors staggered us across the ridge and let a random number of future captives go every ten minutes or so. It's true what is said about learning from your mistakes. When it was my turn, I decided to make a mad dash downhill in the direction of Freedom Road. I was sure my high school track experience would get me there in quick order, outrunning the enemy.

I wasn't more than a hundred yards down the hill when I learned a crucial lesson in evasion tactics—how to cross over a downed tree. "Very carefully" is not the answer. Go around, you idiot. I hurdled over the felled tree with my right leg, but my left foot snagged a carefully camouflaged tripwire as I was about to clear the tree. On my way down, I felt the concussion of a massive explosion on my right side. From a flat-on-my-back position, I saw a bright green cloud rising from a hidden container that had been placed beside the tree.

My position had now been compromised. Instinctively, I checked for wounds but quickly realized that if it had been a real bomb, I probably wouldn't be conscious enough to determine my physical condition. The smoke made it easy for the enemy to converge on my position.

"Oh, shit," I blurted in anger. *Haul ass, Bean! Run! Run!* my mind commanded as I heard the automatic weapon fire getting closer. Hide-and-seek operations were over.

As I tried to evade, I believed that they were firing live rounds at me, not blanks. I was chased and finally caught less than a quarter mile farther downhill. A dusty sandbag was shoved over my head and the cord pulled so tight I was choking. At least two or three heavily accented "enemy" soldiers jostled me around like a rag doll. Eventually, I was thrown down a gully.

Reaching Freedom Road, I was tossed in with other captives. Marching in a hand-to-shoulder line, we were moved off. I couldn't see a thing through the material shrouding my head. We must have walked for fifteen or twenty minutes before I began hearing low-level voices of fellow prisoners. It felt like we were being huddled in a group. I bumped against fellow sailors as the guard pushed me into place. We stood in line for what may have been another half hour.

A dreaded familiar voice sounded from a distance. "Remove your hoods, you worthless bunch of American pigs!" It was the sergeant major!

On order, I removed my hood and looked around. We were in a fenced compound, grouped next to a wood-framed cottage. Across the small open area was a row of decrepit horse stalls. My breath floated away from me in the cold morning air, the bright sun above failing to warm my chilled body. One by one we were ushered into the cottage. Inside, we were ordered to strip down to our skivvies and knit watch caps.

An armed guard shoved a rifle muzzle in my gut. "Take off clothes," he ordered.

Once I had stripped, another guard searched my jacket, pants, shirt, and shoes for concealed weapons and contraband. I danced a jig for a while, desperately attempting to warm up. One of the sergeant major's thugs came into the cottage and pulled out a random selection of prisoners. Lady Luck wasn't with me that morning. He yanked off my watch cap, grabbed me by the hair, and dragged me outside.

I was motioned to one of the horse stalls. Under other circumstances, the sight of half-naked, scared shitless, wannabe Navy commandos would have been hilarious. The situation I was in left no room for humor. It was bitter cold. My body trembled from the frosty air. I started backtracking when I saw the sergeant major coming my way.

"What have we here, comrades?" he asked, glancing at the two guards. "Ah, a religious one!" noting the gold St. Anthony medal hanging from my neck along with my dog tags. His coarse, callused left hand easily wrapped tightly around my neck, lifting me up to my tiptoes. My eyes bulged. "What is your mission, pig?" he shouted into my face, leaving behind a whiff of month-old Limburger cheese.

Classroom lectures earlier in the week came to mind. I knew that under the United States Military Code of Conduct, Article V, my life would be spared. Article V states: "When questioned, should I become a prisoner of war, I am required to give name, rank, service number, and date of birth. I will evade answering further questions to the utmost of my ability. I will make no oral or written statements disloyal to my country and its allies or harmful to their cause."

"Raúl Herrera, Seaman, 997 03 36, November 11, 1946," I replied. The next sound I heard was the splash my bare back created upon slamming into a puddle of murky, frigid water in the middle of the stall. The sergeant major slammed his muddied boot up against the base of my neck. I squirmed and thrashed in agony.

"Where is your primary unit?" he asked, pushing his massive boot harder against my throat.

"Raúl Herrera, Seaman, 997 03 36, Nov—" was all I could utter before a kick to the stomach convinced me death was imminent. I felt helpless and alone. One of the guards reached down and pulled my watch cap over my face. I knew what was next and it didn't take long before a cold splash of water hit my face. My only salvation was to try and guess when the next dousing would occur so that I could take a deep breath and hold it. To my surprise it never happened.

As I began to pray for the torture to end, the sergeant major grabbed my St. Anthony medal again and pulled on it to get me to stand. I accommodated his apparent intention.

"You're a fool," he yelled. "There are no saints. You pray to deaf idols. No one can help you. Now, tell me what I want to know, and you will be punished no more. Refuse—you die!"

Defiantly, I replied, "Raúl Herrera, Seaman—"

"Kill him!" he ordered. His aides grabbed my arms and led me toward a fifty-five-gallon water-filled drum that was capped with a layer of ice.

"997 03 36, November 11, 1946," I exclaimed, as if that should keep me from harm—indeed not. The soldiers lifted me up, over, and headfirst into the drum, breaking the thin layer of ice with my forehead. I was good at holding my breath underwater, just like I used to do back at the YMCA in San Antonio, but the shock of the freezing water forced me to expel my precious stored air supply. Like a San

Antonio River catfish out of its element, I thrashed wildly, arms and legs going every which way. My frantic display was a cue for the soldiers to pull me back up—barely in the nick of time. Water spewed from my mouth and nose as I coughed and gasped for air simultaneously.

My head was spinning with thoughts of escape, torture, and death. I shook and twitched all the way back to the cottage. My half-frozen fingers made it difficult to put on my clothes and shoes. It was hours before I regained my normal body temperature. We were being pushed to our physical and psychological limits.

When prisoner processing was complete, we were marched down a gravel road to what would become our home for the next two days—the POW compound. It was an area about the size of a basketball court and was outlined with a twenty-foot-high chain-link fence, topped with concertina wire. The enclosed area had only one gate and it was guarded by one of the sergeant major's cronies from a watch tower. A large rectangular sandbagged bunker was situated in the middle of the compound. Some of us gathered in small groups, others walked around to stay warm. It didn't take long before a few of the men were called out. They were escorted by armed guards and taken into a small building a short distance from the compound. This process continued for most of the day.

The inevitable came to pass; it was my turn in "the barrel." I was taken to a tiny, all-wood cabin. It was a very crude structure, basically just a shell. The room was bare, other than a desk and chair where the interrogator sat and a single dim light bulb at the end of an electric wire hung directly over the desk. The interrogation officer was young and slender, with slick blond hair and kind features. I had hopes he would be of equal temperament and not be the Jekyll and Hyde type.

"Come, sit there," he invited.

"Where?"

"Sit down!" he screamed.

I saw only a nailed-together, two-piece, T-shaped two-by-four wood piece on the floor, between the front of his desk and the wall, a distance of four feet.

"On this?" I asked, holding it with both hands.

"YES!" he yelled, slamming the desk with the palm of his hand.

I placed the bottom end of the "T" on the floor, the obvious choice, and tried to sit on the flat section.

"How many sailors on your boat?" he inquired.

"Raúl Herrera, Seama—"

He lunged over the small desk and in the same motion, his fist found the middle of my chest. My body slammed against the wall then down onto the floor. My father's

Pancho Mata Gallinas macho genes exploded in me. I jumped off the floor ready to attack *el pinche cabrón*. I came to my senses in time, bent down, picked up the stool and sat on it once again. This time, I leaned forward, tightened my jaw, glared at him with a vengeance, and mouthed, "Seaman, 997 0—"

I was on the floor once again in seconds. This time, I slammed the T-stool down, sat, and screamed, "3 36, Novem—" The son of a bitch punched me on the left side of my face this time, sending me back down to the floor. I was dazed and didn't get up. All is fair in love and war and I was losing this battle . . . the bastard.

His chair scraped the floor as he pushed away from the desk and stood up.

Oh, shit! Now the kicking starts, I surmised.

The next words out of his mouth startled me.

"Training session halt," he announced, but in a welcome American tone.

"Listen," he said, shaking his head in disbelief at my stupid display of foolish pride and Mexican stubbornness, "if you should *ever* fall captive to the Viet Cong and a similar situation occurs, stay down until *they* pick you up. The Viet Cong will interpret your display of resistance and defiance as an invitation for some stress release, at your expense. Never ask for more," he warned.

Holding my jaw, I simply nodded as I got myself off the floor.

"Session over, report back to group," he said, returning to his weak attempt at a German-style accent.

On Saturday, we were all ushered into a large room filled with pictures of Stalin, Hitler, Hồ Chí Minh, and other communist leaders. The room was dark and accented with red lighting cast upon communist slogans and insignias that hung from the walls. A table at the head of the room had a huge basket of fruit, breads, and pastries centered on it.

Czar, the sergeant major's German Shepherd, stood guard at the table's edge. Although a large swastika flag served as a backdrop, my focus was on the basket of food. My mouth salivated with want and desire. I was about to go crazy and make a mad dash for the basket when the sergeant major burst through a side door, bringing the room to immediate silence.

With a large turkey leg in one hand and a frosty mug of beer in the other, he paced back and forth in front of the captive audience while expounding the benefits of communism and mocking our American democratic ways. He gnawed at the turkey leg, taunting us by pointing and waving it in front of our faces. Every now and again he tore a piece off and tossed it to Czar.

His discourse reached a fevered pitch. He began yelling and throwing things. He ran out of things to throw. Then the basket on the table caught his attention. He let out a bellowing howl, grabbed some fruit, and began hurling it at us. At first, we left the food where it fell, thinking if we caught it, we'd surely die. He tossed more, now in a softer manner so as to encourage us to catch the goods.

"Eat!" he said without a trace of his fake accent. "Training exercise terminated, gentlemen," he cheerfully announced.

We all looked at each other, wondering if we should believe him. All at once we hit the deck rummaging the floor for any form of food we could find. I found a banana, peeled it, and in two bites it was gone. I stuffed my face with grapes and cookies, while tears rolled freely from my eyes.

The week of hell at last was over. I had survived SERE.

CHAPTER 7

PCF TRAINING

I took several days, if not weeks, before our SERE-induced aches and pains diminished. Several of us went directly to sick bay upon return to the NAVPHIB Base in Coronado. Some crewmen were treated for pneumonia. I nursed a severe cold for one week. The punishing exercise served its intent well. Our skins grew another layer—a cohesiveness that resulted in the transformation of individuals into a tight Swift Boat crew.

The program's next phase consisted of boat familiarization and cross-training.

At first glance, Swifts looked like tugboats. A closer examination, however, revealed a heavily armed fighting machine. The Navy saved a considerable amount of money and precious time in providing a vessel suitable for use in Vietnam. This was accomplished by taking a type of vessel already in use in the Gulf of Mexico by off-shore oil rigs in transporting supplies, equipment, and personnel to and from shore.

Following the initial construction of thirty-eight aluminum patrol boats, Sewart Seacraft, of Berwick, Louisiana, was awarded additional contracts, bringing the total of Mark I PCFs to 104.[1]

Swifts were powered by twin V-12 Detroit diesels. Their maximum speed was thirty-two knots (thirty-seven mph), a speed that could only be reached by a bare-boned Swift. At best, with calm seas, a PCF on patrol might average twenty-five to twenty-eight knots. During patrol activities, we were advised that an eight-knot speed was favorable. A key factor of this vessel was that it required less than five feet of water to operate. The shallow draft was a major factor in the selection of these boats because of their intended use close to shore.

A cabin was added to the back of an existing pilothouse. It contained two bunks, cabinet space, a small fridge, and a hot plate suitable for food preparation. Below the cabin deck were two compartments for ammunition. A guntub was placed above and behind the pilothouse, equipped with twin .50 caliber machine guns. Behind the engine compartments in the flat afterdeck was an 81 mm mortar with a single .50 caliber machine gun mounted piggyback style on top. The gun was capable of firing in the standard drop and fire method, and it also had the ability to fire via a hand-load, aim, and trigger-fire mode. Each machine gun had the capability to fire 450 rounds per minute, and the mortar could easily drop a round two miles away. Three types of mortar rounds were available—illumination rounds, high explosive (HE), and white phosphorus (WP, commonly called Willie Peter) rounds. This made the PCF ideal for fast ship-to-shore fire support when needed.

In addition to the fixed armament, each Swift was equipped with numerous smaller weapons, including an M79 grenade launcher, fragment, incendiary, and concussion grenades, M16s, and .38 caliber and .45 caliber revolvers and shotguns. Since the patrols were designed for 24-hour periods, the boat was equipped with radar, sea-to-shore radio, a field radio, and oh, yes, a head (onboard toilet). It was quite an impressive combat package, more like a seaborne tank. I was so much in awe of its overall fighting prowess—we would be invincible.

As the weeks went by, we studied the boat from stem to stern. We crawled through the bilges, tracing out all the systems—electrical, hydraulic, and steering. Damage control exercises were conducted regularly. Crew members were cross-trained in each other's fields, so any one of us could operate all aspects of the boat.

Mr. Bergin tapped me with the responsibility of learning the radar and radio functions. The fact that I joined the Navy to take up drafting didn't matter. Working with frequencies, transmitting messages, learning radio protocol, and getting to learn the radar's functions was exciting.

One day, Mr. Bergin advised the crew that we were scheduled for the firing range. Until then, we had only cruised around San Diego Bay practicing boat maneuvers, board and search procedures, radar navigation, and mock mortar fire support. Heading out to the range, which was twenty miles out to sea past Point Loma, was exhilarating. I crawled up into the guntub for the ride. The boat, at full throttle, crashed into each oncoming wave. Water sprayed out from under the bow in dramatic fashion. It felt like I was on top of a bucking bull. On occasion, the spray came over instead of out and drenched all those above decks, giving me a taste of the salty sea.

The Swift's speed and handling justified its reference as the Corvette of the Navy.

The boat handled well in moderate seas, although we were only able to proceed at a maximum speed of twelve knots. We slammed through the five-to-six-foot waves with ease. The only annoying factor was the lack of shock absorbers beneath the hull. My legs recoiled with every impact. We slowly decreased speed and came to a full stop. The boat started riding every wave. As the ocean tossed us from one side to another, my stomach tried to decide which way it wanted to go as my body went in the opposite direction. Within minutes, I found myself feeding the fish.

"Best way to earn your sea legs, Bean."

"It's not funny, Boats. I'm not feeling well."

"Here, eat some saltines. It'll add bulk and help settle your stomach."

Boats was a seasoned sailor. Fourteen years in the Navy left him brinier than a block of salt lick in a Texas pasture. He sported an assortment of tattoos—a naked beauty on his right upper arm, which came alive each time he flexed muscles, twin sparrows that hovered over his pecs, chains on both wrists, and a pig centered in the middle of two laurel wreath sprigs. Carver was not the touchy-feely type, but his second son's birth a year and five months earlier had led him to tattoo the name KEVIN in all capital letters on his left forearm. Boats had a twelve-year-old son as well, Bobby Don Carver Jr., from his first marriage.

I sat on the ammo box in the fantail, holding onto the stanchion with one hand and a box of saltines in the other.

"You okay, Bean?" hollered Mr. Bergin from atop the guntub, preparing to cut loose on the twin .50s. I mustered a horizontal thumbs-up while holding on to the fantail cable railing.

I was the last one to take a turn in the guntub. I climbed in through a base opening in the pilothouse, where the twin .50s were secured in a vertical fashion against the barrel support attached to the radar mast. When I disengaged the lock mechanism, the rotating gun mount and ammo platform unit immediately spun to one side in response to the rolling sea. The instructor, on the pilothouse roof and outside the guntub, stood to my right, quickly reached in, and grabbed the handle, ordering me to grab the opposite one. In a rolling sea, the free-spinning gun mount was difficult to control, and my string bean physique didn't help.

I held onto the vertical wood handles to the outside of each gun, spread my feet apart, and planted them firmly against the base of the guntub. The next step was the most difficult. Prior to firing the weapons, .50 caliber rounds had to be chambered into position. To the outside of each weapon was a horizontal charging handle. I lowered the barrels and pointed them dead ahead, in line with the bow. Mr. Bergin and Boats stood behind me by the radar mast. They cut me some slack by not laughing when I couldn't simultaneously cock back the chambering handles. After helpful guidance by the instructor and support from the crew, I finally succeeded.

I let go of the trigger tabs immediately after my first burst. My entire body shook like a jackhammer operator. In addition to controlling the horizontal spinning motion of the gun mount, I discovered that the recoil action caused the barrels to climb. I felt like a fireman trying to control a hose for the first time. Bullets were flying in every direction. By the time I was able to gain some firing control and enjoy what I was doing, my time was up.

The clatter of the .50s made the hull vibrate with every burst. I'd seen war movies before, but none came close to the full effect weapons of this type had up close. The noise was almost unbearable. I speculated that being at the receiving end of these twin dragons wouldn't be pretty.

We were warned that the enemy would often go dark—that is, invisible. These combatants were known as sappers, special task operators—commandos. They carried out their operations underwater. They had caused the US Navy its first devastating blow of the war.

The sinking took place in the Port of Saigon. During the night of May 2, 1964, two Viet Cong sappers from the 65th Special Operations Group exited a sewer tunnel and swam to the starboard side of the World War II–era aircraft carrier USNS *Card*, each carrying ninety pounds of explosives and timing devices for two bombs. They spent an hour in the water securing the charges against the *Card*'s hull. They set the timing device and swam away.[2] At 0500 hours the bomb ripped a truck-size hole in the engine room compartment, killing five civilian crewmen. The *Card* sank in forty-eight feet of water.

President Johnson insisted on keeping news of the incident out of the public eye, reporting it as only damage to the carrier. To the Viet Cong it was a major victory. To celebrate, North Vietnam created a commemorative postage stamp. The ship was raised and taken under tow by the salvage vessel USS *Reclaimer* and the tug USS *Tawakoni* to the Philippines, where it was restored to full operational status and was able to devote six more years of commendable service.

In the spring of 1967, many crews and boats were already engaged in combat. Of the 104 Mark I Class Swift Boats manufactured, PCF-101 arrived in Vietnam on

December 5, 1966. PCF-102 and PCF-103 were delivered in May and July the following year. The last one, PCF-104, remained on the West Coast and served as a training boat.

Operation Market Time units had successfully detected four enemy resupply vessels since the Vũng Rô Bay incident on February 16, 1965. The trawler attempt of December 1965 in the Cà Mau Peninsula was turned away. Three trawler infiltration missions occurred in 1966. In May another Cà Mau trawler was sunk. In June, a trawler was intercepted and captured fifty-five miles south of Vũng Tàu. In December, another run at the South Vietnam coast, eighty miles northeast of Qui Nhơn, was blocked, and the trawler was turned away.

On January 1, 1967, PCF-71 was operating along the shore, a few miles south of the Bồ Đề River, in the 8-D patrol sector out of Coastal Division 13 base in Cat Lo. At 2115 hours, an unidentified, unlighted contact appeared on radar ten miles off the coast. The seaborne unit was heading easterly, parallel to the beach. Lieutenant Junior Grade Richard W. Dawson set general quarters and proceeded to investigate the suspicious unit.

The Swift directed a flashing-light message at the vessel once it came into visual range. A driving rain and three-foot seas made boat handling difficult, but the crew was ready. All challenges directed toward the vessel were ignored. PCF-71 closed in on the unmarked vessel, illuminated her, and was blasted by heavy automatic weapons fire. After receiving several hits at point-blank range, PCF-71 unleashed her machine guns, riddling the trawler from bow to stern.

Lieutenant Dawson reported to Sepia, radio net control in Vũng Tàu, that his unit was engaging a steel-hulled trawler and requested assistance. During the firefight the skipper and two other crewmen suffered shrapnel wounds. The 71 Boat cleared the area to assess her damage. By the time PCF-71 was able to resume the battle, contact with the enemy trawler had been lost.

At 2130 hours, PCF-68 and the USCGC *Point Gammon* were tied alongside during an attempt to repair the PCF's fathometer when the urgent call for help came in. They left their designated patrol areas immediately. Their skippers assessed the situation while en route to the scene and speculated the trawler was headed toward the mouth of the Bồ Đề river. *Point Gammon* closed on the contact and began issuing flashing light challenges at 2140 hours.

A mile from the unidentified radar blip, Lieutenant Roger W. Hassard, skipper of the WPB, intercepted the evading ship before she was able to make the beach and illuminated her at 2245 hours. It was identified as a seventy-foot steel-hulled trawler with a blue-green hull and a cream-colored superstructure.

Arriving on scene, PCF-68 was directed by the WPB to cut ahead of the trawler and fire warning shots across its bow. PCF-68, with Lieutenant Junior Grade Alex Bass in charge, engaged the trawler in a fierce firefight. Employing white phosphorus mortar rounds in trigger-fire mode, the Swift landed several direct hits, setting the trawler afire before she could reach the safety of the river mouth, less than a half mile away.

A well-entrenched enemy on the beach then attacked PCF-68 using automatic weapons. Lieutenant Bass's crew launched suppressive fire at the shore position. Three secondary explosions were observed as the resulting fires spread toward the pilothouse area. Two hours after midnight, the enemy vessel ran aground. While the Swift Boat alternated her attack between the enemy ship and the land battery, the trawler disappeared into the depths below following an explosion.[3]

• • •

As we heard of these incidents, I realized that my Swift Boat tour of duty would not be a cakewalk. Preventing the landing of armed North Vietnamese resupply trawlers made the possibility of enemy confrontation a high probability. We were heading off to a hot war.

CHAPTER 8

BRAVE SAILORS

PCF-3 and PCF-4 were the first two Swift Boats designated for combat patrol duty in Vietnam. The boats and their crews were sent to Subic Bay for a shakedown and modifications. Lieutenant Junior Grade David McFarland, skipper of PCF-3, and Lieutenant Junior Grade Charles D. Lloyd put their boats and crews through intensive sea trial maneuvers, with focus on boat handling, radar capabilities, and communication reliability. As a consequence, they encountered numerous issues that resulted in changes. Of particular importance, the rudders were too small, so bigger rudders were welded to help steering at slow speeds.

One major modification can be credited to Lieutenant Lloyd. He determined that the standard handheld spanner wrench used in adjusting mortar fuse setting would be difficult during combat or in rough seas. He designed a fixed mortar fuse-setting apparatus. The handle section was removed, and the wrench portion was welded to the top of slanted bases located on both sides of the mortar box on the fantail.

On October 30, 1965, the USS *Fort Marion* (LSD 22) delivered the first two Swift Boats, PCF-3 and PCF-4, to An Thới, Phú Quốc Island, in the Gulf of Thailand.[1] These two Swift Boats were the first of seventeen PCFs planned for Market Time operations in the Phú Quốc Island area. Lieutenant John Dominic Broglio was PCF Division 101's first commander.

The newly established division reported to Commander Task Group 115.4.9, Coast Guard Commander James A. Hodgman, who was responsible for Market Time operations in Patrol Area 9.[2] The two boats tied up alongside the *Fort Marion*. The USS *Krishna* (ARL-38) had arrived at An Thới on September 17 to support Coast

Swift Boat PCF-4 plying the waters around An Thới , Phú Quốc Island, Republic of Vietnam, circa October 1965. (Photo credit: US Navy)

Guard Squadron One operations.[3] It would also serve the needs of the Swift Boat activities out of An Thới. While en route from Subic Bay, modifications were made aboard the *Krishna* to the communication center that made it suitable for Market Time operations.

Shortly after the radiomen mounted the antennas on their boats and fired up their radars, a call came in ordering the two Swift Boats into action. The South Vietnamese Special Forces A-Team camp, near the district town of Duong Dong, was under attack and they needed urgent fire support.

Three hours after being off-loaded, the two Swift Boats and Coast Guard Cutters *Point Garnet* (WPB-82310) and *Point Comfort* (WPB-82317) made their way to the opposite side of the island, approximately fifteen miles along the island's western shore. A "Bird Dog" (Cessna L-91/O-1 Spotter Plane) on scene directed mortar fire from above. Lieutenant Junior Grade Charles Lloyd, PCF-4 Officer in Charge (OIC), and Ensign Theodore "Tony" Wright, PCF-3 OIC, directed their crews to drop mortar fire. The pilot reported 95 percent of the Swift's targets were hit, with nine Viet Cong killed. And so began the Swift Boat story—in combat action from day one in South Vietnam.

Both PCF crews used the *Krishna* as home base for several days while Tent City was set up within the American sector of the South Vietnamese Navy base at An

Thới, fifty feet from the compound limits. Several village huts lined the base of a small hill approximately 100 yards from the perimeter. The VC had a clear shot at the US Navy complex from the top of this vantage point.

A sandy area near the beach was leveled, and wood pallets served as a foundation for flooring. At night, crews slept on cots with mosquito netting, using cardboard boxes and emptied 81 mm mortar boxes as storage for their clothing. Their meals were prepared in a field kitchen and eaten in a mess tent. PCF Division 101 was now officially in-country, albeit on an island.

The patrol schedule was grueling. Initially, the two boat crews alternated twenty-four-hour patrols with twelve hours on base. Off-time was spent sleeping, filling sandbags, and building their own bunker. At night, they slept with a Mark II carbine at their side. The Viet Cong carried out sniper attacks and lobbed mortars on them almost every other night. The base perimeter amounted to no more than a five-foot wire fence. At night, it was guarded by ARVN soldiers.

During the first eight weeks, PCF-3 and PCF-4 patrolled primarily in and around Phú Quốc Island and in the waters between the base and the mainland, fifty miles to the northeast. Patrols were extended to thirty-six hours—two days and one night. Small islands near the mainland provided calm shelter. Late at night, they would anchor, then set a three-man watch standard that allowed them time to sleep. Days were spent inspecting junks and transiting small cargo vessels and familiarizing themselves with native boat traffic in the area.

On Christmas Eve 1965, the USS *Catamount* (LSD-17) delivered six more Swift Boats to An Thới: PCFs 5, 6, 9, 10, 11, and 12, bringing the total to eight. At the start of 1966, Swift Boat crews began patrolling the mainland shoreline. They alternated assignments among six patrol areas spread along the coastline from the southern tip of the Cà Mau Peninsula, northwest to Ha Tien at the Cambodian border. Having only eight Swift Boats, Lieutenant Broglio relied on his boat officers to adjust their patrol limits to ensure the southwest coastline of South Vietnam was well patrolled. Due to the distance from An Thới to the tip of the Cà Mau Peninsula (100 miles), two boat crews and one Swift Boat operated off a Market Time destroyer on a twenty-four hours on, twenty-four hours off rotation.

The eight Swift Boat crews, under the leadership of Lieutenant Broglio, were busy carrying out the Market Time mission and rewriting the on-patrol operational manual based on daily patrol experiences. Reports on lessons learned were immediately sent to Coronado so new crews undergoing PCF training could be better versed on what to expect when they arrived in-country.

PCF-4 Incident

Ending blind speculation of just how dangerous our combat mission in Vietnam was to be, we learned of incidents involving Swift Boat crews already there. Mistakes made in combat by the early crews became invaluable lessons for those of us undergoing training in Coronado. Two and a half months after Swift Boats began patrolling the waters off the coast of South Vietnam, Operation Market Time suffered its first combat loss.

The arrival of six more PCFs increased the show of force along the mainland. As a result, the Viet Cong were compelled to become more creative at moving weapons and men from the mainland to Phú Quốc Island and back. To harass Market Time units and make their presence known in the area, they randomly placed Viet Cong flags on floats or on bamboo sticks driven into the muddy shallows near the shore.

Lieutenant Junior Grade Charles Lloyd and his PCF-4 crew were on station near Rạch Giá, a provincial city, on Valentine's Day 1966. Nothing out of the ordinary occurred during their scheduled twenty-four-hour patrol. The crew had spent their day conducting routine stop and search operations of fishing sampans, basket boats, and transiting cargo junks, manning their general quarters stations each time they inspected a vessel.

Thirty-year-old Dayton Luther Rudisill of Greensburg, Kansas, was behind the twin .50s in the guntub located above and behind the pilothouse. Rudisill's red wavy hair and friendly smile made him easily recognizable. He was an experienced second-class Gunner's Mate with twelve years of dedicated naval service.

Rudisill and Tommy Edward Hill were "tight." Hill was a second-class Boatswain's Mate and the crew's lead petty officer. Hill, two years Rudisill's senior, hailed from Knoxville, Tennessee, and had fourteen years of service in the Navy. Ed Mundy, Hill's crewmate on the USS *Winston*, remembered him being an old-style boatswain's mate, always wearing pressed dungarees, shined boondockers, and perfectly shaped white hat. He had a mature face, a gentle smile, and a distinguished Humphrey Bogart jaw.

Lieutenant Lloyd was born in Atlantic City, New Jersey, and grew up in Steubenville, Ohio. He graduated from Wheeling College in 1963, and since the draft was hot on his heels and job interviews were scarce, he enrolled in the Navy's Officer Candidate School. Graduation day was memorable, for it took place on November 22, 1963, the day President John F. Kennedy was assassinated in Dallas.

Adding to the experience level of Lieutenant Lloyd's crew was Joaquín Charles "Jack" Rodríguez. The twenty-four-year-old Engineman Second Class hailed from Jackson Heights, New York. Rodríguez's Cuban roots weren't as obvious as the New York City look he possessed.

An eighteen-year-old sailor from Woodland, California, was the crew's deckhand. Seaman David Joseph Boyle, only one year out of boot camp, was recruited from Swift Boat Division 101 staff.

Robert Johnson, Radioman Third Class, was PCF-4's Ops Boss. Although only twenty years of age, Lieutenant Lloyd knew he could depend on Johnson for operating and maintaining the communication and radar equipment on board. Born in Coupeville, Whidbey Island, Washington, his family eventually ended up in Medford, Oregon. His father's service in the Navy, during World War II, influenced him to join the Navy Reserve.

PCF-4 was making its way northwest along the shoreline during the late afternoon. Rạch Giá was approximately fifteen miles behind them. It was 1715 hours when they rounded a bend in the shoreline.

"Skipper, VC flag up ahead, off the starboard bow," Rudisill called out from his guntub position.

"Dead in the water, Boats."

Hill pulled back on the throttles ahead of Lieutenant Lloyd's order.

"Skipper, them bastards just keep jacking with us."

"I know, Boats. Luck was with us on our last patrol, remember? We cut down their flag and thank God nothing happened. It was in this same location if I remember correctly."

"Gunner, scan the shoreline with your binoculars. You've got a better view from up there. Look for any suspicious movement."

"Copy, Mr. Lloyd."

The skipper did the same from his position just inside the starboard side pilothouse door.

"Boats, think we should take it down?"

"Yes sir, Skipper. We can't let them sumbitches think their harassment crap will make us pick up our marbles and go home."

Lieutenant Lloyd looked up into the guntub and hollered, "How 'bout you, Gunner?"

"Sure, but I'd first try to trigger any secondary explosion, just in case that's their game plan, Skipper."

Seaman Boyle poked his head into the pilothouse and concurred with the plan to take down the flag.

Lieutenant Lloyd went down into the cabin to gather some concussion grenades from the small arms locker. Johnson was sitting by the radio controls. Lieutenant Lloyd brought him up to speed on the situation and asked his opinion.

"It's not worth it if we're doing it just for chasing down war souvenirs, sir."

"It's a scare tactic. They're hoping we stay away from their territory. Sorry Charlie, ain't gonna happen."

Lieutenant Lloyd went into the pilothouse once again. "Take us in at a crawl, Boats. Stop about twenty yards away."

"Aye, aye, Skipper," Hill responded.

The enemy flag, with its red top, blue bottom, and single gold star in the middle, was secured to a bamboo pole driven into the shallow muddy bottom. The flag waved steadily ten feet above the gentle rolling waves. As the boat inched toward the standard, Seaman Boyle took a position in front of the pilothouse on the starboard side, holding on to the railing that ran along the bottom of the windows. Lloyd stood on the catwalk by the pilothouse door, and Rodríguez, armed with an M16, took station five feet behind him.

Lieutenant Lloyd recalled reading an article in *All Hands* magazine about river operations that often lobbed grenades at VC flags found in the middle of rivers or canals. Assuming this was a trap, the crew fired small arms and hurled four hand grenades to within a few feet of the Viet Cong flag, to detonate any charge that may have been set.

Indeed, it was a trap. The enemy lay well concealed behind the rocky shore, anxiously waiting for the Americans to take the bait.

Having failed to trigger a secondary explosion, Hill cautiously maneuvered PCF-4 toward the flag until it was alongside the starboard bow. At the same time, Johnson went topside through the rear cabin door and walked the starboard-side catwalk, stopping six feet behind Rodríguez. Seaman Boyle cut two lashings from the pole. The boat broke away from the flag and Hill throttled the engines, bringing the pole within Boyle's reach once again. As Boyle was cutting the last two lashings, the Viet Cong detonated the 200-pound mine they had planted earlier.

The explosion was massive.

PCF-4's bow was thrust upward under a gush of seawater, like a breaching whale. The impact ripped a jagged twelve-foot horizontal hole, from the keel to halfway up the starboard side bow. Like an erupting volcano, the fiery ball of metal burst through the sleeping compartment, into the pilothouse, and out the guntub, killing Hill and Rudisill instantly. The impact catapulted Boyle, Lieutenant Lloyd, Rodríguez, and Johnson varying distances behind and outboard the starboard quarter of the fantail.

Johnson blacked out momentarily. Opening his eyes, he saw a mass amount of sea spray all around and suddenly realized he was airborne. He splashed hard into the water. No sooner had he surfaced when the VC flag, still tied to a section of the bamboo pole, landed on his head. The impact didn't hurt as much as his legs, which had been bent backward at the knees from the sudden massive concussion effect of the deck under his feet. He had no control over his legs. Johnson did the best he could with his arms and swam in the direction of the boat. All the while, automatic weapons fire was zinging above his head and making the water spurt all around him.

Three South Vietnamese Navy Coastal Group (CG) 43 patrol junks were operating in an area seaward from Rạch Giá when the detonation occurred. Although the Three Sisters area was fifteen miles northwest along the coast, they heard the immense blast and immediately made their way toward the site. They arrived on scene in less than an hour.

PCF-4 was sinking fast. It was going down in ten feet of water, approximately 250 yards offshore. On his way toward the sinking PCF, Johnson found the youngest crewman, Seaman Boyle. He was floating on the water, face down. Johnson managed to turn Boyle on his back, placed his right arm around his chest, and with the other arm paddled slowly toward the boat. Keeping his eye on the boat, he noticed that the emergency raft had been blown off its topside location.

The aft section of the boat was elevated, and the painted PCF-4 lettering towered above their heads. The zinc plates, normally below the water line, were above the surface. Boyle was semi-conscious and in grave pain. Johnson guided Boyle's hands onto a thin-lip edge of the hull's bottom.

"Hang on tight to this edge, buddy, and don't let go. Help is coming."

Lieutenant Lloyd had been thrown thirty feet in the air and, on impact, plunged five feet below the water's surface. The concussion affected his equilibrium, causing him to stroke through the water horizontally versus attempting to rise to the surface. He too realized he didn't have use of his legs, and that he was in excruciating pain. Still dazed, he discovered he was paddling toward the beach. Using only his upper torso, he pushed onto his back, momentarily floating. That's when he noticed one of his boots was pointing to the side and the other was pointing in the opposite direction, well beyond ninety degrees from normal.

He turned himself onto his stomach, bringing his boat into view. He was horrified to see PCF-4 settling bow first into the soft, muddy bottom.

"Oh, God! It's a disaster," he muttered to himself.

As Johnson neared PCF-4's fantail with Boyle in tow, he heard Lieutenant Lloyd's moans to his right, toward shore. Without regard for his own safety and impaired physical condition, using only his arms, he swam away from the boat in search of his Skipper.

"Everyone all right?" Lloyd asked as Johnson approached.

"Boyle's clinging to the tail section, Skipper. Haven't seen anyone else. Can you swim?"

"Negative. I can't move my legs. Both broken, I think."

Johnson pulled on Lloyd's drab green T-shirt, and together they paddled toward their drowning Swift Boat. Boyle was barely hanging onto the fantail and unresponsive, as the Viet Cong continued raining fire on the downed Swift. The three took cover on the port side of the boat's fantail. For the moment, they were safe.

"Can you get to the Prick 10 [field radio PRC-10] and send a flash traffic Mayday message?"

"I'll try, Skipper," Johnson replied as he felt his way along the edge of the submerged port side catwalk. Getting to the pilothouse door area, he saw that the radio was underwater and the cabin, where the AN/URC-58 single sideband radio was located, was submerged. Communication was impossible. They were isolated from all friendly forces and within reach of enemy hands.

"No-go on the radios, Skipper."

"Get the raft. Put Boyle in it and go as far away as you can. I'll stay here."

"We can't, Skipper, explosion blew it off."

Their options were limited. The beach, although a short 250 yards away, was controlled by the enemy. Villages were absent in either direction along the coastline. Fishing boats were not expected to be nearby. Their best recollection placed Market Time units well beyond the horizon. The three men clung to the boat's fantail, their only option.

South Vietnamese CG 43 Units 43.02, 43.13, and 43.16 came under heavy small arms and machine gun fire from enemy-held positions on the beach when they arrived on scene, an hour after hearing the blast. The Viet Cong force, more than one platoon, had fortified themselves along the rocky shoreline in an effort to inflict heavy casualties on the American craft patrolling the area. Seven Viet Cong were observed entering the water, ostensibly to kill any remaining survivors and recover weapons from PCF-4, which, if captured, would serve their insurgent campaign.

To ensure PCF-4 wouldn't be salvaged, the remains of those killed recovered, or the injured crewmen rescued, the Viet Cong stationed snipers in the tree line and behind rocks at water's edge to impede the recovery. The rescue and salvage operation took place under sporadic enemy fire. Petty Officer Third Class (PO3) Hoang and Seaman (SN) Duong on board CG Unit 43.14 positioned their vessel near the stricken Swift Boat to draw the enemy fire off the other units attempting to rescue the survivors. Armed with an M1 Garand rifle and a .30 caliber machine gun, the two sailors courageously returned hostile fire. Three of the Viet Cong swimmers were killed and the remaining four were forced to withdraw.

CG Unit 43.02, with PO3 Thuong and SN Son, immediately went to the aid of Lieutenant Lloyd.

"No, no," he ordered. "Take my men first."

PO3 Thuong jumped into the water and helped Boyle and Johnson board their patrol boat. Both men were taken aboard the Vietnamese Navy junk and placed on the wooden deck behind the small boat cabin. CG Unit 43.16 approached to assist with the rescue. They tied up to junk Unit 43.02. Vietnamese Navy Petty Officer Third Class Phat and Seaman Ly observed that PO3 Thuong was having difficulty getting Lieutenant Lloyd aboard. They jumped in to assist, and together managed to push Lloyd up and aboard Unit 43.02's deck. Lloyd's pain skyrocketed as the three Vietnamese sailors desperately struggled to get him out of the water.

PO3 Thuong climbed back on board and moved his boat a safe distance seaward where the two Vietnamese sailors bandaged Lieutenant Lloyd's legs and used mouth-to-mouth resuscitation on SN Boyle, who had stopped breathing. Lloyd stretched his arm toward the mortally wounded seaman, seeking to encourage him to hang on, but regrettably couldn't reach him.

Lieutenant Lloyd kept floating in and out of consciousness, the excruciating pain forcing him back to momentary awareness. PO3 Thuong brought a tin cup filled with tea from their cabin. Lloyd managed to only wet his lips with the lukewarm green tea. The sting coming from his lower extremities was overshadowed by a deeper hurt that came from within. Three of his men had been killed in action, and a fourth man lying next to him was about to succumb to his injuries.

CG Units 43.14 and 43.16 remained at the scene to prevent the Viet Cong from recovering any equipment or planting more explosives. They continued providing counter fire against the enemy force until the US recovery and salvage boats arrived. At 1830 hours, two L-19 FACS (Bird Dog spotter planes) came on the scene to assess the situation and identify the source of the persistent enemy fire.

Lying on his back on the wooden deck, Lieutenant Lloyd grabbed one of the sailors' shirt sleeve, pulling him close. "Prick 10, Prick 10," he grunted at the sailor as he raised the other hand, thumb to his ear and pinky toward his mouth. The young man left and returned with the field radio. Lloyd dialed a frequency monitored by the Army.

"Mayday, Mayday, Mayday! Lieutenant Lloyd, Assort Foxtrot 4 sunk. Hit by mine. Three Sisters. I say again, PCF-4 sunk, Three Sisters. Onboard Yabuta, heading to Rạch Giá. Three wounded aboard. Two KIA, one missing. Send Medevac, send Medevac. ASAP. Out."

Lieutenant Lloyd's Mayday call was received in Rạch Giá at the Tactical Operations Center (TOC). In short order, Army helicopters arrived on scene and began taking the rocky shoreline under machine gun and rocket fire. Lieutenant Dunn, an Army medic, and a Navy chief gunner's mate boarded a Zodiac and headed up the coast, racing to get there before the sun fell entirely below the western horizon.

Lieutenant Dunn, skipper on PCF-5, had been on patrol in the Cà Mau Peninsula area. He spotted the circling gunships in the distance and changed course toward them. They were able to intercept CG unit 43.02 that was on its way to Rạch Giá with the wounded Swift Boat crewmen. They came alongside the junk, secured the Zodiac, and rushed to where the injured lay on the back of the junk.

"We're here now, Charlie," Lieutenant Dunn assured Lloyd.

"Take care of my seaman, Gil. He needs your help."

The Army medic checked Boyle for vitals and turned to Dunn, shaking his head.

"He's in a better place, Charlie. Let's see what we can do for you."

Lieutenant Lloyd gritted his teeth, squeezed his eyes, and shook his head, the expression reflecting his agonizing remorse.

Although he was in great pain, Johnson's injuries didn't include leg fractures. His vital signs were normal, and he was made as comfortable as possible. The medic and Dunn placed a tourniquet on Lloyd's left leg and immobilized it by using a rifle as a splint. He had lost a lot of blood from the compound fractures on that leg. A morphine syrette was administered to Lloyd's thigh. The medic secured the expended tube to his T-shirt, a method used by field medics to alert Medevac or field hospital personnel that the patient had already received a dose of morphine. A blood-marked "M" on the forehead was an alternative technique.

Lieutenant Dunn raised comms with the Medevac chopper, advising them they were ready for evac. The junk's radio whip antenna was bent over and secured. The

Military personnel remain with the Zodiac to search for EN2 Rodríguez after PCF-4 succumbed to a Viet Cong mine and sank in ten feet of water, fifteen miles west of Rạch Giá, Republic of Vietnam, 14 February 1966. (Photo credit: US Navy)

pilot lowered the airborne ambulance's skid close to the small cabin. The Medevac medic stepped off the skid and onto the cabin's top. The three men worked hard to get Lieutenant Lloyd to the top of the cabin, the highest point on the junk. Lloyd was in severe pain, even with the dose of morphine. Several attempts were made to lift Lloyd onto the flat deck on the Medevac unit, but each failed. The rolling seas made the transfer extremely dangerous, given Lloyd's condition. The Medevac unit aborted the attempt but returned to extract RM3 Johnson. The medic boarded the craft and departed for the Kiên Giang Province hospital in Rạch Giá.

Lieutenant Dunn stayed with Charlie Lloyd for the ride to Rach Giá. The chief boatswain's mate and the medic transferred back from the Yabuta and onto their Zodiac, remaining on scene to assist in search operations for the missing engineman, EN2 Rodríguez. CG Unit 43.02, with Seaman Boyle's remains aboard, departed the area, and made its way to Rạch Giá.

Recovery of PCF-4 began under a hail of enemy fire. The Coast Guard Cutter *Point Clear* (WPB 82315), LT Jon Uithol in command, arrived on scene at 2000 hours. He called in the US Air Force Douglas AC-47D, known to allied forces as "Spooky," or "Puff" the magic dragon, to suppress the attack, while PCF-3 and PCF-5 attacked the enemy force entrenched along the rocky shore.

PCF-4 sinks in the foreground as PCFs 3 and 10 assist in the search, rescue, and salvage operations off the western shore of the Cà Mau Peninsula, Republic of Vietnam, 14 February 1966. (Photo credit: US Navy)

Divers located the bodies of Hill and Rudisill, both found at their combat stations. The following morning, Rodríguez's body was found floating nearby. The three Swift Boat crewmen were placed in black body bags and taken to the *Point Clear*. Later that morning, a Medevac helicopter lowered a litter rescue basket on to the cutter's fantail. PCF-4's fallen crewmen were hoisted on board the helicopter and departed the scene.

• • •

Days later, on February 18, a memorial service for the four crewmen was held on a sandy beach near Tent City at An Thới. In a show of support for their fallen shipmates, Coast Guard crews boarded an LCM and came ashore at the Swift Boat pier. They joined PCF crews and personnel at the service. Tommy Edward Hill, Dayton Luther Rudisill, Joaquín Charles "Jack" Rodríguez, and David Joseph Boyle became the first Swift Boat casualties of the Vietnam War.[4]

CHAPTER 9

ON LEAVE

T he tragic sinking of PCF-4 and the untimely death of four Swift Boat crewmen was a hard lesson learned. It clearly demonstrated that our craft and crews were not invincible as I presumed. As if this disastrous episode wasn't enough to further convince us of the perils of war that lay ahead, we were told of another tragedy.

PCF-26 Ambush

On March 27, 1966, Lieutenant Murice M. Simer's PCF-26 left Coastal Division 13 Swift Boat base at Cat Lo, approximately forty miles southeast of Saigon, to patrol a known-enemy section of the Đồng Tranh River, seventeen miles southeast of Saigon. They were taken under .50 caliber and .30 caliber machine gun fire from both banks by the Viet Cong. It was the most intense waterborne action of Operation Jackstay to date.

The crew, already at general quarters, returned fire. Engineman Second Class Alton R. Gunter, manning the aft single .50 caliber machine gun, suppressed small arms fire from one riverbank and then swung about and fired at the opposite bank. An enemy shell found its mark, and Gunter was blown off his feet and onto the afterdeck of the Swift Boat.

Although wounded by shrapnel in three places, he managed to get to his feet, man his position, and continue his suppressive fire. His aftermount assistant, Seaman Jack A. Wallgren, was also hit and out of commission. Gunter soon ran out of .50 caliber ammo. Braving enemy fire from both banks, he dodged his way to the ammo locker and hauled out a supply of 81 mm mortars.

The enemy's location was too close for a standard mortar barrage via a drop and lob procedure. Instead, he hand-loaded each round, leveled the mortar to almost horizontal, took aim, and trigger-fired the mortar. Single-handedly, he was able to effectively direct his mortar attack on both banks and thus silenced the VC's guns.

For his bravery and gallant action, Rear Admiral Norvell G. Ward, Commander Naval Forces Vietnam, presented the Silver Star to EN2 Alton R. Gunter at an awards ceremony held in Qui Nhon.[1]

"Men," the instructor resumed, "I relate these events to scare you. That's right, scare your asses into realizing you're not heading out to a picnic. It's war, gentlemen. If you expect to beat the odds on survival and not come back in a pine box, stay alert and learn your jobs well." He continued with details of another combat incident.

Four Boat Ambush

During Operation Jackstay, on May 22, 1966, four Swifts were patrolling near the Rung Sat Special Zone, four miles upriver from Saigon on the Dinh Ba River. The boats were not in sight of each other because of the river's snaking course. Lieutenant Junior Grade Alexander G. Balian, the skipper of PCF-41, was at the after-steering controls on the fantail. At the ready on the forward controls in the pilothouse was a barnacled sailor in his 40s, Boatswain's Mate Second Class Raleigh L. Godley. Radioman Second Class Robert L. Keim was at the portside door, peering at the thick vegetation along the riverbank through binoculars. In the guntub was Engineman Third Class Charles E. Barham.

Without warning, PCF-41 was suddenly hit by a round fired from a 57 mm recoilless rifle. The explosion ripped through the thin quarter-inch aluminum hull at the bow and flashed upward and burst into the pilothouse, killing Godley at the helm. Radioman Keim was blasted onto the narrow catwalk outside the pilothouse door. He momentarily blacked out. Regaining his senses, and unaware that he was severely wounded, he made his way back into the pilothouse and found Godley's body lying on the pilothouse deck. The helm was blown away, and the instrument panel was destroyed.

It is believed that Godley's last action was intended to pull the boat and crewmates away from enemy fire. He shoved the engine's throttles forward, forcing the Swift to race along the river out of control. Another round landed close by, rocking and showering the boat with water, as Balian took control of the after-steering station. His efforts to regain control of the boat, as the rest of the crew continued to return fire, became fruitless as PCF-41 abruptly ran aground.

The skipper anticipated that the other boats would come to their aid immediately. Unfortunately, the dense foliage along the banks had isolated the sounds of the attack. As Keim reported to Lieutenant Balian that the radio was out, he became aware of their dilemma. He wiped sweat from his neck, only to discover that it was blood coming from a shrapnel wound to his head. His right leg had taken another piece of jagged metal. SN Ralph E. Powers and GMG2 Glenn D. Greene, who had been manning the aftermount, were slammed to the deck by the sudden lunge of the Swift when it ran into the sandbar.

Anticipating another assault, the skipper ordered his men to reload their weapons. When the VC did attack, the crew of PCF-41 returned fire, spraying the foliage with increasing intensity. The enemy's fire was suppressed at the right moment, but the crew's ammo had all been expended. The skipper ordered his crew to prepare to abandon ship. The only way out of their predicament was to drift downriver through enemy lines. Lieutenant Balian ordered the wounded Keim inside the small raft, and the crew placed their rifles alongside him. The crew entered the water and clung to the raft, two on each side. It was a difficult decision, but Godley's body was left behind. The crew's training in survival, evasion, resistance, and escape was about to be put to a rigorous test.

If the enemy wasn't enough to worry about, the crew knew they were also surrounded by deadly water snakes as well as crocodiles. The drifting crew passed within earshot of VC patrols and camps. As night fell and the moon broke through the overcast skies, Keim had to be lowered into the water so as not to cast a silhouette. The crew moaned a sigh of relief as a Swift Boat was heard approaching. Yet the engine noise died out as the Swift turned back. They drew some comfort knowing that at least an effort was being made to locate them. Twice the raft with her exhausted crew drifted into schools of jellyfish that flowed in with the tide. As the venom sped through their bodies, their arms and legs began to swell. They stifled cries of anguish lest the VC hear them.

Eventually, another Swift was heard approaching. Barham held up his rifle, and the radar aboard the Swift picked up the metal contact. The crew was saved. The following morning, a salvage team reached the grounded boat, and Godley's body was recovered. The crew regrouped and returned to patrol duties and more confrontations with the enemy in the days and weeks to follow.[2]

The instructor advised us that in addition to combat, Swift Boat crews were an important factor in the MEDCAP mission—Medical Civic Action Programs, best known by US military personnel as "hearts and minds." PCF crews distributed small bags filled with personal hygiene items to the adults in the fishing junks they inspected while on patrol. They also transported medics or doctors to seaside villages to care for individuals in need of medical attention.

One crew assisted an expectant mother in the delivery of her baby. In a non-MEDCAP mission, PCF-61 operating out of Da Nang on May 23, 1966, came to the aid of a fast-sinking junk in heavy seas. Fleeing from the Viet Cong, 157 Vietnamese had left their village. The Swift Boat saved them from drowning, taking all 157 on board and transporting them to the USS *Vance* (DER 387). The villagers were taken to Qui Nhơn and turned over to Vietnamese authorities for transportation to their destinations, Tuy Hòa and Nha Trang.

I had been foolish and naive to think that our crew would spend a year in Vietnam without engaging the enemy in combat. The incidents detailed that day were more than enough for me to question my future. I was too young to be thinking about death.

Training ended on a high note, however. Certificates of completion for PCF crew training were issued on March 31, 1967, and we were granted a short leave before our scheduled departure on April 6 from McChord Air Force Base in Washington. The five-day leave was totally unexpected but immensely welcomed. I looked forward to seeing everyone back home once more before shipping out to the war zone. My heart raced knowing that I'd see Norma one last time. We had pending love matters to address.

Norma was the only one who knew I was coming home for a short leave. Her brother, Jesse, picked me up at the airport. It was late Friday afternoon. With a seabag over my right shoulder, I walked at a brisk pace along the gravel alley toward the house, eager to see my parents. Stepping up the two concrete steps to the porch, I belted out the family whistle and heard mom shout, "¡Mijo, mijo! You're home." I dropped my seabag onto the porch as Mom welcomed me with open arms and tears of joy.

While waiting for Dad to get home from work, Mom and I sat in the shade of the front porch, sipping a cold glass of fresh squeezed lemonade—sweet, just the way I liked it. I heard gravel rumbling up the alley. Dad was home. Seeing him walk from the car, I could tell he had a tough day. Dad wasn't much for hugs; just the same, we exchanged an awkward embrace. Dad took off his white painter's shirt and sat on the gray wooden porch. They expected the next time they'd hear from me would be from overseas. Their eyes expressed relief for seeing me once again before I departed for Vietnam.

When questioned about what I'd be doing in the war, I confessed I was going to be on patrol boats, but in one of the harbors along the coast of Vietnam. They bought into the notion that the war was being fought in the jungles of Vietnam. I knew otherwise. The "In case of" document I had recently signed in Coronado made me gaze at both my parents intently. They had been my security for twenty years. In Vietnam, I would have only their prayers as reassurance I would remain safe.

Time at home was spent visiting family and friends. Norma and I were together every night. We went to the movies, bowling, and ate at Angelina's, our favorite pizzeria. The last opportunity Norma and I had to exchange our personal and private goodbye was Tuesday night. After attending a friend's birthday party, we headed back to the Elmira Motel for a second attempt at sealing the commitment to our blossoming relationship. In Room 44, we pledged our love to each other, forever. I vowed we'd get engaged and begin making wedding plans on my return from Vietnam. Norma promised that she'd wait for me and would be mine, *para siempre*.

The hours and days passed by quickly. The final sendoff at the San Antonio International Airport on Wednesday, April 5, was traumatic for all of us. There wasn't a dry eye in the large gathering of relatives and friends that came to give me moral support on my departure to the war. I hugged and kissed each one, thanking them for their well wishes. My crisp white uniform became wrinkled as I said my goodbyes.

Norma stood next to my father. Tears flowed freely over her rosy cheeks while her bottom lip quivered. She threw her arms around me and squeezed tightly. Her painful whimpers echoed in my ear. I grabbed my white hankie and wiped away her tears.

"Oh, please don't cry, be strong. Don't forget, we've got to plan an engagement party when I get back," I said, attempting to comfort her.

"Promise me you will take care of yourself and please, don't get hurt!"

We held on to each other with outstretched arms, our fingertips refusing to let go.

"I'll write, as soon as I find out where I'll be stationed," I said, our fingers slipping away from each other. "I love you and don't forget your promise. *¡Para siempre!* Wait for me."

"Don't worry. You know I'll be here. *Te espero*. I love you too," she whispered.

I turned to my parents. Mom was already weeping, and Dad was barely holding back tears. I hugged them and felt my mother's trembling hand on my right shoulder. We hugged for several minutes without saying a word. Onlookers wiped their eyes as well, as they witnessed the heartfelt departure of a family member in a sailor's uniform.

"*Mijito*, your father and I want you to have this." My mother handed me a plastic dashboard figure of St. Anthony.

"We had it blessed at Sacred Heart," she reverently exclaimed, as if through her firm belief and Father Matula's blessing, the statue would keep me safe from all danger in Vietnam.

Struggling with every word, I answered, "*Se los prometo*, I'll always keep him with me wherever I go. *Si Dios quiere*, I'll see you back here in a year."

Mom opened her black purse and pulled out a crystal beaded rosary, an heirloom from her mother, Francisca Cavazos Berrones. She grabbed the cross with her right thumb and index finger, gently raised her arm, and made the sign of the cross on my forehead, across my shoulders and chest at least three times while uttering special prayers in Spanish. When finished, she placed it on my lips to kiss the tiny Christ on the cross. Emotionally torn, Mom began losing control. The pain of my departure was too much for her. I had to leave. I embraced them once again and kissed them as other family members patted me on the back. I turned toward the door leading outside to the tarmac.

I could hear my mother's cries get louder as I handed the attendant my boarding pass. I glanced back at the group before going through the door. I shouldn't have. Tía Toñia was helping Mom up as she seemed to be collapsing under the stress. I struggled to swallow as I looked at Norma for a final time and motioned a kiss goodbye. I gritted my teeth, attempting to maintain composure.

My heart grew heavier with each step I took up the ladder to the plane's door. Tears streamed from my eyes as I reached the top.

"Are you all right, sir?" the Continental Airlines stewardess asked.

"Yes, ma'am," I whispered. "I'm on my way to Vietnam."

She bit her lower lip and squeezed my arm as I walked past her. I went on to my seat. From the window, I could see *la familia*, noses pressed to the tinted windows and hands up high, waving ceaselessly. The plane pushed away from the gate and turned toward the taxiway. Their figures grew smaller with the distance and then I saw them no more. I clutched the little St. Anthony statue while straining to keep the terminal in sight through tear-filled eyes, praying to God that He would answer my mother's prayers and bring me safely back home in a year.

CHAPTER 10

JOURNEY

I met up with Gunner at the Seattle-Tacoma International Airport late in the afternoon and we made our way to McChord AFB. Our flight to Vietnam had been canceled. I called my cousin Monica and spent two days with her family in Tacoma. I couldn't pass up the opportunity of seeing family one last time before heading to Vietnam. On Saturday I was back to McChord around noon.

Entering the center, I heard a soft voice on the PA system announce, "Northwest Airlines Flight 117 will be ready for boarding in thirty minutes. All passengers, please proceed to Gate 12."

An ill feeling dug itself deep in the pit of my stomach. My forehead broke into a clammy sweat from the fear that engulfed me. I looked around at others awaiting the flight, wondering how many shared similar feelings.

Some of the men arrived at the center half snockered, their last hoorah before heading to a war zone, I concluded. Others seemed untouched by spending their last hours on US soil, in shock perhaps, each contemplating his future. Together, regardless of branch of service, officer or enlisted man, we had answered the call. Together we were being sent to contribute our share in the fight for the preservation of freedom.

The inevitable notification finally came over the PA system, "Northwest Airlines Flight 117 now ready for boarding." I grew scared. Going off to war was a surreal experience. The last few steps to the boarding ladder were the most difficult. I never realized how comforting, how secure, simply standing on American soil could be.

Gunner and I, having checked in together, were assigned adjacent seats.

"Want the window, Gunner?"

"Nah," he said, "you take it. I'll do the middle seat. I'm gonna cut some Z's."

I enjoyed window seats. Gazing into a soft blanket of clouds always filled me with inner peace. Still a kid at heart, I would press my nose against the tiny window, taking in as much of the scene below as possible. The cabin seemed eerily silent except for the sound of a few men placing their belongings in the overhead compartments.

The flight attendant finished emergency instructions as the plane approached its final turn onto the runway.

"Well, Gunner, you ready?" I asked, taking a deep breath.

"Ready as I'll ever be," he replied, head resting against the seat's high back and eyes closed.

Cleared by the control tower, the engines started to whine, and the plane began its forward thrust. Within moments we were airborne and gaining altitude. The plane leveled off and began a gradual ascent. The captain's voice came over the PA system.

"Welcome aboard, gentlemen. Your final destination will be our fourth stop. Your journey will be long, so stay as comfortable as you can. We'll be headed northwest to Elmendorf AFB, Alaska, then across the Pacific to Yokota Air Base, Japan. From Yokota, we'll stop at Kadena AFB, Okinawa, prior to our last leg of the flight into Cam Ranh Bay."

"Great, Gunner, we're taking the scenic route," I mused.

Porky and Boats made certain the first leg of our flight to Vietnam was memorable. They almost got their asses yanked off the plane by MPs when we landed in Alaska. We learned that Porky had goosed a blonde stewardess one too many times. Too much free time back at McChord, along with a bottle of whiskey they smuggled aboard the plane on departure, led to the mischievous behavior. Mr. Bergin managed to convince the pilot he'd personally see to it his men wouldn't cause any more problems.

Porky and Boats had clicked from day one of PCF training in Coronado. Only three years separated the pair—Porky was twenty-eight and Boats thirty-one. They had eleven and fifteen years, respectively, of seafaring experience up their bell-bottoms, well on their way to becoming crusty old salts. Their only interest was in finding a good time and not trouble. They loyally practiced the maritime tradition of never drunk on duty, never sober on liberty.

Since his early country-school years in Annapolis, Ohio, Porky was never more than one step ahead of chaos. In his freshman year of high school, he managed to get kicked out of every class. At sixteen he proclaimed he knew more than the teachers and walked out of school never to return, opting for life in a poolhall and a different set of friends.[1]

In Okinawa, I had time to walk around the base terminal. I found a newsstand and purchased a postcard to send home. I selected a card that made me think of the marketplace across the Rio Grande, El Mercado in Nuevo Laredo, Mexico. In the picture was a lady in a colorful kimono arranging bunches of gladiolus and daisies. Mom loved flowers; they always brought a warm smile to her face. I knew she'd like the card. I dated the card Monday, April 10, 1967.

As I left the shop, a newspaper caught my attention. The headlines reported a milestone in the Vietnam War. The 500th US airplane had been shot down over North Vietnam.[2] The planes lost represented a $1 billion US investment over the previous thirty-two months. The war was getting closer.

Flight 117 headed into a pre-dawn sky at 0500 hours. My tour of duty in Vietnam would soon begin. Three hundred sixty-five days filled with uncertainties. I reached into my pocket and pulled out my plastic mini statue of St. Anthony, praying that he'd intercede for me and ask God for His protection.

Next stop, Vietnam.

CHAPTER 11

IN-COUNTRY

I was startled out of a deep sleep by the whirring sound of gears opening the doors to the plane's landing gear. They reached their down-and-locked position, creating a loud clunk. The plane reacted to the drag they produced. "Gentlemen, this is your captain. We'll be making a steep descent into Cam Ranh Bay this morning. Please remain in your seats and fasten your safety belts. We'll be on the ground shortly."

I squinted as the sun's golden rays pierced the port side cabin windows. I raised my arms, stretching them to their limit. I looked out onto the South China Sea and saw nothing but the beautiful ocean blue. It looked so tranquil. I prayed the time I'd be patrolling those waters on a Swift Boat would remain as peaceful. In the far distance, I saw the silhouette of a large Navy ship. By that time, I gathered land could be seen from the starboard side windows. Fellow servicemen extended their necks, attempting to catch a glimpse of the land that awaited them.

The plane banked right, in a heading that would soon take us overland. Shortly after it leveled off, I sensed the plane was no longer in a gradual descent but rather plummeting at a sharper angle. An Army sergeant sitting next to Gunner told us that a steep approach was used to limit the chances of the Viet Cong bringing us down with anti-aircraft fire. I didn't know whether to believe him or not. He may have been yanking our chain, assuming we were on our first Vietnam tour.

The plane made a safe landing, and at the end of the runway waited a Jeep with a large white board attached to the back and the words FOLLOW ME painted in large black lettering. As the plane followed the Jeep, it was evident we had landed on a military air base. A train of cargo tugs passed us with loads of bombs, on their way to service awaiting F-4s prior to their next bombing mission. Two F-4 Phantoms rolled by on a parallel taxiway, each carrying a 16,000-pound payload of bombs and rockets.

The plane stopped in an open area of the tarmac. "Welcome to Vietnam," the captain announced. "We'll be deplaning shortly. Try and have a safe visit, gentlemen." No one said a word. We had reached our destination, the Republic of Vietnam. It was Monday, April 10, 1967.

The pilot broke in once again, "A quick reminder, we are now in the Indochina time zone. Turn back your watches by two hours." It had seemed more like dawn, but my Timex displayed 0830 hours. Six-thirty matched the daybreak conditions.

A convoy of what looked like eighteen-wheel cattle trailers pulled up alongside the plane. The troops weren't in a rush; deplaning was taking longer than I expected. Reaching the exit at the back of the plane, I discovered the reason. We were greeted by a blast of hot, muggy air. The smell of diesel exhaust was strong and the loud noise of jets taking off was constant.

Gunner and I followed the crowd. I was stunned to discover the trailers were for us—we were fresh meat being loaded onto cattle trailers. Surprisingly, the inside was modified to include bench seats along the sides. We were taken to a large open hangar.

"Hey, Bean. Let's head that way, a bunch of swabbies over there. That must be our group."

"Makes sense, Gunner," I replied. Our enlisted man white uniforms made it easy to identify the branch of service. It was safe to say sailors made up approximately ten percent of the new arrivals, if not less.

A Navy JG with a clipboard in hand was calling out roll. All present and accounted for, we jumped aboard two cargo trucks—deuce-and-a-halfs—for the ride to the Swift Boat base. A third truck was used to haul our seabags and suitcases. The M35, a 2 1/2-ton military vehicle, was introduced in 1950 and got its nickname from the older World War II GMC CCKW.

Mr. Bergin managed to call shotgun and rode with the driver on our truck. The ride through the base seemed to go on forever. Cam Ranh Bay (CRB) had militarily served the Russians and Japanese as well as the French during various conflicts since 1905. For the United States, as early as 1966, CRB took on the role of a major supply center. Its bay provided superb natural anchorages, and the numerous off-loading docks were ideal for cargo freighters and Navy transport ships. The long runways could handle the Lockheed C-141 Starlifter and the larger Lockheed C-5 Galaxy, both excellent mass transport aircraft. Cam Ranh Bay was also home base for a squadron of P-2 Neptune aerial surveillance aircraft. They too were an integral part of Operation Market Time.

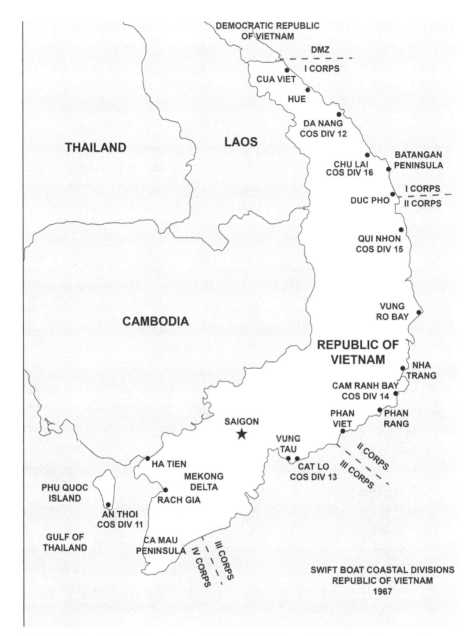

Swift Boat Coastal Division locations—Cam Ranh Bay is located in II Corps. (Image credit: Nathan C. Ryan)

The Swift Boat base was established as PCF Division 104 on April 11, 1966. Eight months later, on January 1, 1967, it became Coastal Division 14. Located in the southern portion of the Second Coastal Zone (II Corps), it was the fourth Market Time Swift Boat base to be set up. After PCF Division 101 was established at An

Thới on October 30, 1965, PCF Division 102 in Da Nang was set up on January 23, 1966, followed by the base at Cat Lo near Saigon, PCF Division 103, on February 12, 1966. The fifth Swift Boat base was established at Qui Nhơn, in the northern half of the Second Coastal Zone (II Corps), as PCF Division 105 on May 2, 1966.

The base complex with all its paved roads was soon left behind. We were now in open country. A group of eight low-flying UH-1 Huey Iroquois helicopters whirled directly over us. The thump-whopping sound their two-blade main rotor made in flight was unique. It was my first real impression of war. I was glad it wasn't the sounds of machine gun fire or explosions. The area had small scrub brush, tree clumps here and there with sandy patches throughout. As we drove further on a hard-packed bumpy road, we entered a dense wooded area. Apprehension set in among the passengers.

Gunner yelled out, "Anyone have a weapon?" All shook their heads. "What the hell are they doing sending us down this road without an Army patrol escort?" I hadn't thought about our unarmed situation, and Gunner's remarks worried me. Every now and again we'd ride next to the shoreline, and just as quick we'd be back in the woods. I wondered if we'd get shot at by a Viet Cong sniper as we traveled the open road.

We approached a pass between two hills. Reaching the crest, the bay appeared in the distance, with its emerald-green waters glistening and beckoning. We drove through another, smaller pass, and a dirt road veered off to the left. It led to the Swift Boat pier. Five PCFs were moored side by side on either side of the pier. Rounding a bend, the naval complex came into view. Not far from base was a white sandy beach. Some were playing volleyball while others swam in the cool surf. My assumption of what the battlefront would look like was shattered—in a good way. For the moment, I felt my tension and apprehension fade.

Long two-story, cream-colored wood barracks, smaller officers quarters, Commander's Division 14 Headquarters (Cos Div 14), and off-duty clubs lined the beach side of the sandy "boulevard." Across the street, larger buildings housed the Naval Support Facility offices and the mess hall. The trucks stopped in front of Cos Div 14 Headquarters. We proceeded to the truck carrying our seabags. Names were called out and each man retrieved his gear. We mustered in front of the headquarters building, where we were received by Lieutenant Edward R. Farrell, Division Commander. To ensure all were present and accounted for, one of his staff called out roll.

"Welcome to the 'Any Time Any Place' Swift Boat Division, gentlemen. My Cos Div 14 staff will be available to answer any questions you may have after you process.

But first, get your morning hunger pains squared away. Mess hall is down the road on your right. Muster back here at 0900 hours. Your gear will be safe. Carry on."

There were no MREs for us sailors. No sir, C-Rats were not on the menu this morning. It was a typical Navy breakfast chow line—scrambled eggs, bacon, sausage, toast, biscuits, grits, and of course the famed "shit on a shingle." SOS, as well known by most who have served in the military, was a quick hot meal consisting of chipped beef in a creamy sauce over toast. Coffee, milk, and orange juice were also available.

At 0900 sharp, Lieutenant Farrell came out to greet us. "Gentlemen, most of you are on transit status. Expect to be here two or three days. After you are dismissed, my staff will take you to an assigned barrack. Drop your gear and proceed to Disbursing, where you will convert all your greenback currency, change included, to MPC, Military Payment Certificates for those of you not familiar with the acronym. US bills, greenbacks, are forbidden in-country. We don't want Charlie to get his hands on them and buy the weapon that's gonna kill you. Next, stop by sick bay and get your shots records verified and updated if necessary. Oh, and don't leave without getting a supply of anti-malaria pills. For now, you all have on-base liberty until otherwise ordered. Officers, meet back here at 1400 hours for a Market Time briefing. Carry on."

My shots were all in order. The medic gave me a supply of the anti-malaria orange horse pills. I took the pills but stashed them deep down inside my seabag. I heard they produced two or three days of diarrhea. I decided since I'd be on the coast and not in the jungles, I wouldn't need them.

At Disbursing, I turned in all my greenbacks for MPC. Everyone called it Funny Money. Series 641 MPCs, issued on August 31, 1965, were available in one, five, and ten-dollar bill equivalents. Loose change was also converted to notes in corresponding amounts of five, ten, twenty-five, and fifty cents. The twenty-dollar MPC wouldn't be released until Series 651 was issued on April 28, 1969. Issue dates were always kept confidential to prevent neighboring countries from using it as primary currency, forcing devaluation elsewhere. This would also keep people from hoarding large sums. On conversion day, C-Day as it was called, all previous MPC series bills became worthless.

It was noon by the time Gunner and I made all the rounds, picked a bunk at the barracks, and settled in for the time being.

"Let's get some chow, Gunner. After lunch we can head down to the beach."

"Great idea, Bean. We may as well take advantage of this vacation. It might be the last time we can take in some relaxation."

Prior to joining the Navy, the only beach I had ever been to was Padre Island along the southern Texas coast. There was no comparison. This beach was straight out of a Bahamas travel brochure. Like the absence of combat upon our arrival, however, something was missing on this gorgeous white sandy beach . . . girls, females, chicks, *rucas*. We made the best of the afternoon, playing volleyball, swimming in the bay, and beachcombing.

After evening chow, we caught up with Mr. Bergin. He had me fetch Porky and Boats before they bellied up to the bar at the Acey Deucey, a club for E-5 and E-6 enlisted men.

"Did you get a chance to go down to the beach?" Mr. Bergin asked.

"Bob and I went, sir. Had a great time."

"After the officers briefing, I went down to the far end. Found an extremely large cone shell. The water is clearer here than those in Puerto Rico." Mr. Bergin paused and turned to look at Porky and Boats. "I expect you to be on your best behavior. I can't afford for our crew to be left behind. Am I clear, Boats?"

"Yes, sir," Boats replied.

"Don't think for one minute that we're safe here either. Lieutenant Farrell advised us that Korean Marines swept a peninsula above here recently and three VC were captured. The enemy is always at striking distance, so stay alert, crew."

"I thought all of this was part of Cam Ranh Bay—you know, inside the perimeter?"

"It is, Bean, but the enemy still sneaks in and blows things up. They're called sappers. Lieutenant Farrell also told us about a VC lieutenant who surrendered. He told them he was angry at his commanders because they wouldn't give orders to blow up specific targets on base. He knew the complex well, pointing out every bunker location, guard posts, and patrols. Hell, he even stayed to watch a movie one night. So, heads up, men."

During the day Vietnamese workers on base carried out barracks-cleaning chores, operating the laundry facility, and washing dishes in the mess hall scullery. Any one of them could be a VC operative. The North Vietnamese Army troops (NVA) wore uniforms, but the VC dressed the same as all common villagers did—loose-fitting black silk pants called *quần lãnh* and thin black button-down long-sleeve shirts. The ladies often wore light pastel button-down long-sleeve blouses in addition to the basic black. Most notable were their conical hats called *nón lá* (leaf hat). Their footwear generally consisted of various styles of sandals, including their favorite which had tire tread soles. I didn't find it comforting to realize that the only thing distinguishing these smiling Vietnamese workers from VCs was a K-44 rifle.

Our mini vacation was over. For Swifties, in-country travel between major facilities was via cargo / troop transport carriers like the C-47 or the C-130. On Friday, we and two other crews boarded a "Bou" for the 290-mile ride north to Da Nang.

"Bou" was the nickname used for the twin-engine C-7 Caribou. We had been assigned to Coastal Division 12 in the First Coastal Zone (I Corps), South Vietnam's northernmost sector.

From the air, Da Nang appeared to be a thriving city. The air base was located at the southern edge of a huge bay called Vung Da Nang. Son Tra Peninsula was a prominent landmark that defined the southeastern side of the bay. In 1966, the Air Force began operating a tactical control center for all air missions over North Vietnam. As early as 1965, American troops began calling it Monkey Mountain because of the abundant number of unique monkeys called red-shanked doucs who found the forested mountain a natural habitat.

After gathering our gear, we boarded a haze-gray Navy bus for the twenty-minute ride to the Swift Boat base. The bus was like the ones school kids rode back home, with one other major difference—the windows were screened with tight wire mesh. VC sappers were known to drive by fast on motorcycles and toss hand grenades through the open windows.

The drive through the base facility did not take as long as it had in Cam Ranh Bay. Inside the base, the sights and sounds were familiar. Diesel exhaust fumes were becoming the most prevalent war zone essence during my first four days in-country. As we left the base perimeter, we saw Vietnamese actively going about their business. Men on bicycles carrying produce fought for space with cars, trucks, and buses.

At many of the small markets and open-air stores, women sold their merchandise from an odd-looking squatting position, their bottoms resting on their heels. Men assumed this position as well, not only while working but also as they drank a beverage or smoked with friends. If I attempted to assume that posture, I know I'd roll onto my back instantly.

We reached the downtown area, and two- and three-story buildings appeared on both sides of wider streets. Beautiful high school girls dressed in white *áo dàis*, the country's traditional attire for women, walked in groups with books clutched in their arms. I'd never seen anything like this before. It was a two-piece garment consisting of a form-fitting top with a mandarin collar and long sleeves. Slits on both sides of the ankle-length bottom created panels front and back that flowed with the breeze, exposing the young ladies' white silk pants. Although the *áo dài* entirely covered the young lady's body, it had a unique way of displaying everything.

Some wore conical-shaped hats with colorful chin straps. Others allowed their silky-smooth black hair to flow naturally past their shoulders. Many of the younger women on the streets in Da Nang carried a marked French influence in their appearance.

The driver pulled over to the side of the road and stopped shy of the entrance to what appeared to be a US compound. "This is Camp Tien Sha," he said. "It's an old French base, now being used as a Navy housing compound. Drop by later and check out what's available on base. If you can overlook the occasional sniper fire and the hit-and-go mortar rounds, you can relax and enjoy time off there."

Within minutes we turned left onto a road leading to the US Navy piers. Three vessels stood out from the rest: two-story barges that resembled Noah's ark. "APL-5 on the far end will be your sleeping quarters—officers and enlisted," the driver informed us. "So that you FNGs don't assume that I'm only a brainless slug bus driver, I'll have you know the official Navy designation is Auxiliary Personnel Lighter (APL), but we call it the 'Apple.' Tell the master at arms you're the new Swift Boat crews checking in, and he'll get you squared away."

On my way off the bus, I stopped and asked the driver, "By the way, what's an FNG?"

He broke into laughter. "Oh, that's what we call all in-country 'fresh meat.' You know, Fucking New Guys!"

Each APL was maintained by a crew of six officers and sixty-six enlisted men. There was berthing for 583 personnel. Heads and showers were located along the outer bulkhead areas. In the middle, rows of sling-fabric bunks, stacked three high, served as bedding. The berthing areas were capable of handling stacks of five racks, but only three were being used. The bottom and top racks were used for storage.

The officers took up residence in the Chief Petty Officers area. There, the bedding arrangement was like that for the enlisted. Scuttlebutt had it that one distinguished JG from the Boston area, not happy with the accommodations, requested a private room with a bay view, but his request chit never made it up the chain of command. The APL was a floating hotel, complete with mess hall, infirmary, barbershop, and laundry. Best of all . . . it was air-conditioned. What a war!

Mr. Bergin took our orders and turned them in to Personnel at the Cos Div 12 office, located on an adjoining barge, the YR-71. It was a non-self-propelled floating workshop. A larger floating repair facility, the YFNB-2, was moored to the same pier behind the YR-71. Both were responsible for all necessary repairs the Swift Boats and eighty-two-foot Coast Guard cutters required. The sea tug USS *Tillamook* III (ATA-192) had towed these two floating repair facilities from Subic Bay, reaching Da Nang in December 1965. Coast Guard Division Twelve had arrived in Da Nang on July 21, 1965.

Swift Boat Coastal Division Twelve's motto was "For Freedom We Fight." Established first as PCF Division 102 on January 16, 1966, Daniel J. Houton commanded the first six Swifts, PCFs 13 through 18. By the end of July, there were seventeen Swift Boats operating in nine patrol areas out of Da Nang. Coastal surveillance responsibilities along the 250-mile coastline extended south from the DMZ to approximately sixty miles north of Qui Nhơn, which coincided with the southern limit of the First Coastal Zone's (I Corps) tactical zone.

Due to the distances to reach the farthest patrol areas from Da Nang, two detachments were created. The Chu Lai Detachment, fifty-five miles to the southeast, was established on May 15, 1966, with Lieutenant Patrick S. Grafton in charge. The Huế Detachment, fifty-three miles to the northwest, was established on August 20, 1966. By early December, there were nineteen Swift Boats assigned to Cos Div 12. Lieutenant Joseph Lawrence Sestric took over as division commander on October 29.

The division office wasted no time in tossing six strips of fresh bacon into the frying pan. Our crew was scheduled to start patrolling individually as extras with experienced crews the following day. I spent the rest of the day getting settled into my confined space. I was surprised to learn that my footlocker had arrived along with my seabag. The rack I was assigned was located against the back side of a row of lockers. The top of the metal locker was a perfect place for my green trunk.

"You brought a record player, albums, and 45s to the war, Bean?" Gunner asked, laughing in disbelief.

"Hell yeah! I can't be without my Chicano music, dude. I've got oldies too!"

On one of my trips back to San Antonio, I had purchased a portable, battery-operated radio-phonograph. In Coronado, we were advised that in addition to our seabag, we could ship our belongings in footlockers. They didn't have to tell me twice. I wasn't aware we'd be living in a floating hotel. Regardless, the possibility of living aboard a Swift Boat and toting along a clumsy footlocker hadn't fazed me a bit.

As evening came, I grew apprehensive, not knowing what to expect the next day. I wondered if we'd engage the enemy in a firefight on my first patrol. My stomach reacted to unending morbid scenarios that crossed my mind. I searched my seabag and found the plastic St. Anthony statue. It would have to save me now.

CHAPTER 12

THE 79 BOAT

The day I went on my first Swift Boat patrol was April 15—Tax Day. After morning chow, I made my way across APL twenty-seven and thirty and onto the dock. It was a short walk to the pier where the YR-71 and YFNB-2 were moored. PCFs and Coast Guard WPBs were tied up outboard these repair vessels. I went to my assigned boat, saluted the officer, and went aboard. The crew was busy with underway preparations. The OIC called to his radioman and directed him to run me through the pre-patrol duties for the radio and radar. He suggested I shadow him and ask all the questions I wanted on this patrol. There would be one more dry-run patrol where I'd be carrying out the equipment checks under his watchful eye.

Departing Da Nang harbor, we commenced a northwest heading toward the One-Delta patrol area. Its northern limit was the Perfume River, the entrance to Huế, Vietnam's imperial capital until 1945. It was approximately a fifty-mile trip. Approaching the river mouth, I found the shore was like the Texas coast, made up of narrow irregular-shaped islands with sandy beaches all along. In sharp contrast to the Texas shoreline, however, an abundance of palm trees and lush green foliage sprang up beyond the sand dunes.

The day was spent stopping and inspecting fishing junks. Before the first one the crew put on flak jackets and helmets and proceeded to their battle stations. Mount (MT) 51 was the twin .50 caliber machine gun station. The over-under single .50 caliber machine gun and 81 mm mortar was called MT 52 and was manned by two crewmen. Another crewman was designated to man the wheelhouse, or pilothouse as the crew called it. The OIC stood on the narrow catwalk, next to the after-steering on the port side. The fifth crewman held an M16 at the ready and stood on the bow, by the pilothouse window. The port side door was always secured and windows on the port side were closed to prevent a grenade from being tossed into the boat. If a Vietnamese Navy liaison officer was onboard, he would stand near the OIC.

The boat's siren sounded as we approached the junk at minimum speed. The helmsman pulled back on the throttles momentarily, bringing the PCF to a full stop a short distance away from the fishermen. The OIC motioned to them to come alongside. Stretching his arm out, palm down, and bending his hand at the wrist in a rapid up and down paddle movement, he said, "*Lại đây. Lại đây mau!*" As ordered, they maneuvered toward the PCF quickly.

The fishing vessel was a narrow twenty-five-foot weathered-wood boat with a flat board deck. An opening in the center exposed a small engine. Four males were on board, one standing thigh-high in the middle of their nylon fishing nets with four-inch red and blue elongated floats attached. Three young adult men wore black long-sleeve button-down shirts, black shorts, and were barefoot. The fourth was perhaps twelve years old and wore a blue-and-white-checkered shirt and black shorts. He stood motionless, looking anxiously at his family members. The one next to him patted the boy's shoulder, uttering presumably calming words.

Using a stern tone, the young Vietnamese Navy liaison officer demanded documents from each one of them. The lead fishermen slowly reached into a box and pulled out a large plastic bag containing their papers. His hands trembled as he struggled to get out the documents. Our liaison officer yelled out names, and each one of the fishermen responded accordingly. He then asked them questions. With fear in their voices, they each took turns responding. Satisfied, he handed the credentials back and allowed them to return to their work. Grateful to be released, the fishermen clasped their hands in prayer fashion, thanked the boat officer by bowing toward him repeatedly saying, "*Cảm ơn Ông, cảm ơn Ông.*"

My mood changed from trepidation to sadness during the board and search procedure. Vietnamese fishermen endured this routine day after day. All they were doing was trying to earn a living and feed their families. On the other hand, these innocent-looking fishermen could very well be VC sympathizers, transiting the area, attempting to deliver arms or Viet Cong troops along the coast. The enemy was known to threaten to kill a fisherman's parents, grandparents, or children if they refused. This routine Market Time task was anything but safe.

I lost count of the number of boring runs we made from one end of the patrol area to the other and back again. Under those monotonous conditions, it was easy to become lax in our stop and search posture. Halfway through one of the patrol area runs, the OIC pulled away from shore and headed for the open sea, where he placed the throttles in an idle position. We went dead in the water. Sandwiches kept in the small reefer (fridge) in the cabin were passed around along with "bug juice" (Kool-Aid) or coffee.

Soon the sun dropping behind the western horizon cast long shadows off the trees along the shoreline. A train of faint lanterns from village-bound junks blinked near the river mouth like fireflies on a hot summer night back home. I was given the okay to crash on one of the racks for a while. I hadn't been asleep long before the loud order of general quarters thrust me to my feet. Dazed, I managed to put on a flak jacket and a helmet. On the way out of the cabin's back hatch, I grabbed an M16. Countless numbers of times I had practiced this procedure in Coronado, but this night adrenaline engulfed my body. I anticipated the clatter of machine guns at any moment.

We were heading south at top speed. I struggled to see anything in the darkness beyond the bioluminescent glow of the saltwater spray, created by the bow as it crashed through two-foot seas. It was a captivating sight. The leading outward edge of the splash was a brilliant white, and below it was a vibrant, glowing emerald light. The twin props also left a temporary shimmering path behind the boat. I took up a safe position by the recessed rear cabin hatch, between the two vertical engine room ventilation louvers.

The OIC pulled back on the throttles, allowing the sea to bring us to a stop. Two crewmen assigned to MT 52 removed the gun mount cover. One of them lifted the mortar storage box lid and made ready two 81 mm illumination rounds and five High Explosive (HE). While this was going on, the OIC, driving the boat from the pilothouse, turned us about and placed the bow into the oncoming waves.

Streams of red tracers pierced the darkness from right to left, while sporadic bursts of enemy green tracers sped horizontally across the sky in the opposite direction. It was a bitchin' sight to see, and I was glad we were off the beach and out of harm's way. I wondered what the soldiers on the ground might be feeling, though.

The OIC, MT 51, and mortar captain communicated with each other via voice-activated headsets. The assistant held a flashlight as the MT 52 captain lowered the back of the mortar and set the vertical angle provided by the boat officer. He swung the mortar mount 90 degrees to port, facing inland. The loader grabbed the first illumination round and made setting adjustments. On order, he raised it above his head and gently positioned the fins into the barrel.

The OIC throttled the engines, placing the boat at the correct heading, then called out the "Fire" command. The MT 52 captain repeated the order aloud, "Fire," and the assistant lowered the projectile farther down the tube, then released it, lowering his head away from the mortar barrel at the same time. The aluminum deck trembled as the round blasted out of the barrel. Harnessed to a parachute, the illumination-round floated toward the ground, leaving behind a small smoke trail. The bright glowing flare hovered in the sky, casting an eerie amber glow on the immediate ground area below. Following the second round of illumination, the OIC directed the MT 52 team to discharge the five rounds of HE at will.

The OIC walked along the port side and hollered at the crew, "Secure GQ. Bravo Zulu, well done, men." Both gun mounts were covered, mortar canisters were thrown over the side, and we continued our routine patrol. Either the enemy retreated, or they were killed by the HE rounds fired by our crewmen. Regardless, the green enemy tracers ended. I did not feel any remorse about the enemy soldiers who died by our fire support action. Green tracers were the enemy, and we had stopped them. Nine days after arriving in-country, I had finally seen war.

I climbed atop the boat cabin and sat up against the backside of the guntub. I lost my desire to sleep—combat will do that to you. As the PCF cruised in a northerly direction, I witnessed isolated firefights in different areas farther inland. Rockets fired from attack helicopters left bright red trails against the dark sky. Being part of a combat boat crew in action gave me a sense of euphoric invincibility.

I remembered a story we were told two weeks prior to the end of our training. A Swift Boat had claimed a victory over a North Vietnamese steel-hulled resupply vessel. The class became ecstatic upon hearing the news. You would have thought Navy had just beat Army in football. After all, intercepting and capturing a North Vietnamese resupply trawler was at the top of the Operation Market Time priority list. We were all pumped up, eager to engage the enemy on the high seas. I fantasized being aboard that Swift Boat, PCF-78, when the capture took place.

March 14, 1967 Trawler

At a quarter past midnight, Patrol Squadron 46 aerial surveillance patrol aircraft detected an unlighted surface contact approximately forty miles east-northeast of Cù Lao Ré Island. The island, only fourteen miles from the mainland, was used as a navigational landmark by ships of all kinds. The contact was running darken ship and on a northwesterly heading. The Market Time aircraft maintained surveillance on the suspicious seaborne unit.[1]

Five months shy of his thirty-sixth birthday, Lieutenant Commander Charles P.

Pfarrer Jr. was the commanding officer of the USS *Brister* (DER 327). He ordered his ship to set a vector course to intercept the vessel using coordinates provided by the Market Time aircraft. During the next several hours, the contact erratically changed courses and speeds. The *Brister* Combat Information Center's (CIC) radar picked up the suspicious unit at 0403 hours, ten miles southeast of Cù Lao Ré.

Lieutenant Commander Pfarrer requested the Coast Guard Cutter *Point Ellis* (WPB-82330) and Swift Boat PCF-78 head toward an area north of Mui Batangan, a peninsula in Quảng Ngãi Province. Based out of the Chu Lai Swift Boat Detachment, PCF-78 was on the northern patrol limit of this area. The unidentified vessel changed course again at 0420 hours. It was on a heading of 285 degrees and making an apparent run for a sandy stretch of beach north of the Mui Batangan Peninsula. The surveillance plane dropped flares over the contact at 0430 hours and identified it as a steel-hulled trawler.

Engineman Second Class Kenneth E. Gooding Jr. was at the helm in the pilothouse of PCF-78. Standing to his right was Radioman Third Class Andrew Bunk. As they began heading south, Gooding sent Bunk down into the cabin to alert PCF-78 Skipper Lieutenant Junior Grade Frank Kelly McCutchen Jr. Gooding quickly brought their skipper up to speed on the developments. Observing the illumination seaward of their position, McCutchen ordered Gooding to set course inward of the descending flare. On the PCF-78 radarscope, a large contact appeared seaward of a smaller blip. The larger return was presumed to be the destroyer.

The *Brister* challenged the suspected communist aggressor using flashing light signals but drew no response. They fired warning shots across its bow and still no counter reaction. With the enemy trawler entering shallow waters, the *Brister* directed PCF-78 and the *Point Ellis* to challenge and intercept.

Unaware that the contact had ignored challenge attempts and warning shots across its bow, EN2 Gooding maneuvered PCF-78 into a position astern of the contact at 0540 hours and closed on the vessel. At fifty yards from the target, OIC McCutchen ordered Gooding to illuminate it with their spotlight, mounted on top of the pilothouse. This action drew an immediate response from the North Vietnamese gunrunner: it turned hard to port. Eight to ten crewmen ran to various positions on the vessel. On the fantail, a couple of seamen were busy around a large, covered object.

Gooding, suspecting it was a crew-served weapon being uncovered, hollered at his crewmates to take cover, as he turned the wheel hard to starboard and slammed the engine throttles forward. They were moving away fast from the enemy ship when a recoilless rifle round was fired, narrowly missing them. The PCF, however, was hit by twelve rounds of automatic weapons fire. The loud impact of the machine gun rounds in various parts of the PCF and engines at full throttle awoke the remaining crew, sending everyone to their designated battle stations. They donned combat gear, uncovered MT 51 and MT 52, and prepared for action.

"Article, Article, this is Ledger India 78, receiving fire from a steel-hulled trawler, north side of Batangan," the skipper screamed into the mike.

Lieutenant Junior Grade Anthony "Tony" R. Taylor, OIC on PCF-16 and patrolling the adjacent area south of Mui Batangan, heard Gooding's call to radio net control in Da Nang and immediately ordered his crew to their GQ stations and headed north at full speed to render support.

At 0612 hours, the trawler opened fire on the *Brister*. Seaman Denis Baker, the weapons yeoman, was on the fly bridge. Using a sound-powered headset, he passed firing information from Lieutenant Commander Pfarrer to the 3"/50 battery. Baker also manned a machine gun and directed .30 and .50 caliber machine gun fire at the enemy ship. The gunrunner ran aground five minutes later, one mile south of Phước Thiện village and approximately sixty miles southeast of Da Nang. PCF-78 and the *Point Ellis* took the steel-hulled vessel under heavy machine gun and 81 mm mortar fire.

On Lieutenant Commander Pfarrer's order, the boatswain's mate of the watch piped "All Hands" via the 1MC, the ship's internal intercom, and announced, "Away the steel-hulled boarding party." The crew, comprised of a junior officer and seven enlisted men, mustered topside on the starboard. The coxswain, engineer, and bow hook boarded the motor whale boat. The remainder of the team stood by, waiting for the "Launch Motor Whale Boat" command to be given. Only one crewman was missing, a boatswain's mate.

The ship's electronics tech–radar and communications specialist, ETR2 Dan Embree, was loaded down with gear—helmet, flak jacket, .45mm revolver, bayonet, flashlight, clipboard, PRC-10 radio, and a Mae West (the moniker given to the first inflatable personal floatation device, so called because once inflated, the air-filled compartments made the person wearing it look well-endowed like the famed actress).

The missing bosun had been asleep and didn't hear the call on the 1MC. The order to launch was finally issued at 0630 hours. The *Brister* took position, port side to the beached trawler, protecting the motor whale boat and crew. Secured at the bow and stern by davits, the boat was carefully moved over the side and partially lowered to match the deck level. The remainder of the crew went aboard the boat, each one grabbing onto the monkey ropes hanging the length of the small boat as it began its descent.

Their goal, in addition to boarding the captured vessel and retrieving valuable intel documents, was to secure towing lines to the trawler so it could be taken out to deep water where salvage operations could safely take place.

At 0655 hours, the motor whale boat was about to cross the *Brister*'s bow when a huge blast occurred. Lieutenant Taylor's PCF-16 was rounding the tip of Mui Batangan at the same time. His crew heard the explosion, looked north, and happened to catch the detonation cloud rising in the distance. Debris showered the deck of the *Brister.* Had the boarding party been lowered immediately when called away, they would have been alongside the trawler and surely all would have been killed by the massive self-destruct charge.

As the Swift Boats and the *Point Ellis* collected salvageable debris, Puff—the Air Force AC-47 attack plane—took the area behind the beach under immense machine gun fire, having observed personnel running through a clump of trees. When Puff departed the scene, "fast movers" came in and dumped bombs and napalm in the same location. Lieutenant Taylor continued laying suppressive machine gun fire for the next forty minutes, while waiting for another Swift Boat from Chu Lai to arrive with an underwater demolition team (UDT) aboard. They found very little in the surf line: the largest piece of the trawler was a seven feet by fifteen feet portion of the hull.

Recovered smuggled goods included: one heavy machine gun, one 57 mm recoilless rifle, thirty sub-machine guns, one case of claymore mines, 1,200 carbines, 5,000 hand grenades, detonation devices, assorted ammunition for small arms, recoilless rifles, a 60 mm mortar, and a variety of medical supplies.

My first experience aboard a Swift Boat turned out to be more than I expected. I hoped to see destroyers conducting gunfire support missions, or attack helo gunships' red tracers and rocket trails in the night as they hit ground enemy positions. Little did I know I would get a firsthand opportunity on that initial patrol.

The war became personal. I was on a Swift Boat that actively participated in a gunfire mission. I witnessed the muzzle flash of 81 mm mortar rounds being fired and heard the excitement in the voices of the sailors on the boat as they prepared the rounds and dropped them into the elevated barrel in rapid succession.

It was an exhausting twenty-four hours. Regardless, going out with an experienced crew proved beneficial. It helped me get a feel for what to expect when our crew went out on our own twenty-four-hour patrol. I was eager to carry out a hands-on attempt at pre-check procedures. I would get that opportunity the following day.

Both PCFs and WPBs were moored portside to the YFNB's starboard side and facing the quay wall less than fifty feet away. My assigned boat was on the outside rear corner of the boat nest. The crew's radioman stood by me as I went through all my assigned duties. Upon completing my task, he gave his approval. I reported to the OIC that all radio, radar, and fathometer checks had been completed and we were ready to get underway. The OIC took control of the after-maneuvering station helm after all patrol ready reports were made. I stood by the starboard side vertical engine vent at the rear of the main cabin.

"Take in all lines," the OIC ordered.

"Bow line on deck, sir," hollered the seaman from the bow.

"After line secure, sir," the engineman said, wrapping the mooring rope to the port-quarter cleat.

The skipper spun the helm left full rudder, checked for boat traffic behind him, then placed both hands on the throttles. A notch inside the throttle housing kept both engines in the vertical neutral position. He tapped the starboard engine handle forward to a second notch that placed the shaft in gear at idle speed. He simultaneously did the same with the port lever but in the aft direction. The fantail swung about toward starboard. The rudders were brought back to center positions and, with his right hand on the wheel, the boat officer pulled back on the starboard throttle, placing it on the aft notch. The boat slowly backed away from the PCF nest and sailed into maneuverable waters.

The engines rumbled as the skipper pushed forward on the port engine and turned the wheel hard to starboard. The bow eventually pointed us toward the open bay. Soon we were beyond the harbor. The patrol was boringly routine—no detainees, no contraband, and no calls for fire support from friendly units ashore.

We returned to base the following morning, carried out post-patrol duties, and ordered to secure by the leading petty officer (LPO). I found myself more relaxed, having carried out most of the radio communications while out at sea. I felt I was part of the crew. I could write home to my parents and tell them: I was now officially a Swift Boat sailor.

April 20, 1967, was a milestone for Swift Boat Crew 74-A. It marked the day we went out on a crew qualifying patrol. I was ready. Nonetheless, I felt like I was back at Holy Cross the night before a final exam.

"Get your lazy ass outta that rack, Bean," Boats rumbled. "You too, Gunner. Shower up, get some chow, and head down to the PCFs. We're getting qualified today." Navy-issue milk-glass coffee mug in his right hand, Carver walked away but stopped and turned. "Oh, Bean. Pass by the galley and pick up stores for the patrol. Get food for seven."

"Got it, Boats," I moaned as I took my last stretch. "Let's go, Gunner, gotta hustle."

"What's the rush, Bean? They won't leave without me, I'm the gunner, remember?"

"Smart ass. Radioman or gunner, we need to get down there on time."

After chow, Gunner went on ahead while I gathered sandwiches, chips, bug juice, fresh fruit, and ground coffee for the twenty-four-hour patrol. Arriving at the assigned boat, I noticed the crew was already on board, including a new face.

"Mornin', Skipper," I said, saluting Mr. Bergin.

"Bean, this is McNamara. He's our sixth crewman."

"Hey, my name is Raúl."

"Like hell you are," Boats chimed in from inside the cabin. "You're Bean and that's all there is to it."

"I'm Tim, but everyone who knows me calls me Mac."

He grabbed some of the stores I was carrying, and we both headed down into the main cabin. Without being asked, he began organizing things.

"Just get in-country, Mac?"

"Nope. Been here a year already. I extended," he firmly stated.

"Extended?" I exclaimed. "What the hell drove you to stay in this miserable place for twelve more months, man?"

"Long story," he said and left it at that. He seemed flustered by my remark, and I decided to leave well enough alone. Besides, I had work to do.

Having checked the lubricating fluid level in the radar motor housing, I went to the fantail. The twin General Motors V-12 Detroit marine diesels were humming. The two exhaust flaps at the waterline on the fantail were busy playing their standard rumble and clanking tune. Next to the mesmerizing smell of expelled diesel fumes, the rhythmic clatter of the exhaust flaps on the fantail waterline made Swift Boat sailors feel right at home.

Porky was sitting on top of the ammo locker. A half-smoked Lucky Strike hung from the corner of his mouth.

"Onan fired up, Porky? I need to get the radar and radios going."

Porky's unique conversational skills danced between cynical and sarcastic notes. I found his dry sense of humor entertaining.

"Do bears shit in the woods, Bean?" he replied.

"Good. I'll light 'em up, then."

I fired up the Decca D202 radar unit in the pilothouse. It was located to the right of the helmsman's seat, and a black rubber bonnet surrounded the scope. The shroud helped keep glare off the screen during the day, and it toned down the orange glow in the dark of night. The unit had a maximum range scale of twenty-four miles. Steel-hulled trawlers could be 90 percent detected at a five-mile range. Verifying the operable condition of the Raytheon DE176A Fathometer was also one of my assigned tasks. The 240-foot maximum-depth capability would never be of use to us. Instead, patrolling the shoreline required accurate shallow depth readings, as the navigation charts didn't always prove accurate. The last thing we wanted was to run aground within firing range of the Viet Cong.

The 3.0 kW Model 3DJA-1E Onan generator ran our radios, radar, fathometer, and running lights. It also kept food in our small reefer cold. There were two radios aboard each Swift Boat. The main unit was the AN/URC-58 single sideband radio. It was shelf-mounted in the main cabin on the starboard side bulkhead. A remote speaker and microphone were installed in the pilothouse. Swift Boats on patrol used this radio when communicating with base net. Article was the Northern Surveillance Group's call sign, and it had radio communication control over all Market Time units in I Corps.

A field radio, the AN/PRC-10/25 FM unit, was our secondary means of communication. The Prick 10, as we called it, was used in establishing comms with adjacent patrol boats, shore units, and aircraft. My final task was to conduct a radio check with Article.

I was finishing my pre-underway checks when Mr. Bergin called us to the fantail.

"Crew, this is Lieutenant Herriott. He'll be our evaluator on this patrol."

"Glad to be along for the ride, Ed. Gentlemen, we're headed to the first patrol area north of the harbor entrance. I don't expect to meet up with Charlie today, so relax. Carry on as usual."

"Bean, Mac, prepare to cast away lines forward and aft," Mr. Bergin ordered.

After releasing the aft mooring line, I went into the cabin and raised Article on the AN/URC-58 single sideband radio, advising them we were headed to the One Echo patrol area.

While well underway, Boats passed the word down from Mr. Bergin for us to stay sharp. Our evaluator, Lieutenant Jack Adair Herriott, happened to be the Coastal Division 12 Executive Officer and served as the Division Operations Officer.

The patrol included emergency steering procedures, navigation chart practice, radio communications and frequencies, nighttime radar navigation, knowledge of decoding message procedures (CAC), junk inspection, and mortar illumination. In addition, we learned the location of Vietnamese junk base locations, identification

of friendly large contacts on radar, combat tactics, simulated general quarters procedures, and conducted man overboard exercises.

At the end of our patrol the following morning, Mr. Bergin took the after-steering
controls and brought us alongside one of the PCFs in the nest of Swifts tied up next
to the YFNB-2. Lieutenant Herriott mustered us on the fantail.

"Congratulations, Mr. Bergin, you and your crew did well on your qualifying
run. You will learn more each time you're out on station. I'm recommending that
you are ready to assume full patrol duties. Bravo Zulu. Oh, one last thing, don't relax
your combat-ready posture, no matter how many junks you inspect in an hour, in
one afternoon, or all day. Carry on."

"Well done, crew," Mr. Bergin acknowledged. "Boats, when all post-patrol assignments are complete, you can release the crew."

Since the establishment of PCF Division 102 in Da Nang in mid-January 1966,
crews were assigned boats for each patrol. One and a half crews per boat was determined to give adequate down time for crews between patrols, twenty-four hours
on, twenty-four hours off. The crew–boat rotation arrangement soon led to poor
boat maintenance, though. Exhausted crews, returning from patrol, would leave
the boat without a post-patrol cleanup or required maintenance—it wasn't their
PCF. On August 6, that same year, the division commander, Lieutenant Daniel
Joseph Houton, initiated a new strategy. Seventeen senior Swift Boat officers were
assigned their own PCFs. Henceforth, the crews developed a special pride in their
boats, maintaining them in the best operational shape possible. Junior OICs who
took these boats out on patrol ensured the PCF was returned in the same condition
it was in when taken out.

At the end of our crew-qualifying patrol, Porky let me, Gunner, and Mac know
during evening chow that Mr. Bergin wanted us to meet at the YFNB-2 the following
day at 1300 hours. No other details were given. Since patrols went out in the morning,
the order piqued my curiosity.

Mr. Bergin and another boat officer were waiting for us on the catwalk outside
the repair facility barge. "Crew, this is Lieutenant Junior Grade Ray Michilini."

We took turns saluting him as our Skipper introduced us. He continued, "Now
that we've been qualified, we're being assigned our own PCF. Mr. Michilini is here
to turn his boat over to us."[2]

"Afternoon, men. My crew will be here shortly to go over weapons, electronics,
and all other boat particulars you should be aware of."

The mobilization of Swift Boats had been experiencing growing pains. Lieutenant Michilini and other OICs were advised their PCFs were en route to Subic Bay in the Philippines. PCF-79 was one of the boats taken aboard the USS *Gunston Hall* (LSD-5) along with their crews. The 78 and 79 were placed in the well deck, port, and starboard sides accordingly. After making several stops to unload crews and boats at various Swift Boat bases along the coast, PCF-79 and Lieutenant Michilini's crew arrived in Da Nang on July 30, 1966.

Below us alongside the barge were nine Swift Boats tied up to each other, three by three. Occupying the front row were PCFs 16, 56, and 75. Like a boy shopping for a new car with his father, I grew impatient.

"Which one's ours, Mr. Bergin?" I blurted out.

"Oh, sorry, crew," Mr. Michilini interjected. "The 79 Boat will be yours for the next eleven months. You'll be the boat's second crew. Look there, she's the one in the middle row, behind Lou Masterson's 75 Boat."

Michilini's crew arrived, and we all made our way down to the boats. There were only two marked differences between them: the boat number and the paint. Some were weathered and in need of upkeep, but other than that, they were like a school of dolphins, each identical.

Porky crawled into the engine compartment to inspect the propulsion system. Gunner climbed into the guntub, and I stepped down into the cabin with the radio-man to test the radio, followed by the radar system. Mac and Boats checked all boat equipment, including damage control supplies, raft contents, and emergency steering.

Boats Carver and Mac were on the fantail with the boat officers when the radio-man and I finished our checks and joined them.

"Where you from, Ray?"

"New York, born in the city in '41."

"What year did you graduate from the academy?" Bergin asked.

"Ah, you noticed I'm a ring knocker," Michilini chuckled, looking down at his shiny gold Naval Academy ring on his right hand. "Class of '64. I was on a second Med-cruise when I got a surprise set of orders to Swift Boats while we were in port in Malta. There were around twenty crews at the base when I reached Coronado. We were the first group of Swift Boat non-volunteers."

"The boat looks in good shape, Ray. Your crew took good care of her. You must be going home loaded with memories."

"Some good, some God-fearing. In early January, a guy from the Red Cross found me when we got in from patrol. My wife sent a telegram announcing the arrival of our daughter, Christine. That was a great memory.

"On the near tragic side, we met head-on with what was at least a thirty-foot rogue wave during the monsoon. There was no way of avoiding it. We met it straight on. We were part of a support operation up north at Cửa Việt. Exiting the channel, the crew was in the pilothouse wearing life jackets. The wave was so high, it crashed over the guntub. All three front windows were blown out."

"That's a lot of ocean going into the boat, Lieutenant," I stated. "Did you start sinking?"

"No. We managed to get farther away from the turbulent channel entrance and into calmer seas. The bilge pumps performed as they should, and we managed to limp our way south to Huế for repairs."

"Looks like we're in for an adventure," Mr. Bergin remarked.

"Adventure is what you'll get if you're sent south to Chu Lai—that's Indian country. Victor Charlie doesn't give a damn if you're a ring knocker or not. He wants you dead. You stay safe down there."

"I will, Ray. And we'll keep her in good shape—Boats Carver will see to that."

"Well then, the seven-niner is all yours. Let's head ashore," Lieutenant Michilini called to his men.

We stayed on the boat, each of us examining our equipment a bit more and taking note of what was lacking. Mr. Bergin went to the division office with Mr. Michilini to sign boat turnover documents. On my list, I noted the need for new combat charts of the I Corps area and a new logbook. It would be my responsibility to maintain accurate deck log entries for each patrol.

Ten days after landing in Da Nang, April 24, we were en route to area 1-Echo to carry out a Market Time patrol on our own boat. The saga of PCF-79 and Swift Boat Crew 74-A had begun.

During the day, the greater percentage of our time was spent stopping and inspecting fishing junks. Holding an M16 at the ready didn't remove my apprehension. I kept recalling stories about how grenades could be tossed at approaching Swift Boats. I felt tense each time we called a fishing junk alongside.

After lunch, we pulled away from the beach two to three miles, put the bow into the wind, and went dead in the water. Mr. Bergin wanted to test-fire the machine guns on MTs 51 and 52. During the test one of the barrels in the guntub flew out of the support housing.

"What the hell happened, Gunner?" Mr. Bergin yelled. "You didn't set the head spacing correctly, Middleton."

"Like hell I didn't. I know what I'm doing. These are my guns, got my spacing gauge right here. All three barrels were calibrated before we left base."

"Has to be the spacing," Bergin insisted.

Gunner grew livid. "Ever hear of gun barrel fatigue? Barrels develop cracks in the bore near the breech. They've probably never been replaced."[3]

"Don't get testy with me, Gunner."

"Just telling you what I know, Skipper."

Bob's Italian ire was showing. At 6'1" and 180 pounds, he was accustomed to doing the pushing around. He got kicked out of high school twice for fighting. Gunner was a gentle giant, friendly but also stubborn—just like me. Although he was a third-class Petty Officer and I was a seaman, we got along well.

Gunner joined the Navy a year before I did. He volunteered for combat duty on Swift Boats after learning of his close friend's death in Vietnam. SP4 Dominic J. Preira Jr. was killed in action during Operation Masher–White Wing on February 18, 1966. Bob sought retribution for the death of his good friend, also from Burlington, Connecticut. Ironically, one of the shoreline patrol areas out of Chu Lai was in Quảng Ngãi Province, where SP4 Preira died.

That night after dark, we took harassment fire from enemy positions on the beach. Not wanting to push his luck, Mr. Bergin had Boats take us another half mile out to sea. Two miles from the beach placed us at a relatively safe position.

It was getting late, and most fishing junks had already headed back to their villages. For that reason alone, an unlit fishing junk, two miles out to sea, was cause for suspicion. Inspection of the junk found it to be clean, free of any contraband. However, our Vietnamese Navy liaison officer had us detain two of the five men on board. They carried no identification. He suspected they were Viet Cong being transported to another area along the coast. We shackled them to the stanchion posts on the fantail.

Early the next morning, prior to heading back to port, we turned them over to the nearby South Vietnamese junk base. It occurred to me that I could have been face-to-face with the enemy. Their small frail stature was not imposing. They didn't have a killer look about them. I saw them as poor village fishermen, a dangerous misconception.

Upon arrival in port, Lieutenant Bergin was called to the Div Com's office. The crew was about finished with post-patrol cleanup details when Mr. Bergin returned with disheartening news. He mustered us on the fantail.

"Crew, we're being shipped off to Indian country. We've been assigned for a one-month temporary rotation tour to the detachment down south at Chu Lai."

"When do we shove off?" Boats asked.

"Have the boat and crew ready by 0900 hours. Take only necessary gear for four weeks. We'll be coming back to home base after our temporary assignment. Carry on."

We left the Da Nang Swift Boat nest on April 26. It was 1030 hours by the time we pulled away from the YFNB-2. The fantail was loaded with spare parts, supplies, and mail destined for the Chu Lai Swift Boat detachment. I placed the new combat navigational charts for the trip south on the map table in the pilothouse. General reference placed our destination fifty-six miles southeast of Da Nang.

Mr. Bergin was at the helm in the pilothouse while we navigated through Da Nang harbor and out to open water. "Boats, take the wheel. Set course one-five-zero and bring us up to 1850 RPMs."

"Aye, aye," Boats replied, grabbing the helm and pushing forward on the black knobbed throttles. He glanced at the port and starboard RPM gauges, slowly increasing speed until the needles pointed to 1850 RPM. PCFs had no speedometers. We headed south at approximately 21 knots, a tad over 24 mph. As the engines whined, the thrust raised the bow skyward. Ocean spray arched outward on both sides each time the boat slapped through the waves.

Carver leaned back in the elevated, foam-cushioned helmsman's chair and turned toward me. He motioned his right fist in my direction, index finger and thumb bent inward, hand twitching.

That nonverbal order meant that Boats wanted coffee. My ass would be grass if I dared wash his coffee mug—ever. Everyone knew which mug was his. It was the one with the crusty, dark-brownish stain throughout the interior.

Porky was in the cabin, searching the reefer for something to eat. Hooks underneath the wood cabinets above the hot plate held the coffee mugs. It didn't take long to find Carver's.

"Shit, this is disgusting!" I remarked, looking into what had to be his cup.

"Don't you go to washing that one," Porky warned.

"You'd drink out of this?" I asked, tilting the mug toward him. "There's gotta be gnats stuck to the brown tar at the bottom."

"Deck apes are like that, Bean. If there ain't no coffee, just add hot water and you're good to go."

"Okay, I'll bite, what the hell is a deck ape?"

"Got lots of seafaring to learn ya, fella. Navy rats have nicknames—Bosuns are called deck apes. Their job is to keep the ship squared away. I'm engineman, so I'm called a snipe or a grease monkey. You already know Bob Middleton goes by Gunner. They're also called cannon cockers."

"Yeah, Porky, so then why does everyone call me Bean?"

He chuckled, "Well, that's easy. That's a personal handle. Bobby Don baptized you with that name back in Coronado. You remember. If he didn't think much of ya, he wouldn't have done that."

"Does he go only by Boats?"

"I call him Chunky and it doesn't seem to bother him. But if I were you, I'd stick to Boats."

"Yeah, and so radarmen . . . ?"

"Scope dopes. Sparky, or sparks for radiomen."

"I better get this mud up to him before he starts throwing a shit fit."

"Now, don't go to callin' him a deck ape, Bean, or he'll poke you smartly in your snot locker."

Walking toward the pilothouse, I laughed to myself thinking of how in the barrio the *vatos* also used nicknames. We had guys that went by La Pera, Slim, Tomaté, Pee Wee, Moco, and La Mosca.

"Here's your coffee, Boats—black, no sugar, and . . . I didn't wash out your cup," I told him, climbing back into the pilothouse.

"Well, ain't you a darlin'. Thanks, Bean. Now come over here and sit on your sea daddy's lap and be my sea chicken," he begged in a sardonic tone.

"Damn it, Boats, leave Bean alone," Bergin ordered with the start of a gentle smile.

Boats glanced at me and winked. Having never been assigned ship duty since joining the Navy, I was not familiar with the traditional harassment that goes on between crusty seadogs and pollywog sailors aboard ship. There must have been a "Kick Me" sign taped on my back. I kept my disdain towards Boats hidden. Still green in the gills, I knew my place in the Navy's pecking order.

Bobby Don Carver was a beer-bellied, thirty-one-year-old barnacled sailor from Leesville, Louisiana, next door to the Fort Polk Army Base. Bobby Don ran the countryside as a youngster. Like most families in the area, his farmed the land. He attended Simpson Elementary and struggled to maintain average grades. He spent a great deal of his time fighting on the playground.

Bobby Don attempted high school but quickly decided it was not for him. When he wasn't helping a local tree-stumping company, he enjoyed hot-rodding the backwoods around Leesville, often rolling over into ditches next to loose-gravel roads. His father decided the military was the only hope for setting him straight. Boats' parents signed a waiver allowing the Navy to take him at the age of 16.[4]

"So, Boats, how'd you get to be such a hard-ass?" I asked. "Are all bosuns in the Navy like you?"

He laughed. "Mom blamed it on my great-grandmother, Sarah Ann Russell

Carver. She told me Indian blood ran through my veins. Grandaddy'd tell me and my sisters he'd often hear her jabberin' Indian when she'd get ta fussin'."

"What tribe was she from, Boats? I learned about Indian tribes when I was a Boy Scout. What tribes were in Louisiana?"

He glanced at the radar and took a sip of his coffee. "They weren't from our parts. Mississippi, I think. Sister thought Chickasaw or Houma."

It surprised me we were having a civilized conversation. He had a devilish look as he proudly boasted, "Hell, I even chased my sister, Patty Rae, 'round the kitchen with a knife one'st, just to see her get to goin' batshit crazy."

Finding him in a jovial mood, I tested his tolerance. "Well, you best cut me some slack then, or you'll get my Aztec blood to boiling," I teased. "They cut out beating hearts, you know."

"I'm scared already, fucker," he said mockingly. "Now get busy and tell me how far it is to Chu Lai."

I looked at the chart and checked the radar. Several land contacts appeared off our port bow fourteen miles ahead. They were a cluster of small islands leeward of one larger one called Cù Lao Chàm. Our destination was thirty-six miles farther south. Depending on sea conditions, trips to Chu Lai took two hours or less on average. We probably wouldn't make it in time for noon chow.

CHAPTER 13

INDIAN COUNTRY

C hu Lai was a relatively new location on US combat charts in I Corps. It came
into physical being in late April 1965 when the 9th Marine Expeditionary
Brigade was afloat off the coast of Da Nang. They had been activated
and placed on standby in response to the Viet Cong attacks on US advisors in
South Vietnam.

Leading the Marine war effort was Lieutenant General Victor H. Krulak. On
March 1, 1964, he became the Commanding General Fleet Marine Force, Pacific.
Recognizing that I Corps would be the blocking force of an invasion from the north,
he calculated the need for another air base in the northern section of South Vietnam.
Secretary of Defense Robert S. McNamara approved the plan on March 30, and US
Navy ships carefully entered the shallow bay waters of Vũng An Hòa and began
unloading the two-by-twelve-foot aluminum runway matting.

On June 1, the first Douglas A-4 Skyhawk touched down and was brought to a
halt by mobile arresting gear. General Krulak had his air base. That's correct, *his* air
base. Chu Lai is not a Vietnamese word or village name. Rumors abound as to how
the name came about. Long story short, most agree on the myth that claims he used
the Mandarin characters representing his name, Chu Lai.[1]

Our transit to Chu Lai continued. We passed the Sông Cua Dai south of Da Nang,
and except for a gentle ten-mile curve in the shoreline, the beach formed a straight
southeasterly line for the next twenty miles. The only things missing from view were

beach umbrellas and college kids catching rays. Every now and again, small villages peeked through the partially dense tree line beyond the beach.

Two hours after leaving Da Nang, Mui An Hòa lay ahead off our starboard bow. The thin neck of land, which pulled out to sea about a mile and a half, resembled a hammerhead shark on the combat chart. Several dark vertical boulders dotted this area. The strip of land formed the northern edge of Vũng An Hòa. It was a small bay, more like a cove into which the Sông Trường Giang met the South China Sea.

"Boats, the channel entrance is a bit more than a mile past the south end of the peninsula. Watch out for two small outcrops off starboard."

"Good catch, Bean," Mr. Bergin remarked.

"Hey, you might turn out to be a good navigator, after all," Boats added.

After passing a channel buoy, Carver turned the large metal helm to the right. The boat surfed on the crest of each four-foot wave. Carver's handling of the rudders and engine throttles kept the boat from gliding sideways and placed the bow on course down the middle of the channel.

Mr. Bergin stepped out of the pilothouse. "I'll take her in from the fantail, Boats, once we're in the bay."

"Copy, Skipper," he replied. "Bean, Mac, man the fore and aft mooring lines."

Mac headed for the bow and I to the fantail. Rosemary Point was the name of the peninsula on the south side of the channel. It was laced with jagged dark red rocks that resembled huge volcanic pumice. This part of the Chu Lai military complex was home to Naval Support Activity Detachment (NSAD) personnel and to the Cos Div 12 Detachment Swift Boat crews.

The area was totally free of vegetation. Most of the buildings were long two-story unpainted wood structures, presumably barracks. They appeared to be newly constructed. The tin roofs shimmered under the bright sun. The buildings had no windows. Instead, they had louvered wood runs with screen material on the inside. The perimeter was lined with concertina wire and sandbagged bunkers, one for each building. Nearing the end of the channel, I noticed an odd-shaped structure past the last building. It resembled a large, elongated tribal hut with a tall, thatched roof.

Mr. Bergin rolled the helm rapidly from one side to the other, signaling Boats that he had the conn on the fantail. He eased up on the throttles to idle speed and made his final approach toward the floating steel dock, where six PCFs were moored side by side, fantails to the pier. Aboard every boat, crewmen carried out upkeep tasks. Most of the sailors were not wearing the standard Navy work uniform of the day: bell-bottomed dungarees, chambray shirt, blue work cap, and boondockers. Instead, they were shirtless, wore cut-off dungarees, and some wore shower shoes. It must have been obvious to them that we were FNGs from Da Nang since we were uniform of the day compliant. Compared to the by-the-book operation in Da Nang, Chu Lai Swifties seemed to march to their own drummer. After all, it was the entrance to Indian country.

Mr. Bergin worked the throttles and wheel, carefully sliding PCF-79 up against the nearest boat in line.

"Bean, make fast the portside mooring line to the dock cleat," Mr. Bergin ordered.

"Yes, sir," I replied and jumped onto the dock, taking the stern mooring line with me as the fantail bumped gently against the black tire dock fenders. The dock cleat was large enough to support two tie-down ropes, the adjacent PCF and ours. I stepped over to the starboard side, grabbed the mooring line, wrapped two figure-eight turns around the cleat, followed by twisted two half-hitches, one on each end.

"Fantail lines secured, Skipper."

Mac yelled out, "Sideline secured on the bow."

"Porky, shut us down."

"Can't do that, Skipper," Porky responded as he lifted the heavy engine deck cover over the starboard engine. "My girls have to cool off a spell. They've been running hard for the last two hours."

"Roger that, Porky."

A crewman on the adjoining PCF spotted Carver exiting the rear cabin door and called him over.

"Boats, have the 79 patrol ready before releasing the crew," Mr. Bergin ordered.

Carver walked across to the boat alongside without acknowledging the skipper's instructions. He had to have heard our boat officer's order. This wasn't the first time I witnessed Carver's apparent frustration at being told what to do. He didn't seem to take kindly to a JG ordering him around, especially one five years his junior.

Mr. Bergin's eyes narrowed. He grabbed his gear and brown leather briefcase and went ashore. Lieutenant Harold Cowan Griffin Jr. was waiting for him. He had been assigned OIC of the Chu Lai Detachment since mid-April. The two walked to an awaiting Jeep on a terracotta dirt road. The entire area was a dusty reddish-brown.

Mac and I off-loaded the supplies we brought from Da Nang. Without needing introductions, some of the crewmen from adjoining boats helped us. One of them let us know our barracks was the one next to the Straw Elephant, the tribal-looking hut. It was the base EM Club, where E2s, E3s, and third-class petty officers could drink and take in USO shows when they performed. Indian country wasn't looking as bleak as I presumed it would be.

We had the boat squared away with plenty of time to get settled in the barracks prior to evening chow. Gunner and I took up residence in a ten by fifteen cubicle on the ground floor. We quickly broke down the stacked bunks; Gunner took the one by the outside wall and positioned my rack against the hallway partition.

Chow was good, but the mess hall didn't have air conditioning like the APL back in Da Nang. *¡Panza llena, corazón contento!* With a full stomach and a happy heart, it was time to tend to nature's needs. I quickly learned construction on the barracks was not finished—the heads and showers were in place but not functioning. A deluxe ten-seater outhouse had to suffice.

When we arrived, there were only three patrol areas out of Chu Lai. Friday, April 28, was our first patrol. We were assigned the Charlie area, right outside the harbor and to the north, a relatively safe patrol sector. Seven patrols later, most of them back-to-back patrols, we still had not seen any action. On May 12, Lieutenant Junior Grade Lou Masterson, on PCF-75, was in the Delta patrol area. Once again, we had been assigned the Charlie area, and we were approaching our southern patrol limit when we heard radio clatter. It was mid-morning and Lieutenant Masterson, working with a Bird Dog (a spotter aircraft), lobbed mortar rounds and sank an evading sampan. The day had just begun and already they'd made contact with a persistent enemy.

The day was spent inspecting fishing sampans and cargo junks transiting our area. Larger vessels carried produce from small villages along the coast to major markets in places like Quảng Ngãi, Da Nang, and Huế. One of the most unique products transported originated in Phú Quốc Island in the Gulf of Thailand and Phan Thiết, a coastal city northeast of Saigon. The product was a putrid-smelling fish sauce called *nước mắm*, a staple of Vietnamese culture. Layers of sardine-size fish and salt were placed in barrels. Over time, the fish broke down, with the solid pieces falling to the bottom. The final process involved the removal of this matter and passing the liquid through numerous filtering operations. The resulting reddish-amber liquid is *nước mắm*. If we were approaching a cargo junk going north, we knew right away that barrels of *nước mắm* were part of their cargo.

During the night, the radio came alive with excited chatter from home base—Chu Lai was under mortar and recoilless rifle attack from the shoreline across the bay, 600 yards from the Swift Boat dock. It was a hit-and-run attack, short-lived but deadly. One sailor was killed and three were wounded. The enemy had targeted the officer-country barracks, but fortunately, the mortars missed their mark. One other casualty took place on the Swift Boat dock. The washing machine on our pier took a direct hit from a recoilless rifle round.

At daybreak, while approaching our southern boundary, we found a crudely arranged floral wreath floating on the surface. Mr. Bergin speculated that a Viet Cong sympathizer had honored their comrades killed the previous morning in the mortar attack led by Lieutenant Masterson and the crew of PCF-75. The memorial tribute pointed to the probability that at least one of the enemies killed was a supply officer or high-ranking Viet Cong leader. The other possibility was that the Viet Cong were trying to play a game of cat and mouse with us. The wreath could be a trap, anchored to a mine submerged out of site. We circled about and headed north. As we reached the channel into Chu Lai, Lieutenant Masterson reported taking an evading Viet Cong sampan under fire at the mouth of the Sông Sa Kỳ. Mr. Bergin set course south to Mui Batangan.

Gunner spotted the 75 Boat north of Mui Batangan and heading toward us. I climbed atop the pilothouse and sat in front of the guntub. They went dead in the water as we approached. Carver took control of the boat from the fantail. He circled them off their portside, around their stern, and approached their starboard side. Porky and Mac stood by the mooring lines, fore and aft.

I noticed a Navy blanket covering what appeared to be a body lying on the deck, up against the ammo locker on the 75 Boat.

"Bob, check it out, man . . . is that a dead gook on the fantail?"

"Sure as hell looks that way, Bean."

Mr. Bergin stepped outside the port door and looked up toward the guntub. "Bean, that's the last time you or any of my crew uses that term to identify our enemy, dead or alive. It's dehumanizing, same as calling them slopes or dinks. It's not acceptable."

"I hear it all the time in the barracks and on the boat dock, Skipper."

"Me too, but that doesn't make it right, Bean. That prejudicial behavior can lead to abuse or even atrocities. Keep it in check."

"Aye, aye, Skipper."

Lieutenant Masterson came aboard our boat to talk with Mr. Bergin about the incident. Stretched out, face down on top of the pilothouse, I was able to listen in on their conversation.

"Take a seat, Lou. Anyone wounded on your boat?" Mr. Bergin asked.

"Negative. They weren't armed, except for the explosives they were hauling."

"So, what made you take them under fire?"

"We were close to shore, so I had the crew dressed in flak jackets and helmets just in case we got sniped at. It's happened to us before, you know. I was coming around the north end of Mui Batangan. The Sông Sa Kỳ river mouth came into view as we cruised in at quarter speed. There was an unusually large number of fishing sampans at the entrance."

"That's rare, Lou. I've never seen them congregate at that location," Mr. Bergin noted.

"Must have been at least sixty small sampans and basket boats. They stretched from my port hand all the way back into the river mouth, almost to the area that opens into what looks more like a bay than a river.

"My gunner, GMG3 Jim Jones, was up in the guntub, and BM1 Dave Lambert along with EN2 Jerry Zehr were manning Mount 52 on the fantail. Seaman Marlin Jones was at the helm, and I was standing by the chart table. I had our deckhand on standby, ready to supply ammo to both battle stations."

"So what made the junk crew suspicious?" Bergin asked.

"I would have just moved in slowly and started inspecting junks at random, but one caught my attention. It was a larger sampan, maybe a ten- or twelve-footer at the far right, separated from the group. It started heading upriver."

"Is that when you opened up on them, Lou?"

"Nah, I was still too far away. I blasted the siren once and they ignored it. They began paddling faster, telling me they had something to hide. Had they stayed in the middle of the large, spread-out group of fishing boats, I may have missed them. I picked up speed and sounded the siren a second time. They headed for the entrance to a small bay. That's when I hollered at Jones to fire warning shots across their bow. They didn't stop. I had Jones hit 'em again. They were about thirty yards from their destination. I was afraid we were getting suckered into an ambush.

"I ordered Jim to take them under fire. Jones opened up with the twin .50s, walking his rounds into the sampan, then back down through the sinking boat literally obliterating it and its passengers. I saw one attempting to swim to the southern shoreline. I walked out the port side door and yelled at Lambert, my LPO, to take down the swimmer. He grabbed his M16, took aim, and did the guy in."

"That him on your fantail?" Mr. Bergin asked.

"That's him. I eased the boat to where the sampan went down and found nothing but chips of wood and blood-tinged emerald water. The swimmer was floating face down nearby. Lambert dove in and wrapped a rope under the guy's arms. The crew pulled him to the boat and hoisted the remains aboard. He was a young man, probably in his early twenties. Lambert dove back down and recovered two six-by-four-inch destructive charges. The four-inch-thick putty-looking mass had a yellow-grayish color."

"That sounds like C4 explosives, Lou," Mr. Bergin commented.

"I'm certain they are. They were wrapped in plastic, had fuses, and looked ready for immediate use," Lieutenant Masterson added.

He crossed back over to the 75 Boat and proceeded to Chu Lai. Mr. Bergin wasted no time in turning us around, and we headed south to Mui Batangan. We discovered that the fishing club was gone as we headed into the Sông Sa Kỳ.

"Bean, take the wheel, put us at idle speed while I get to the fantail."

"Aye, aye, Skipper."

Moments later, Mr. Bergin had the conn from the fantail. He pulled back on the throttles, bringing us to a near stop.

"Boats, take the conn and keep us at this location. I'm going in. There's got to be more contraband down there that Lou's crewman didn't get."

"Don't take too long. Masterson's firefight may have alerted the VC, and they might be nearby, Skipper," Carver warned.

"I don't like it either, Boats. I won't be down there long."

Mr. Bergin went into the cabin and retrieved his goggles and a pair of flippers. He came back up to the pilothouse, checked the radar, and looked at the spot Lieutenant Masterson indicated where the sampan went down. From the fantail, he maneuvered the boat a short distance and then returned the throttles to the upright position.

I stayed by the pilothouse door, listening for any radio comms. The water was so clear, I could see the bottom. Mr. Bergin put on the diving mask and flippers and jumped in. While in high school at Ramey Air Force Base in Puerto Rico, he spent his free time spear fishing and free diving. This fifteen-foot dive for him was like snorkeling in a bathtub. On the rocky and sandy bottom, he swam around, looking from side to side. He spotted something to his left, came up for air, swam a short distance away, and dove down again. Carver maneuvered the boat closer to him at idle speed.

Mr. Bergin came up with a splash. "I found them. More explosives."

He dove once more and soon came back up, holding what looked like C-ration cans welded together and fused, presumably packed with TNT. He also found blasting caps and sticks of dynamite, marked with the flaming bomb logo and "United States Army Ordnance" printed on them. Lieutenant Masterson was correct: the three KIAs were Viet Cong. What they planned to do with the explosives remained a mystery, but one thing was certain, they would have been used against friendly forces.

We exited the river and turned to port, heading north to rendezvous with our relief and then to Chu Lai. The Mui Batangan area was just what Lieutenant Michilini had called it—Indian country.[2]

Mail finally caught up with us several weeks after arriving at Chu Lai. Each time we'd come in off patrol, I'd check for mail before heading for the outdoor shower. The barracks' master at arms would make a daily run to the Chu Lai mail distribution center to collect our Swift Boat detachment's packages and letters. The first ones I received were from my parents and from Gloria, the Marine sergeant friend back in San Diego. No mail from Norma. Several more weeks went by and still no mail from Norma. I trusted her word, *para siempre*, she promised to be mine forever. Wondering if she didn't get my address correctly, I wrote her again, clearly noting my address: Crew 74-A, Box 280, NSAD Chu Lai, FPO San Francisco, Calif. 96696.

During the next several weeks I met up with several Chicanos on base. I went to the Disbursement Office to make arrangements for my parents' subsidy allotment. Julio Castro, a disbursement clerk and from SanAnto, assisted me with the forms. A percentage of my already low salary would be taken out and added to what the government sent them monthly. I was glad I could increase the amount they were receiving. After all, it wasn't like I needed the money to go out on dates.

One night at the Straw Elephant Julio introduced me to Doc, the base Mexican American medic. The quirk about Doc was, being from California, he was a bit Spanish deficient. In SanAnto the *vatos* called dudes from Califas who couldn't, didn't, or wouldn't speak Spanish, *pochos*. Mexican Americans from Califas were different. Their gang members were known as *cholos*. In SanAnto they were known as *pachucos*, or *chucos*. Regardless, in Vietnam we were all *carnales*, brothers. The three of us got together every chance we could. For a little while, war and the fear of being wounded or killed in combat took a back seat.

Around midday, while we were out patrolling the Charlie sector, flash traffic over the radio broke the boredom. Same Drink Delta was calling for Medevac south of Mui Batangan. The radio transmission was filled with loud static and then went totally silent—no static, no voices, nothing. I went down into the cabin and checked the frequency. All looked good, but we weren't receiving any further updates on the firefight down south, or from any other Market Time units in the area.

"Article, this is Same Drink Charlie, over." I got no reply.

"I say again, this is Same Drink Charlie, radio check, over."

We lost radio comms. I used the Prick 10 and attempted to raise Same Drink Sierra, the 82-foot Coast Guard cutter maintaining surveillance seaward from the Chu Lai patrol areas. They confirmed my radio checks were not heard by their unit. Immediately, I reported the situation to Mr. Bergin. He conducted radio checks as well, with the same results. Fortunately, we were not far from the entrance to Chu Lai. We headed back to port where we were issued a new PRC-25 radio.

Our Da Nang detachment at Chu Lai became Coastal Division 16 on June 16, 1967. Before the month ended, Mr. Bergin had designed our division logo. It was a black shield with a large yellow circle and three red horizontal stripes, representing the Republic of Vietnam's flag. In the middle was a large black ace of spades with a white skull in the center. White arcs top and bottom read COASTAL DIVISION 16–NO QUARTER, our division motto. A four by nine-foot plywood logo was located on our barracks exterior stairs. Plank owner certificates were issued to all personnel.

Firefight at the Co Lay Corral

The action never stopped on the Delta patrol area. Enemy action was on the increase in Quảng Ngãi Province. Lieutenant Junior Grade Robert "Bob" Bolger, a 1964 Naval Academy graduate, was the skipper of Swift Boat crew 17A, assigned to PCF Division 102 in Da Nang, South Vietnam. They were given charge of a brand-new Swift Boat, PCF-99, and subsequently deployed on temporary rotation to the Swift Boat detachment at Chu Lai. Once there, fellow officers welcomed him by bestowing upon him the Non-Dancing Ray moniker, connecting him to Hollywood actor / dancer Ray Bolger of the '30s and '40s.

On May 14, Swift Boat crew 17A received a special assignment—a psychological operation (PSYOP) mission in the 2D patrol area, straddling the forbidding Batangan Peninsula. Patrolling the cape and getting shot at was to be expected. However, running a PSYOP mission on Victor Charlie's front yard was like kicking dirt in the face of a bull. Lieutenant Bolger, paraphrasing Joseph Conrad's novel, coined a term for this territory—the Tactical Heart of Darkness.[3]

The 99 Boat was scheduled to leave Chu Lai before 0800 hours. On board was a PSYOP team made up of a US Marine Corps sergeant and an ARVN sergeant. Lieutenant Bolger's crew helped bring the PSYOP team's equipment on board. It consisted of massive speakers, an amplifier, and a portable tape deck, complete with a variety of Chiêu Hồi (Open Arms) pre-recorded tapes.

In Vietnam, the US government spent millions of dollars on psychological warfare programs. President Lyndon B. Johnson, meeting with US and South Vietnamese leaders in Hawaii in February 1966, stressed the need to continue with President Kennedy's vision of pacification and began a Win Their Hearts and Minds campaign. On the ground and in the air, propaganda booklets and leaflets as well as broadcasts via speaker systems called on the enemy to put down their weapons and defect. A leaflet could be used by a *hoi chanh*, the name given a defector, to provide for a safe passage when turning himself in to authorities.

The boat being relieved was waiting for them north of the Batangan Peninsula. The OIC reported all things normal—no VC-NVA activity in the 2D area over the last twenty-four hours. The crew of PCF-99 spent the morning hours inspecting fishing junks in the area and conducting open-ocean PSYOP activities. The sergeants handed out Chiêu Hồi pamphlets and fliers, hygiene packets, trinkets for children, and fruit. The crew also administered first aid to anyone in need of treatment.

After lunch, Lieutenant Bolger prepared the crew and PSYOP team for the real mission. He planned to start the run along the beach from a location on the south side of Batangan and down toward the mouth of Sông Trà Khúc, approximately three and a half miles. Building seas from the southeast, however, forced Lieutenant Bolger to change his plans. They began their northbound PSYOP run a half mile north of the river mouth. Centered in this stretch of beach were three numbered Co Lay hamlets. Resulting from the high number of sniper and ambush attacks on Chu Lai Swifts from this location, the hamlets were collectively tagged the Co Lay Corral. The team quickly relocated and secured the speakers to the port-side hand railing along the top of the main cabin.

Behind the wheel in the pilothouse was Quartermaster Chief James D. "JD" Wiggins, a twenty-eight-year-old quartermaster with nine-and-a-half years of naval experience. He was born and raised in Cross City, Florida. Although he dropped out of school in the ninth grade, by the age of 16, he had created and operated his own pulpwooding business in Lake City, Florida. The same personal drive that made him succeed as a teenage entrepreneur was also the reason he secured his high school equivalency diploma while in the Navy. As the crew's LPO, Chief Wiggins was a man whose judgment and leadership Lieutenant Bolger relied upon completely.

The skipper stood in the pilothouse, port side, by the chart table. GMG3 Jonathan "Jon" Douglas Daves Sr. was behind the twin .50s in the guntub. The engineman, EN1 Michael Malacky, and QM3 Joseph Theep were manning the Mount 52 on the fantail, Theep behind the machine gun. RM3 Lavon Greathouse was monitoring the radio in the main cabin, ready to provide assistance or haul ammo to both battle stations. Two large metal hatches on the cabin deck gave access to the ammunition stowage locker. The PSYOP team was also in the cabin, standing by with their audio system.

"Chief, steer toward the north side of the river mouth," Lieutenant Bolger ordered.

"Copy, Skipper," replied Wiggins, glancing into the radar bonnet. He pulled to within 200 yards of the beach and turned with right full rudder, bringing both Detroit V12 diesels a nudge forward of idle speed.

Lieutenant Bolger got a thumbs-up from the PSYOP crew, signaling they were ready to broadcast. For the propaganda tape to have any effect, the 99 Boat had to ply along the shallow waters near the beach at loitering speed while keeping the boat parallel to shore. He didn't particularly care for this tactic, but that was their mission. Rules of Engagement called for holding fire until fired upon.

Their initial PSYOP run was underway. It began abreast of Co Lay 3, the first of the three Co Lay hamlets. The scene was right out of an Elvis Presley *Blue Hawaii* movie poster: white sandy beach, lush green vegetation, palm tree–lined sand dunes, and scattered puffy white clouds.

The speakers blasted away a pre-recorded Chiêu Hồi message: "Do you want to get out of this living Hell? Do you want to live instead of dying? If you want to live, then answer the call to Chiêu Hồi. You have just two choices—death or Chiêu Hồi. Death or Chiêu Hồi." The message played on a continuous loop and invited the enemy to lay down their arms and reunite with the government of South Vietnam.

Lieutenant Bolger had devoted a great deal of time cross-training his men in one another's assigned duties, and he knew he could depend on them to fulfill their mission, no matter the circumstances. The Mount 52 GQ station captain slot belonged to Chief Wiggins, with the engineman, EN1 Malacky, as the loader. Seaman Theep, whose GQ station was pilothouse helmsman, requested permission to man a weapon the next time they were at GQ close to the beach. On this day, the young sailor got his wish and switched stations with Chief Wiggins.

Nerves tightened as PCF-99 approached Co Lay 2. All eyes scanned the dunes for movement. The loudspeakers continued broadcasting the message: "You have just two choices—death or Chiêu Hồi. Death or Chiêu Hồi." They reached Co Lay 2 without drawing enemy fire. One mile ahead was Co Lay 1. A half mile farther north, outside the northern boundary of the Co Lay Corral, was the southern edge of a large village known as Mỹ Lai. Friendly ground forces in the area code-named the Viet Cong stronghold Pinkville, as that was the color it was shaded on the combat charts.

Halfway between Co Lay 2 and 1, the Viet Cong opened fire on Lieutenant Bolger's Swift Boat. Automatic weapons fire raked PCF-99's aluminum hull from stem to stern. Ricocheting bullets danced all around as Daves and Theep strafed the sand dune with a barrage of .50 caliber machine gun fire.

The PCF was under attack from three bunkered positions along the sand dunes. Automatic weapons fire bore down on Crew 17A and the PSYOP sergeants like they were sitting ducks at a shooting gallery. Their speakers were not damaged and continued blasting away the pacification message at the adversary, "Death or Chiêu Hồi."

As trained, Greathouse stepped into the pilothouse and relieved Chief Wiggins on the helm, who then darted along the starboard side catwalk, while bullets whistled by overhead, to man the Mount 52 position on the fantail. Everything was happening at lightning speed. The noise from the twin .50s was unbearable. The pilothouse vibrated from the recoil of the Ma Deuces.

The crew knew Lieutenant Bolger's counter battery tactic well—flank speed and stay broadside to the line of fire in a manner that gave the two machine gun mounts' firepower maximum effect. The firefight at the Co Lay Corral became fierce.

Greathouse pushed the throttles forward in quarter increments until they were at all ahead full. He began executing the standard maneuver, working his way along the beach, allowing Mount 51 and 52 to engage the entrenched enemy, laying down a ferocious blanket of suppressive fire.

On the fantail, Chief Wiggins stood tall behind the unprotected over-under machine gun / mortar mount, firing short bursts of .50 caliber rounds at the bunkers. If he maintained the butterfly triggers depressed, he knew he'd be out of ammo in short order and would not be able to continue suppressing the enemy fire.

Wiggins shifted his attack from the machine gun to the mortar. He set it to trigger-fire mode and hollered at Malacky, the engineman: "Mike, load a round of HE."

The engineman raised the lid of the ammo box, pulled out an 81 mm tube, carefully slid the round out and dropped it, fins first, into the elevated barrel. "Round in, Chief," Mike hollered. Wiggins leveled the barrel, took aim, and pulled the trigger. The round burst into a ball of debris and sand on the beach. He went back to the machine gun, pumping .50 caliber lead at the three Viet Cong positions on the beach. Theep grabbed an M16 from the cabin. PCF-99 was still well within the 600-yard effective firing range. He fired several clips toward the adversary.

Once past Co Lay 1, Lieutenant Bolger ensured his crew was intact and both battle stations were armed and ready. "Turn us around," he ordered. Greathouse executed an Anderson turn to port, pulling back on the port throttle to neutral, turning the wheel hard left. The 50-foot combat boat made the standard 75-yard, 180-degree turn until its bow faced south. The gun mount crewmen turned their weapons to starboard, facing the beach. The crew, filled with fiery attitude, was locked and loaded for payback.

"Fire at will, fire at will," Bolger ordered.

Greathouse placed the engines at half speed, giving him more control of the boat as they crashed into three-foot seas, trying to maintain a level posture suitable for the gunners' accuracy. Malacky had two HE mortar rounds ready. While Daves strafed the three bunkers and enemy automatic weapons fire was suppressed, Chief Wiggins trigger-fired the rounds at the bunkers and then returned to firing the single .50 as they passed the last bunker. From the starboard side pilothouse door, Lieutenant Bolger thumped off M79 grenade rounds as Theep unleashed more M16 rounds at the beach.

As PCF-99 neared the southern boundary of the Corral, Greathouse turned the wheel to port and increased speed while continuing a zigzag maneuver away from the beach. Out of firing range, the throttles were placed in a neutral position, eventually allowing the sea to take over the boat's movement. Lieutenant Bolger and crew checked their boat for damage and personnel injuries. Aside from numerous new ventilation holes, PCF-99 was still battle worthy.

Theep and Greathouse carried ammo to the two gun mounts. The two battle stations were re-armed and ready to continue the fight. It was standard operating procedure (SOP) to submit a Market Time Spot Report (MTSR) for combat operations. Lieutenant Bolger grabbed the mic and reported, "Article, Same Drink Delta. FLASH TRAFFIC, over."

"Same Drink Delta, Article, send your traffic, over."

"Roger. Mike Tango Sierra Romeo, 2-Delta, 14 May, Number 1. Received fire from three shore Alpha-Whiskey positions. Single One-two-decimal-seven millimeter and one, possibly figure two three-zero caliber Mike-Golfs. Returned fire, no casualties. Request position one Same Drink unit for possible assistance. Encrypted position to follow, over."

"Copy, Delta. Stand by. Out."

A short time later, Article directed Same Drink Delta to repeat the PSYOP mission. In short, you found the enemy, take him out. Lieutenant Bolger's call for backup arrived. PCF-19 took up position on PCF-99's stern port quarter, allowing enough distance between them for the boat's support fire when needed.

GMG3 Daves climbed back into the guntub. Theep was at the wheel with Lieutenant Bolger by the chart table. Chief Wiggins manned the single .50 on the fantail, set the mortar back to trigger-fire mode, and had EN1 Malacky load an HE round in the mortar barrel. Greathouse stayed in the cabin, monitoring the radio and standing at the ready by the forward magazine.

Lieutenant Bolger drew comfort knowing PCF-19 had his six, while additional Market Time units were on their way to provide support. Daves' and Wiggins' anxious thumbs rested on the butterfly triggers of their weapons, barrels pointed at the positions they had received fire from on their first run.

Malacky leaned toward Wiggins. "I can see them setting up at the dune line, Chief."

"They'll be eating an HE sandwich if they open up on us again," Chief Wiggins proclaimed. He pointed the mortar barrel at the suspected target and, using caution, tapped the trigger with his right index finger. Aware of the immediate danger, he called to Malacky, "Run forward and tell Skipper to get us the hell outta here. We're about to get ambushed again."

Before Malacky took a step, the well-known pop-pop-pop sound of semi-automatic rifle fire rang out from the beach. The enemy was firing for accuracy. Once they calibrated their aim, they opened up in fully automatic mode on PCF-99 and her crew from the same three bunker positions.

Chief Wiggins pulled the trigger. The fantail deck shuddered as the mortar barrel recoiled. A high-explosive round hit the base of the tree line next to the sand dunes. Enemy fire halted momentarily, allowing Wiggins time to unleash another burst of .50 caliber machine gun fire. Green tracers sped toward the 99 Boat as red ones went out. Incoming rounds zipped past them making odd sounds, some shrill, others tumbling thud-like noises. At any moment one could find its mark. The twin .50s went silent. Wiggins turned to his right, looked at the guntub, and didn't see Daves. The Chief turned to his engineman only to find he was flat on his back on the deck.

Malacky's right hand took a small arms round through the palm. He placed the hand over his chest, blood spewing upward two feet high. The Chief yelled to the PSYOP crew in the cabin, "Grab him and take him in." They did not respond. When the bullets started hitting the boat, they both hit the deck and stayed there, not wanting to expose themselves to intense enemy fire. Wiggins continued his suppressive attack, but also noticed the speakers had gone silent. That enabled him to hear the clatter of the cover boat's machine guns pouring devastating fire on the beach.

Chief Wiggins glanced back again at Malacky and noticed his eyes were open. "Can you move?" The wounded crewman nodded in the affirmative. "Then get your ass below." The engineman sprang to his feet, sprinted behind Wiggins and across the open deck, bullets flying overhead, and literally dove into the cabin.

Hot .50 caliber brass casings rained down into the pilothouse from the guntub, some bouncing off Theep's flak jacket, when the Ma Deuces' staccato abruptly stopped.

"I'm hit, I'm hit. The fuckers got me," screamed Daves as he fell through the guntub opening and onto the deck in the pilothouse, landing at Lieutenant Bolger's feet, blood gushing from his right hand and crying out in agonizing pain. Greathouse ran out the back cabin door yelling at Wiggins, "Daves' been hit, he's down."

The crew simultaneously reacted to the situation, individually taking necessary action in rapid fashion. Greathouse hit the throttles, pushing them to max speed, pulling away at forty-five degrees from the beach in a zigzagging maneuver. This tactic allowed Chief Wiggins on the fantail to keep pumping lead toward the enemy bunkers, suppressing their fire.

"Article, Article. Same Drink Delta receiving heavy Alpha-Whiskey fire, same coordinates as before. Figure two Whiskey-India-Alpha's on board. PSYOP system destroyed. Out."

Lieutenant Bolger's message was brief and to the point. For now, that was the extent of his second MTSR. At this critical moment the crew didn't need a boat officer. PCF-99 was under heavy enemy attack, and it needed another gunner.

Daves grabbed his skipper's pant leg with his hand as he was climbing over him. "The right barrel is out of commission, Boss," Daves uttered. Lieutenant Bolger nodded and continued his climb into the guntub.

As Bolger prepared to unleash the twin .50s on the beach, he noticed an AK-47 bullet hole had borne through the right ammo belt housing, rendering the right-fifty inoperable. In all probability, the resulting shrapnel from the exploding round was what hit Daves' right hand. Lieutenant Bolger took the beach under aggressive fire as the boat continued increasing speed and moved past the last bunker position. The twin diesels were pushed to their limit, taking PCF-99 and her crew out of harm's way.

QM3 Theep had joined the Navy to become a hospital corpsman. While undergoing medical training in Balboa Naval Hospital in San Diego, he dropped out because he discovered he couldn't handle the sight of blood. Instinctively, he overcame that idiosyncrasy and jumped into action to save his crewmate's—his brother's—life.

During normal open-sea junk inspection operations, the crew wore their Chu Lai renegade-style uniform of the day—shirtless, cut-off dungarees and boondockers or shower shoes. On close to shore activities, in particular up in the guntub, they wore the standard Navy issue dungaree bell-bottoms, chambray shirt, and deck shoes. The last thing you wanted was hot brass dancing all over your bare legs and feet.

On this day, GMG3 Daves was also wearing a metal helmet, flak jacket, and flak pants. There was nothing fancy about the latter. They were bulky, oversized briefs lined with the same protective material as the flak vest. Intended to protect a person from artillery or rifle fire shrapnel, they weren't designed to stop bullets. The quarter-inch aluminum surrounding the machine gun emplacement was not a design flaw in PCF construction. Armor plating was never a consideration. All battle station positions aboard the Swift Boat were vulnerable.

Wiggins secured Mount 52 and dashed into the cabin. He found Malacky, stretched out on the lower port side bunk, in great pain, his gritted teeth holding back profanities. The Marine sergeant, with help from his Vietnamese counterpart, had been working on Malacky's injured right hand. They tore any shirt they found into strips, created two compresses, and applied them to both sides of the wound, applying pressure. A ligament was ripped apart and it rolled up into a ball near his elbow, knotting up under the skin and resembling a marble.

"Chief, can you light me up a smoke?"

Wiggins popped a Winston between Malacky's lips and lit the cigarette. Grabbing the first aid kit from the small arms locker, Chief Wiggins pulled out a bandage. He tore open the packet, held one edge, and shook it about.

"Here, let me help you, Chief. You look nervous," Malacky said, casting a James Dean smirk at Wiggins.

"Asshole, just trying to shake the bandage out. Be still so I can patch you up, buddy. Let us know how you're doing when you get back to the Land of the Big PX," Wiggins replied as he wound the bandage around the engineman's hand.

"I will, Chief. Leave me here for now, I'll be okay," Malacky said, sitting up at the edge of the bunk. "Daves needs help, man. See what you can do for him."

In the pilothouse, Greathouse turned the helm to starboard, taking PCF-99 farther away from the beach. Lieutenant Bolger and Theep began comforting Daves. Chief Wiggins helped Lieutenant Bolger and Theep remove the flak pants and vest off Daves. The three carried the wounded gunner down into the cabin and placed him in the middle of the deck.

Tendons and shreds of muscle were all that was keeping his hand attached to his forearm. He was losing blood at an alarming rate. Daves, screaming in pain, used his left hand to hold onto his right forearm. Shrapnel from an automatic rifle round had severely torn up his right wrist. He suffered numerous less critical shrapnel wounds to his arms and legs from rounds that pierced the guntub.

"Did you get the bastards, Skipper?" Daves asked.

"We put it to them, Guns," Lieutenant Bolger said. "The 19 Boat is in there now givin' 'em hell, and two more boats will be here soon to assist. Be still while we bandage you up."

Theep grabbed the first aid kit, pulled out the tourniquet, and wrapped it below Daves' elbow. Although the flow of blood slowed, he had lost so much that each time the boat rolled, blood sloshed over the deck from bulkhead to bulkhead. Theep administered a morphine syrette to Daves' left arm, while Lieutenant Bolger and Wiggins covered the severe wound with rags and bandages. Bolger and Theep held the crewman's arm and hand steady over a wood splint as Wiggins wound the bandage until the almost severed hand was immobilized.

Lieutenant Bolger assessed the situation. Both GMG3 Daves and EN1 Malacky needed immediate medical attention. The transit back to Chu Lai was over twenty miles and would take too long. He went back into the pilothouse and grabbed the mic.

"Article, Article. Same Drink Delta. Request Dust Off my location now. Have two, repeat two Whiskey-India-Alpha's on board. Over."

"Roger, Delta. Stand by. Out," was the reply. I Corps Market Time radio net control in Da Nang contacted the 498th Medical Company in Qui Nhơn.

"Delta, this is Article, over."

"Go ahead, Article," Lieutenant Bolger replied.

"Delta, Dust Off Six One (61) is on the way."

"Copy, standing by."

Lieutenant Bolger stepped outside the port side door and looked south, searching the sky. Hearing machine gun fire from the beach, he turned toward that direction and saw PCF-19 making a firing run on the enemy position. The gunners were walking their .50 caliber machine gun rounds up the sandy beach and hitting the top of the dunes. Their suppressive fire pinned down the enemy, silencing their weapons.

Two more Swift Boats arrived on station. PCF-75 and PCF-76 continued to take the three enemy bunker positions under machine gun and mortar fire. The exchange was fierce. Charlie wasn't giving up easy. Both units received half a dozen hits each of small arms fire, and PCF-75 lost one of their radio antennas during the engagement.

"Engines stop," Lieutenant Bolger instructed Greathouse. "Keep her steady, bow into the seas. Dust Off will be here in ten to pick up Daves and Malacky."

"Copy, Skipper, steady and into the seas."

The OIC asked the crew for a personal injury report. On quick examination of blood-stained clothing and areas that noticeably hurt, Lieutenant Bolger, Chief Wiggins, and Theep found they had suffered minor shrapnel wounds.

Hearing the familiar whup-whup-whup sound of helicopter blades, Lieutenant Bolger grabbed a hand flare purposely without checking to see what color it was. The chopper was off the mouth of the Sông Trà Khúc. Lieutenant Bolger set the Prick 10 to the Dust Off frequency.

"Dust Off Six-one, Same Drink Delta, over."

"Delta, this is Six-one, Batangan ahead of me, over."

"Copy, Six-one. Stand by for smoke," Lieutenant Bolger informed. He popped the flare and a brilliant flash arched into the sky, leaving behind a thick red cloud trail.

"I've got two reds ahead of me, Delta."

The Viet Cong had popped the same color flare as well, attempting to trick the air ambulance unit with the intention of taking them down if they chose the wrong marker. It was a tactic used often in the field during combat.

"Feet wet or dry, Delta?" the pilot asked.

"Six-one, Delta. Feet wet, feet wet. Victor Charlie and November Victor Alpha are dry. Have two souls standing by aft."

"Roger, heading to you now," the pilot replied.

To eliminate the possibility of the helo's tubular struts getting tangled in the fantail stanchion cable, they were taken down. All mortar containers, brass shell casings, and black metal ammo belt links were thrown over the side. The forceful down draft from the rotor blades could make projectiles of any loose material on deck. Dust Off 61 consisted of two pilots, a flight medic, and a crew chief. They began their descent.

The first open-ocean PCF Dust Off extraction was underway. The chopper, not having a personnel lift basket capability, had limited options, none of them good. The injured sailors would have to climb aboard through the open helicopter door without the use of a safety harness. Swift Boat training in Coronado did not include this death-defying procedure.

The pilot slowly lowered his craft, starboard side to the boat's port stern. This gave him full visual of the approach. The blades kicked up a stinging salty sea mist. The maneuver was extremely hazardous. Too low and everyone standing on the fantail was in danger of being sliced to bits by the blades. On the first attempt the PCF's fantail rose suddenly in response to a larger swell from the rolling sea, forcing everyone to their hands and knees.

Lieutenant Bolger figured the best approach in transferring his wounded crewmen was starting with the most able, EN1 Malacky. The pilot tried the stern corners with no success. The crew next attempted to utilize the height of the ammo box. The lid was three feet off the deck. Malacky climbed atop the box, assisted by Chief Wiggins, who was already on top and in a crouched position. Theep and Lieutenant Bolger grabbed onto their legs attempting to keep them steady on top of the box as the boat swayed side to side.

A loud snap, followed by an eerie whipping sound, startled the men. The unexpected occurred. The Dust Off rotor blade cut the URC radio antenna in half. Their direct communication line over the horizon to Da Nang was severed. The radar mast was feet away. Had that been hit, it would have resulted in a catastrophic disaster. The pilot pulled away instantly to regain control of his airship. The pilot resumed the rescue attempt. As the chopper came closer it was difficult to determine who was riding the waves. To Chief Wiggins, the helicopter looked like a giant yo-yo going up and down, but in fact it was the Swift Boat that was bobbing on the crest of three-foot seas.

Wiggins and Malacky found themselves sidestepping to avoid being knocked overboard or onto the deck by the helicopter skids. They dropped to their knees, crouching to avoid being crushed by tons of airborne metal. The pilot was doing his best to maintain step with the dancing boat. The flight medic and crew chief aboard the helicopter, harnessed to the sides of the open door, stood by ready to receive Malacky. Without coaxing, Chief Wiggins gave Malacky a huge shove the next time the deck of the helicopter was even with the ammo box, and in he went. The two men in the helicopter grabbed hold of his blood-soaked uniform and held onto him as the air ambulance shifted away from the Swift Boat's fantail.

"Ready for Daves," Wiggins called out to his skipper. Theep and Lieutenant Bolger, with the help of the Marine sergeant, brought Daves out from the cabin. The morphine had taken effect. His legs were like spaghetti al dente. The transfer was going to be more of a challenge than Malacky's. At least the pilot's control of the airship improved. Theep knelt on Daves' left side, attempting to stabilize him on the ammo box by holding onto his waist. Chief Wiggins knew there was no time to waste. If the pilot saw Daves' unstable condition and judged that the boat to helicopter transfer was questionable, he might abort. Wiggins stood behind Daves and as before, waited for the boat to climb on a wave.

"You can do it, mate. Next time the door gets even with us, I'm tossing you in, buddy."

Daves' head wobbled in an odd affirmative nod.

On impulse, Chief Wiggins grabbed him under the armpits and, mustering all the strength he could, tossed his crewmate into the awaiting arms of the two men on the helicopter, three feet away. Lieutenant Bolger's remaining crew celebrated their success, as Dust Off 61 banked to the right and climbed skyward. The door closed as the helicopter circled south en route to the field hospital at Đức Phổ. The impossible had been achieved.

One week later, we were back in Da Nang. Our Onan generator could not be fixed by the Chu Lai enginemen, so it would have to be replaced. While the work was being carried out, I was called to the division office. They had a bag of mail for the crews back in Chu Lai. I took the bag down to our boat. Anxious to find something from Norma, I dumped the contents of the bag onto the top rack in the cabin. I pushed the packages aside and gathered all the envelopes. One by one I scanned their fronts, hoping to see my name.

Middleton was also in the cabin, checking the small arms locker. "Here's one for you, Gunner," I called out.

"Who's it from, Bean?"

"Home, Bob, home," I remarked.

Halfway through the stack I found one for me. It was from my sister, Martha. I shrugged, put it aside, and kept looking. I became disheartened—none from Norma again.

I continued my search. After forty-one days, the letter I had been waiting for finally arrived.

"I got it, Gunner, I got it," I hollered at him. "Norma finally wrote."

I left the stack of mail on the bunk and headed out onto the fantail, smelling the envelope for the scent of Occur. It had none. I climbed up on top of the pilothouse and sat down, resting my back on the guntub. I expected the pages to be splattered with lipstick kisses.

Instead, I was shocked at what I read.

> Dear Raúl:
> My brother is forcing me to write this letter to you. By the time you get this letter, I'll be married.

It had to be a joke, a prank, anything but a Dear John letter. Norma promised me that she'd be mine, *¡para siempre!* I stared in disbelief at the words. The longer I gazed at the page, the more the pain in my heart deepened.

We were scheduled to head back to Chu Lai the next day. In a fog I went ashore, walked down to the dock and then on to the main road, Norma's heartbreaking letter crumpled in my fisted left hand. I strolled aimlessly alongside the paved road, head hung low. Every now and again I'd kick up a cloud of dirt. Lost in the memory of our two years as a couple, I found myself sitting on a stone block, looking at small waves slapping against the rock dike at the Vietnamese junk base.

Finally, I trudged back to the APL hoping that the next time we got into a firefight with the Viet Cong, one or more rounds would take me down. I couldn't live without her in my future. Back in Chu Lai, I frequented the Straw Elephant with hopes of drowning my sorrows in alcohol. Dear John letters received in a war zone are devastating, I concluded, and shouldn't be allowed. *¡Pinche Norma!*

The rift between Boats and the skipper grew bigger. Receiving orders from a JG was not sitting well with the older enlisted man. Carver pushed the envelope of insubordination at every turn. Mr. Bergin wanted to count on his leading petty officer's experience and leadership, but Boats didn't see it that way. He was bent on pushing

back on our officer in charge. In the heat of battle, this defiance could prove disastrous to our crew. The matter would have to be resolved, sooner rather than later.

EN2 Rinehart was in line to be the crew's LPO because of his length of time as a second-class petty officer, but he didn't want the job. Mr. Bergin assigned the position to boatswain's mate Carver. That vote of confidence didn't move the disgruntled bosun's support needle in a favorable direction. The skipper went as far as extending a field promotion to First Class Boatswain's Mate E-7, when he became eligible. Boats' rebellious attitude persisted, however.

After Carver's second refusal to follow orders to get the boat cleaned, fueled, and rearmed prior to releasing the crew, Mr. Bergin called Boats up to Officer Country for a dressing-down session. For the record, he went through a list of possible charges the bosun could be written up on, but also let him know that he preferred not to do that. Mr. Bergin made him an offer—duke it out or arm wrestle.

Lieutenant Bergin won the arm strength match. He opened the fridge in the officers' lounge and pulled out a couple of bottles of Ba Muoi Ba 33 beer. He issued new orders to his second-in-command. The 79 Boat belonged to the boatswain's mate when it was moored to the pier. When the skipper came on board and Carver reported the boat was ready for patrol, PCF-79 belonged to Bergin.

To ensure everyone was in step, Mr. Bergin issued his standing orders. They always required one man in the guntub with an M16, sound-powered phones at the ready, and machine guns uncovered except in inclement weather. General quarters would be sounded when within 1,500 yards of a beach. The boat would stay 1,000 yards clear of any hazard to navigation. Radar contact at two and a half miles warranted caution and alerting the OIC. Finally, in the absence of the OIC, the Boatswain's Mate would assume positive control of his watch section.

The order placed the OIC as sole responsible party for the crew's actions and their welfare. He expected each of the crew to keep him informed and act correctly when the situation arose. Each member of our crew signed the document.

CHAPTER 14

SKUNK ALPHA

Gunner and I sat on the open deck of the fantail, each cradling an 81 mm mortar on our lap, sipping a Coke, munching chips, and watching the war. Three months in-country had shaped us into a well-balanced and responsible crew, allowing us to carry out patrols with confidence. Familiarity with the numerous patrol areas out of Chu Lai helped us maintain a high degree of patrol effectiveness.

Task Force Oregon forces, operating south of Chu Lai, pushed the enemy toward the beach during the previous night. We pulled away a good distance from the beach to await further mortar support instructions. It was during this nighttime fire support mission I witnessed Puff the Magic Dragon in action for the first time. Some knew it as Puff, others called him Spooky.[1] The modified USAF Air Commando Douglas AC-47 appeared to morph itself into Vulcan—the mythical Roman god of fire.

Its modifications were made by a young officer, Captain Ronald W. Terry, who traveled to Vietnam in 1963 with a US Air Force team to assess the needs for a five-year limited-war commitment. A modified Convair C-131 tested the weapon system in the United States prior to modifying two C-47s at Biên Hòa, Vietnam. A camouflage paint job and an "A" prefix designated it as an attack version. The planes proved their capability under actual combat conditions. Structurally secured to the aircraft's left side, three electric GAU-2B/A, 7.62mm minigun barrels protruded out Spooky's cargo door and two open windows. The miniguns carried the commercial name of Vulcan—quite befitting. Each gun fired, Gatling-style, at a rate of 6,000 rounds per minute—enough to fill a football field with a round in every square yard in sixty seconds.

The violet red tracer rounds fell towards the target as if from the end of a garden hose spray nozzle. They resembled the furling red stripes of Old Glory in a gentle breeze. Under concentrated fire, Spooky worked in a counterclockwise course around its target, tearing a bright red funnel into the velvet black sky. The red rays resembled a laser light show. It was morbid to feel entertained by Spooky's work. Regardless, Gunner and I took pleasure in witnessing the awesome display of firepower.

In addition to the standard coastal surveillance responsibilities, we provided fire support for ground troops near the beach. Our 81 mm mortar had a range of two-and-a-quarter miles, so we could stay at a safe distance of one-half mile off the beach.

We provided fire support twice more that night before resuming normal patrol activities in our area. As dawn approached, more fishing junks and sampans than normal appeared throughout our patrol sector. We attributed the increase to the Task Force Oregon sweep of the area. Mr. Bergin ordered general quarters, and we began inspecting fishing boats, one after the other. By the time we were relieved on station, eighteen Vietnamese were detained for questionable or missing identification papers. On the way back to port, Mr. Bergin placed me in charge of guarding the detainees. Porky and Boats shackled the fishermen who had no form of identification and resisted the most to the base of the mortar mount.

I sat on the ammo locker while guarding the detainees. As I held a loaded M16 on them with a round in the chamber, they squatted on the fantail deck wearing the same timid look displayed by any other Vietnamese fisherman we ever questioned.

In port, I learned that five of the detainees were draft evaders from the Republic of Vietnam Army, and eight were confirmed Viet Cong. The news startled me. I was face-to-face with the enemy and never suspected it. I wondered how many similar encounters with our adversary I had experienced. Realizing the potential danger left me determined to stay alert and always be ready. I was aware that the early part of July 1967 produced a significant increase in vessel detections and inspections in the Chu Lai Market Time coastal zone. Inspecting junks day and night, one patrol after another, became boring and routine, opening the door to a potential ambush.

During our training in San Diego, we had learned how a crew's carelessness resulted in severe boat damage and injuries to the sailors aboard a Swift Boat while making a typical boat inspection in Vietnam. The junk hadn't appeared suspicious to the crew. Although at GQ and combat ready, someone overlooked one crucial standard boat inspection procedure. The pilothouse door remained open. When

Navy Patrol Plane Commander Lieutenant Commander Max G. Branscomb, Cam Ranh Bay, Republic of Vietnam, circa July 1967. (Photo credit: Max G. Branscomb)

the Swift pulled up alongside, someone in the junk tossed a hand grenade inside the pilothouse.

Suspicious Trawler Detected

On Tuesday, July 11, 1967, a chain of events began that would culminate in a day of glory for Operation Market Time.

Navy Lieutenant Commander Max G. Branscomb and his four-officer flight crew hopped on a base transport vehicle for a quick ride to their scheduled noon Market Time aerial surveillance patrol. Like his father before him, who served in Navy coastal patrol operations in the Caribbean and on the Eastern seaboard during World War II, thirty-two-year-old Branscomb flew surveillance aircraft along the coast of Vietnam. Commissioned as an ensign on April 6, 1957, he received his wings the following day. After several duty stations, he received orders to VP-1, Patrol Squadron One. Lieutenant Commander Branscomb's squadron section arrived in Vietnam on May 31, and they operated out of the Naval Air Facility in Cam Ranh Bay (CRB), one of three major ports, the other two being Da Nang in the north and Saigon in the south.[2]

Branscomb served as the Patrol Plane Commander (PPC) of a P2V7 Neptune surveillance aircraft. His officer crew consisted of four lieutenant junior grade officers. Copilot Steve Netherby and third pilot Carl Spangler also served as navigators. Vern Jones occupied the Tactical Air Coordination and Control Officer (TACCO) slot. Gary Elliot sat next to the TACCO and monitored the search scope radar.

The group arrived at the squadron office around 1030 hours. Lieutenants Jones and Elliot received an intel mission briefing from the squadron air intelligence officer. He advised them of various large Chinese commercial ships seen in the area recently. Staying alert for steel-hulled coastal cargo trawlers, known to transport weapons made in China and destined for the enemy forces operating in South Vietnam, remained highest on the list of standard operating procedures. The intel officer handed Jones copies of numerous North Vietnamese trawler silhouettes for use in quick identification.

The nine-man enlisted crew carried out pre-flight checks under the leadership of the plane captain, Edward A. McLaughlin. Mac, as the crew called him, supervised the loading of 3,650 gallons of aviation fuel. With fifteen and a half years in the military and a superb knowledge of reciprocating engines, he also served as the lead mechanic. At takeoff, he sat on a jump-seat between and behind the two pilots in the cockpit, where he monitored engine RPM and temps and maintained an accurate fuel consumption log.

The last of the pre-flight deliveries came from the base ordnance department. Hays and two other crewmen carefully worked as a team in loading parachute flares, short burning smoke lights, and other explosive ordnance. A .50 caliber machine gun rounded out the airship's armament. The copilots ensured all the weapons and flammable ordnance were stored safely and wired correctly.

Given the green light to take off, Lieutenant Commander Branscomb eased up on the brakes and YB-10 rolled onto runway 02/L. Once cleared for take-off, all pilots were expected to get moving and airborne ASAP because there was always a flight on final, ready to land. The 10,000-foot runway lay straight ahead; beyond it was the South China Sea.

In a matter of minutes, YB-10 climbed to the normal surveillance operating altitude range of 2,000 feet. At this altitude, the APS-20 radar covered a 200-mile range. YB-10's patrol area covered an area east of Cam Ranh Bay to 100 miles out and north, twenty to fifty miles off the coast, where most seaborne traffic took place.

Binoculars in hand, Netherby made visual scans of the surface below. Mechanic John Gwinn alternated with King at this lookout position throughout the flight. The observation station, although isolated, played an important role. A nose observer saw a flare fired by a downed pilot in the Tonkin Gulf, saving his life. On another occasion, a crewman at the station spotted a large barge carrying a heavy-duty crane, which broke away from a sea-towing tug during heavy seas.

"PPC, Radar. I have a contact. Recommend a closer look." Lieutenant Jones marked the contact on his radarscope. It was synchronized with the smaller screen in the cockpit. The contact was approximately fifty-five miles east-southeast of Chu Lai.

"Copy, Radar. Break. Crew, man rigging stations," Branscomb ordered over the ICS. He turned the plane toward the contact, and it began its descent. Netherby pointed off his starboard bow. Branscomb banked right and spotted the contact.

"PPC, Radar. Contact ten miles out."

"Got it in sight, Radar."

Branscomb positioned the plane in line on the vessel's wake.

"Crew, PPC. Approaching contact on its stern."

Although late in the afternoon, enough daylight remained for pictures to be taken. The first suspicious observation was the ship's course. She headed into the sun, west toward the coast, with no port in sight. The sun's rays fell on the steel hull's port side.

"Vessel will be off starboard, watch for its wake," Branscomb informed the crew. Each man had a specific observation order to focus on—vessel number, name, electrical and radar gear, flag of country origin, ship length and color, location of wheelhouse, crewmen above deck, and noteworthy items on deck. YB-10 dropped to 100 feet above the rolling waves. The trawler was small, and they had to be low to the water to get a good aspect photo.

"Coming up on the starboard side, course two-two-zero, speed ten," Lieutenant Commander Branscomb informed the crew.

"Stand by, starboard side, now, now . . ." Branscomb added power and rolled left. Cutting across its bow would have been an aggressive and unfriendly display, according to maritime tradition. Branscomb didn't want to raise suspicions and force the trawler to rethink its mission.

Branscomb turned to Netherby and said, "That sure looked a lot like the Chinese trawlers we're supposed to be looking for."

"Affirmative," replied the copilot.

YB-10 circled the contact from above at 1,500 feet. The PPC called Jones on the ICS, requesting the photos given him at the intel briefing. While Lieutenant Jones gathered the pictures, Netherby polled the crew for the Rigging Report. They described an olive-green fishing trawler, bow number 459, 120 feet long, running darkened ship, flying no colors, and no signs of a radar. Limited code phrases caused the use of the inclusion of "boxes on deck." Running darkened ship was not alarming

Composite photo of suspicious trawler and Operation Market Time surveillance aircraft YB-10, fifty-five miles east-southeast of Chu Lai, Republic of Vietnam, 11 July 1967. (Photo credit: Vern Jones)

since it was just before sunset. The concern to the officers at Market Time headquarters in Saigon was the trawler's course of 220 degrees.

Captain Ralph Di Cori, Market Time Commander, sent an urgent message to the Coastal Surveillance Center (CSC) in Da Nang. When advised of the details, Commander Charles R. Stephan, Market Time Task Group Commander in I Corps (CTG 115.1), placed CSC at general quarters. A CSC radarman plotted the trawler's position on the DRT tactical plot table. Its projected course placed landfall south of Chu Lai. The USS *Wilhoite* (DER-347), on its southern patrol barrier and closest to intercept at the time, was ordered to maintain its station.

YB-10 received several messages in a short period of time. Jones and Elliot deciphered them. Headquarters directed Branscomb to make another run on the trawler before sunset to check any deck activity along with its current location, course, and speed. On this run the contact had its running lights on and had changed course to 120 degrees in a southerly direction and parallel to the coastline.

Around the same time, Backdoor 7 reported their departure from CRB. YB-10's relief was on the way.

YB-7's PPC, Commander Phil Hawkins, contacted Lieutenant Commander Branscomb to initiate patrol handoff. Lieutenant Jones provided contact information to Lieutenant Netherby for radio transmission to YB-7. What had been a standard patrol ended on a high note for Crew 10. They had detected a probable North Vietnamese gunrunner.

Marathon Chase Begins

During mid-watch from midnight to 0400 hours, in the dimly lit *Wilhoite* Combat Information Center (CIC), Radarman Second Class Dave Payson took over controls of the surface radarscope. His good friend, RD3 John Wayne Bohon, from Sedalia, Missouri, took his station next to him at the DRT plotter table.

Payson donned his sound-powered phone headset and went to work on the contact. The glow of the surface radarscope painted an eerie green tone across his face.

"Skunk Alpha bears 090 degrees, eight miles, base course 120 degrees speed ten knots."

"Roger," Bohon replied. "Zero-nine-zero, ten miles, one-two-zero at ten." He meticulously pinpointed the exact location of the destroyer and the trawler on the grid-marked sheet, labeling it with the letter A.

In the Navy, an unidentified surface radarscope contact is labeled a "Skunk." The first of the day, beginning at midnight, is assigned the letters of the alphabet, beginning with A. Although noted as Skunk A, it is pronounced Skunk Alpha. Subsequent Skunks are labeled B (Bravo), C (Charlie), D (Delta), and so on. Payson relayed the information.

"Bridge, Radar. Skunk Alpha bears 090 degrees, eight miles, base course 120 degrees, speed ten knots."

"Roger, Radar," replied the messenger of the watch on the bridge. He posted the report in the ship's deck log.

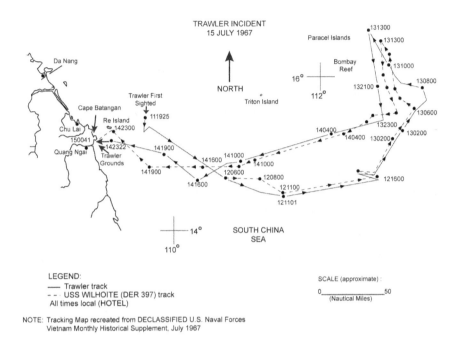

Marathon trawler tracking chart. (Image credit: Gabriel R. Herrera)

During the next several hours, the two radarmen continued tracking the trawler. Skunk Alpha, in no apparent rush, cruised at a constant ten knots, her captain and part of the crew presumably asleep below deck.

Commander Stephan directed the *Wilhoite* to close the contact at daybreak, make a visual inspection, and take pictures of the steel-hulled vessel. Lieutenant Commander E. W. Hays, *Wilhoite*'s skipper, left his sleeping quarters at 0400 hours. He stopped by CIC to review the latest position on Skunk Alpha prior to going up to the bridge, where a hot cup of coffee awaited him.

At 0450 hours, he ordered a final approach on the trawler. An hour later, at 0554 hours, Lieutenant Commander Hays turned to Lieutenant Junior Grade G. L. Peterson, officer of the deck (OOD).

"Mr. Peterson, sound general quarters."

"Aye, Captain." The OOD in turn relayed the order to the boatswain's mate of the watch.

The bosun leaned against the bulkhead by the Klaxon and the 1MC—the alarm control box and the ship's intercom. The small chrome boatswain's pipe hung from a lanyard around his neck. He flipped the lever on the 1MC, raised the instrument to his lips, and piped the shrill All Hands alert, then issued the order.

"General quarters, general quarters. All hands, man your battle stations. Up and forward on the starboard side, down and aft on the port side. General quarters, general quarters."

The bosun engaged the Klaxon and a repetitive short horn blast echoed throughout the ship for fifteen seconds.

"General quarters, general quarters," he repeated, followed by another fifteen seconds of the Klaxon. A third and final round of GQ Klaxon sounded.

At the appearance of the 300-foot US Navy war ship, Skunk Alpha went dead in the water. The *Wilhoite* circled the suspicious vessel twice, taking pictures, as did the VP-1 Market Time aircraft on station. Three crewmen walked topside. One was on the small fantail behind the wheelhouse. The other two crewmen stood by draped fish nets amidships on either side. All three appeared to be checking the nets hanging over horizontal bars. Not once did they glance at the destroyer.

To give the impression they were headed back to their patrol station along the coast of Vietnam, Lieutenant Commander Hays ordered his ship to head west.

Hays sent a situation report message to CSC Da Nang. It included the trawler's features—no official flag signifying country origin; bow plate number 459; 120-foot, olive-drab steel hull; pilothouse aft; no navigation radar; and fish nets scattered topside. The boxes on deck that aircraft YB-10 had reported were not observed.

The *Wilhoite*, upon reaching a distance placing it beyond the horizon and outside of the trawler's visual range, came about and initiated a clandestine radar tracking of Skunk Alpha. The radar picket ship maintained covert surveillance from 10 to 12 miles away as it continued its random easterly course.[3]

From Saigon, Captain Ralph Di Cori, Market Time Task Force Commander, via an encrypted message to CSC in Da Nang, made it known he wanted Skunk Alpha shadowed back to its home port, Haiphong, if necessary.

Throughout the morning of the twelfth, position reports kept coming into CSC in Da Nang, and radiomen marked the trawler's positions on their tactical plot. She maintained her southeasterly course, carrying her farther away from the coast of Vietnam. As ordered, the *Wilhoite* continued its covert surveillance of the presumed gunrunner. By 1100 hours and approximately 235 miles east-southeast of Chu Lai, Skunk Alpha changed course to an east-northeast heading.

Five hours later, she changed direction again. This time, at 1600 hours she took a west-northwesterly heading. The vessel maintained this heading for twenty miles. She appeared to be returning to the Vietnam coast. In an abrupt move, she reversed her track. Once back to her initial course change, she settled on a consistent north-northeast heading.

Skunk Alpha maintained this course for the remainder of the day and into the night, making only minor changes. The *Wilhoite,* monitoring the trawler's every move, relayed the information to CSC in Da Nang. The stealthy marathon pursuit continued.

On Thursday, July 13, at 0600 hours, Skunk Alpha began seven hours of radical course changes, culminating at 1300 hours with anchoring on the east side of the Paracel Islands, 230 nautical miles east-northeast of Chu Lai, presumably debating on a course of action. Would they permit themselves to be ridiculed and perhaps be condemned to death should they decide to return to the mainland? Or, perhaps realizing they had been detected, could they be awaiting further instructions from Hanoi?

Lieutenant Commander Hays kept his ship to the east of the Paracel Islands, beyond visible sight, and continued to monitor the trawler. RD2 Payson monitored the surface radarscope station once again. Skunk Alpha's radar blip became lost amidst the many small inlet rock outcrops peppering the edge of the larger island. Payson stared at each sweep of the scope, hoping to see a shift in one of the tiny contacts. He feared the trawler slipped away without his noticing. Lieutenant Commander Hays spent more time than normal in CIC, breathing down Payson's neck as he peered into the radarscope. Payson grew tense.

Before the end of his afternoon watch, the young radarman sprang up in his cushioned seat, blinked twice, and moved his face closer to the radarscope. He thought he saw something different. The radar sweep came around again and this time he did note a blip variation. He slid to the edge of his chair. One of the tiny specs appeared to have shifted. Payson observed three more sweeps before exclaiming to Bohon, "She's moving, she's moving. Skunk Alpha is on the run."

"Bridge, Radar. Skunk Alpha is on the move. Repeat, trawler is on the move."

"Copy, Radar."

It was now 1600 hours. Skunk Alpha heaved anchor, moved clear of the islands, and began moving in a south-southeasterly direction. Before long, Lieutenant Commander Hays dashed into CIC to observe the trawler's movement.

"Well done, Payson," the skipper said, patting him on the shoulder. "Keep up the good work, Bohon." Lieutenant Commander Hays, pleased with what he saw on the radarscope, returned to the bridge.

The radiomen plotted Skunk Alpha's movement a while longer before being relieved. By 2100, the trawler moved south of Bombay Reef. Skunk Alpha, now on the move for the past seven hours, made a decisive course change. At 2300 hours she turned to a southwesterly heading. If she stayed on this course for a good stretch, it could be assumed her second infiltration attempt had begun.

On the evening of July 12, Commander Stephan gathered his Northern Surveillance Group (NSG) staff to begin studying intercept options. Should the suspicious contact respond to the *Wilhoite*'s warning shots once inside the twelve-mile territorial waters of the Republic of Vietnam, a motor whale boat would be used to send a boarding party to search the vessel. They stood the risk of being cut down by camouflaged gun mounts. The destroyer also ran the danger of being damaged or possibly sunk if the trawler's crew detonated a self-destruct charge, typical to previous unsuccessful infiltration attempts. The gunrunner could attempt evading by turning back out into international water and escape.

A task group of vessels, positioned seaward of the infiltrator, seemed the best plan. Commander Stephan had the benefit of knowing landfall would be in the vicinity of Mui Batangan, based on Skunk Alpha's dead reckoning track (DRT) projection.

The March 14 trawler had beached north of this location. That fact added positive speculation the North Vietnamese naval commanders favored this coastline. Commander Stephan calculated landfall by 2000 hours on Friday 14, but because the moon would still be up at that time, he surmised Skunk Alpha would slow down to reach shore after midnight and make her final run under the cover of a moonless night.

The NSG staff meeting continued late into the evening. Plan development was fluid, growing rapidly. The *Wilhoite* occupied the lead role. The group welcomed the coincidental but opportune arrival of a new US gunboat. The USS *Gallup* (PG-85) had reported for Market Time duty earlier in the evening. The *Gallup* had already been scheduled for patrol the following day, south of Mui Batangan on the Quảng Ngãi coast. Her crew hadn't anticipated a debut of this magnitude, but nonetheless, Lieutenant Commander Bill Spane and his crew welcomed the opportunity to prove her worth.[4]

In June 1965, the *Gallup* was launched as the first class of high-performance small craft designed by the Navy since World War II. Their tasks included patrol, blockade, and surveillance for unconventional and guerilla warfare. Under normal underway steaming conditions, this gunboat used its two geared diesel engines, but because of the latest advances in naval engineering, its single but powerful gas turbine jet engine could be pressed into service for additional speed. The two systems combined allowed this type of vessel to reach speeds of forty knots in a short period of time. Her armament included four .50 caliber machine guns and 3"/50 and 40 mm gun mounts.

Considering the *Gallup*'s speed, Commander Stephan decided to stay in Da Nang until late Friday afternoon, at which time he would transit down the coast with ample time to transfer to the *Wilhoite* as the OTC (Officer in Tactical Command). Staying in Da Nang allowed him time to continue observing Skunk Alpha's DRT. He chose the *Wilhoite* as command center during the final stages of the operation because of her superb CIC and radio communication teams.

Since the establishment of the coastal surveillance operation on March 24, 1965, trawler attempts had all culminated in the demise of each vessel. Although Market Time units received credit for the infiltrators' destruction, the boats had been sunk by a self-inflicted blow. It was a known fact that a network of self-destruct charges lined each trawler's cargo holds. A detected gunrunner, certain its mission had failed, had two options—fight to the death or activate the delay-timer mechanism. The latter might allow the crew time to abandon ship before the vessel blew itself up. Given this strategy, the NSG intercept plan called for the inclusion of an Explosive Ordinance Demolition (EOD) specialist.

The meeting ended with a discussion on the need to add one or two Swift Boats to the mission. The PCF's ability to load the 81 mm mortar on the fantail, level it off, and fire it in the direct trigger-fire mode made the inclusion of the Swifts imperative. Selection of the PCFs depended on which patrol sector the trawler made its final approach. One of the Swifts on either side of the steel-hull's track would be called upon to join the task group.

On Friday morning, Commander Stephan awoke to learn Skunk Alpha was continuing her projected DRT course toward the Vietnam coast. To keep the trawler from aborting her mission, he called off the VP-1 Market Time aircraft, leaving covert surveillance in the hands of the able radar crew on the *Wilhoite*. In addition, US Navy, Coast Guard, and Republic of Vietnam seaborne units in southern I Corps received orders to stay clear of any suspected trawler infiltration attempt, unless otherwise directed.

Mui Batangan belonged to the Blue Dragons. The Korean Marines were available to suppress attempts to unload the trawler's cargo should she manage to make the beach. Commander Stephan alerted their commanders, Chu Lai–based US Army Task Force Oregon, as well as the III Marine Amphibious Force. If the trawler had the peninsula as its destination, it would land in their Tactical Area of Responsibility (TAOR).

The commander of Explosive Ordnance Disposal Unit Two, Commander A. Sokolowski, sent GMG2 Edward A. Knaup on a temporary duty assignment with the Northern Surveillance Group. He arrived at NSG headquarters at 1300 hours. Commander Stephan set a 1700-hour departure for the gunboat, allowing for a rendezvous with the *Wilhoite* at dusk for their transfer.[5]

At 1309 hours, CSC received a message from the Market Time commander in Saigon. Captain Ralph Di Cori ordered all units involved to proceed to a point astern of Skunk Alpha and form an intercept. In the hour that followed, Commander Stephan revised the NSG plan and had the station assignments encrypted for transmission later in the evening.

To avoid delays, he sent a message to Lieutenant Commander Hays, ordering him to bring the *Wilhoite* out onto Skunk Alpha's starboard bow to expedite the scheduled rendezvous. Commander Stephan, apprehensive there might be an attempt to infiltrate two trawlers, placed all units in I Corps on the alert. The Swifts in southern I Corps were placed on a special barrier.

Friday morning, as Gunner and I headed for breakfast, a call came in from Mr. Bergin. He often called me, prior to a scheduled departure, to give me specific meal requests for the 24-hour patrol. This time, however, he called to inform us our area had been changed. Our assigned area was now the Two Delta November patrol. This was not uncommon.

Mr. Bergin stopped by the Swift Boat operations shack to pick up the KAC codes for use in sending and receiving encrypted radio messages while on patrol. While there, Lieutenant Farrell informed him two additional passengers were assigned to our patrol. With the high potential of a trawler attempting landfall in one of our areas, he believed it best to take our Vietnamese Navy liaison petty officer, Nguyễn Văn Phát, commonly called the Fox. He and the senior US naval advisor with Coastal Group Fifteen, Lieutenant Junior Grade Philip Heidinger, joined us on patrol.

After breakfast, Gunner headed to the boat dock to begin his weapons check. I stayed behind to gather stores for the patrol. Halfway to the pier, a Jeep pulled onto the edge of the gravel road.

"Hop in, Bean!" Mr. Bergin hollered.

"Thanks, Skipper. The overloaded box is getting heavy. I should have called Mac to come help."

Reaching the fantail of the 79 Boat, Carver extended a brush-of-an-eyebrow salute to Mr. Bergin as we went aboard.

"We about ready to get underway, Boats?"

"Middleton is just about done with the guns. Mac and I have the boat squared away."

Porky climbed out the snipe-locker, wiping his greasy hands with a red rag he always draped over his rear pants pocket. One at a time, he lowered the heavy engine hatches. They slammed shut on the deck as he let them fall the last four inches. He turned, nodded his head in Mr. Bergin's direction. "Skipper."

The expected manner of addressing him was always "Mr. Bergin" or "Skipper." Mr. Bergin was Old Destroyer Navy, where the common phrase in that shipshape force, "familiarity breeds contempt," applied. So for me, it was "Yes, sir, Mr. Bergin" or "Yes, sir, Skipper."

"Engines ready?" Mr. Bergin asked.

"Now, you know my twin girls are always warmed up and ready for patrol by the time you come on board, Skipper."

"Good man, Porky. You never fail me."

"I'll fire up the radio and radar, Skipper. It shouldn't take long," I said.

"Mac," Boats called out. "Take the stores from Bean and get them squared away."

Fifteen minutes later, I reported to Mr. Bergin. "Radar and radio are a go, sir. I'll give Article a radio check when we're past Rosemary Point."

After placing his brown leather satchel in the cabin, Mr. Bergin took the after controls while Boats and Porky pulled in the aft mooring lines. PCF-79 pulled away from the pier. We were on our way south toward the Batangan Peninsula.

Three quarters of an hour later, we rendezvoused with PCF-56, already heading back to port, and relieved her. By 1135 hours we were on station within the Two Delta November patrol area, twenty-four miles south of Chu Lai. We established a three-mile barrier from shore, as directed by patrol op orders. Call sign Article (CSC Da Nang) controlled radio comms of all Market Time units operating in I Corps. More specifically, it was Commander Stephan's call sign when ashore.

At Chu Lai, Coastal Division 16 Commander, Lieutenant Farrell, used Home Plate as his call sign. Once on station our call sign became Same Drink Delta November. For the sake of brevity, we often transmitted as Delta November.

At 1200 hours, the officer of the deck, Lieutenant Junior Grade L. H. Bell, radioed CSC in Da Nang, giving the *Wilhoite's* position. The trawler maintained a course of 245 degrees and speed of ten knots. As the two vessels continued their westward track, both were east-southeast of Mui Batangan.

Patrol activities in the Two Delta November patrol sector were normal. We spent an hour inspecting junks around the river mouth of Sông Sa Kỳ, at the tip of the peninsula. I found it strange Mr. Bergin didn't move us south to inspect junks at the mouth of Sông Trà Khúc, four and a half miles south of Batangan. Typically, we'd patrol the length of our area and back again. We'd learn why soon enough.

Finishing the inspection of a tiny circular basket boat, Mr. Bergin maneuvered us south around the point where seas were calmer. At a safe distance from shore, he put the throttles to idle and called the crew to the fantail.

"Bean, let's chow down. What's for lunch?" Mr. Bergin asked.

"Well, today we're having beef Stroganoff, buttered carrots, bread rolls, and your choice of wine or beer."

"Don't be a smart-ass, Bean," Boats snipped. "I'm hungry, so whatcha bring?"

"Your favorite, Boats. Horse-cock sandwiches." Everyone laughed and thought I was pushing my luck with the response. But it *was* Carver's favorite. On occasion, he tried giving it a French flare by calling it *fillet de mule tool.*

"I'll pass," Lieutenant Heidinger declared, displaying a sour look.

Boats looked at him and explained, "Bah-loney, with lots of mayo. It's a Louisiana thang."

I prepared the sandwiches and Mac helped pass them out. Potato chips and soft drinks made the rounds as well. Mr. Bergin stood up from the small, elevated platform of the after steering station and moved us farther out to sea at a slow speed. He placed the throttles to idle position again, walked over to the mortar mount, and gathered his thoughts.

"Men, I've got important information for you. There's a trawler out there. Lieutenant Farrell gave us intel indicating the potential for a steel-hull infiltration attempt after dark is high. A month before we arrived in-country, one beached north of us, in the Two Delta patrol area."

Porky removed his cap, wiping sweat off his forehead. "Is it coming our way?"

"It hasn't been confirmed, but Killer Lou and I believe that because of recent occurrences at the mouth of the Sông Sa Kỳ, we determined a trawler could remain undetected as its cargo is unloaded deep inside the river."

"When will we find out if it's coming our way, sir?" I asked.

"Don't know, Bean. We're ordered to remain on high alert. I'm going to rendez-vous with Delta and Echo to set up a plan, just in case. Meanwhile, monitor the radio for any traffic from the big boys farther out and our Coastie friends in the area."

"Will do, sir."

Mac collected the cans and paper goods while I squared away the galley. Middleton climbed into the guntub. Boats, Porky, and Mr. Bergin went to the pilothouse.

I took a seat in front of the radio in the main cabin, grabbed the logbook and a pencil, and stood by for radio traffic of any kind. Although we weren't at general quarters, there was excitement in the air.

Mr. Bergin called the adjoining OICs via the Fox Mike, and soon the two PCFs arrived. Mac and I tipped the tire fenders over the side as did crewmen on the approaching Swifts. They moored either side of us and their OICs stepped onto our fantail.

I stood by the stepladder at the back of the cabin and listened to the three skippers talk about the possible infiltration attempt by a North Vietnamese gunrunner into one of our areas. The officers decided that if a trawler came into our area, the other two would come in and support us as well as cover our flanks. If it went north of us, we'd move in to assist, while Echo would cover our Delta November sector. Similarly, we would move south to assist Echo if it went into their area. They agreed any attempt at running the beach would take place at night. Radio reports would provide the earliest alert of an infiltration attempt in our area. The officers returned to their boats and departed to their assigned patrol sectors.

"Bean, call the crew to the fantail."

"Yes, sir," I replied.

I stepped into the pilothouse and called out, "Skipper wants us on the fantail."

Gunner jumped out of the guntub onto the top of the pilothouse. He stepped down the ladder on the starboard side of the cabin, then made his way back to the fantail where the rest of the crew was waiting.

Mr. Bergin glanced around to confirm the crew was present.

"Okay. Nothing is certain yet. We need to be fully prepared to engage the enemy. Boats, Porky, break out mortars—five HE, four illumination, and three Willie Peter. Remove the tapes off the canisters. Gunner, check mounts 51 and 52. Calibrate each fifty and be sure the mortar is ready for action."

It was a wise move. If we did go up against a trawler, every second counted. Preparing mortar rounds during combat, especially at night, would impede our combat efforts.

"What do I do?" asked Mac.

"Break out eight ammo boxes for the twin fifties and five boxes for the fantail. Place them in the cabin, but out of the way. Oh, and help Gunner take out the weapons from the small arms locker. He can tell you what else to do."

Gunner and Mac went off to carry out their assignments. It was a battle scenario we had studied over and over again in Coronado. Several months of intense combat training in Coronado was being put into action. It was no longer a drill.

Mr. Bergin continued, "Porky, give everything the once-over in the snipe locker and make sure the Onan generator won't let us down."

"Got it, Skipper."

"Boats, when Mac is finished helping Gunner, check emergency steering equipment and ensure you have everything you need."

Boats started walking away.

"Wait. Boats, one more thing. Double-check the damage control tool bag and put it on the lower bunk in the cabin." Boats nodded.

"Bean, it's been a while since you've cleaned the contact connections to our sound-powered-phones. You know dried up sea moisture can disrupt clear communication."

"Yes, sir. I'll take sandpaper and make sure they're clean."

"Have Mac help you sound-check the units in the pilothouse, guntub, and here on mount fifty-two."

"Is that it, Mr. Bergin?"

"No. Check radar reception. Verify the cabin and pilothouse night lights are working. And break out flashlights and change the plastic lens covers to red for night-vision use. Lay them out on the top bunk in the cabin."

"Aye, sir," I answered and went about my business.

Mr. Bergin cruised the patrol area at a slow pace from the pilothouse while folding the combat chart of the Batangan area for maximum range of coverage display. There was nothing Lieutenant Heidinger and the Fox could do but watch all the combat-readiness tasks being carried out.

Swift Boat crews, officers and enlisted, patrolling the southern coastline of I Corps were still unaware of any trawler intercept plans, much less that they were undergoing a major change. At the end of the NSG meeting the night before, the strategy included a task group of three Market Time vessels. The *Wilhoite* and *Gallup* would trail the infiltrator as it approached shore. Skunk Alpha had three alternatives: go dead in the water and surrender, turn port or starboard and be met with devastating force, or proceed on course and face unfavorable odds in an ensuing battle with one or two Swift Boats.

Earlier in the day, Lieutenant Victor G. "Pete" Reiling Jr., First Coastal Zone Psychological Operations Officer, approached Commander Stephan with a recommendation to include a PSYOP speaker team in the NSG trawler intercept plan. Reiling believed a surprise message could force the crew to surrender. The speakers could serve the operation in the event it reached a boarding stage.

Commander Stephan gave an unfavorable response. After offering several alternatives, Lieutenant Reiling's final suggestion met conditional approval. He recommended the PSYOP team board a Coast Guard cutter (WPB) and transit south to the intercept zone. The aluminum-hulled vessel's size could accommodate the speaker team and their equipment.[6]

The cutters replaced the wooden-hulled, eighty-three-foot, gasoline-powered cutters built during World War II. At general quarters, the crew of two officers and nine enlisted men manned the controls and five .50 caliber machine guns on deck. The cutter's armament included an over-under 81 mm mortar with piggyback-mounted .50 caliber machine guns on the bow, two "waist" guns amidships, and two more on both aft quarter slots.

Commander Stephan approved the plan on the condition that one of the WPBs available in port would volunteer for the job. Lieutenant Reiling's confidence unyielding, he went on to gather his equipment in preparation for a mid-afternoon departure. His poised disposition served as a foretoken of the positive outcome resulting from Commander Stephan's meeting with Lieutenant Commander John Friel, Coast Guard Division 12. He placed high confidence in his men, making it easy to volunteer one of his boats for the operation. The *Point Orient* (USCGC 82319) finished its routine upkeep, making the selection of a cutter best suited for the job an easy task.[7]

Skunk Alpha began a southwesterly course, altering her track away from the suspected destination—Mui Batangan. Regardless of the motive, the *Wilhoite* continued its marathon chase of the suspicious contact from beyond the horizon, as she had for the past three days.

Commander Hays, still unaware of an intercept plan, considered it a strong possibility his destroyer might have to challenge, engage, or even board the enemy ship on its own. At 1409 hours, he set general quarters, putting his crew through various combat scenarios, including board and search exercises. The *Wilhoite* secured from GQ at 1459 hours. The destroyer continued her covert surveillance of Skunk Alpha as she maintained her DRT course toward the Quảng Ngãi coast.

Aboard PCF-79, the waiting began . . . the hardest part of an anticipated battle.

CHAPTER 15

SKY HOOK

The *Point Orient*, under the command of twenty-four-year-old Lieutenant Junior Grade Norman T. Saunders, from Amityville, New York, departed the Da Nang Market Time pier at 1545 hours. His executive officer, Lieutenant Junior Grade Kenneth J. Morris, maneuvered the eighty-two-foot Coast Guard WPB through the no-wake zone near the piers and then on toward the harbor entrance. Lieutenant Reiling climbed the ladder into the pilothouse.

"Lieutenant, in the rush and excitement, I forgot to give you this from Commander Stephan. Not too late, I hope," Reiling said.

"Well, I'm sure it will confirm what you've already told me—we're off on a jolly trawler hunt," Saunders exclaimed, opening the message-routing envelope.

The orders, also sent by radio to the *Wilhoite* at 1545, announced the activation of Task Unit (TU) 115.1.9, code-named Sky Hook. The seaborne task unit consisted of the *Wilhoite, Gallup, Point Orient*, and a Swift Boat. The trawler's projected landfall was Mui Batangan. It allowed Commander Stephan to tentatively select PCF-79 as the fourth vessel in the intercept group. The 79 Boat would be advised later in the evening when it became certain Skunk Alpha's destination was Sông Sa Kỳ.

The *Point Orient*'s destination, Cù Lao Ré Island, lay seventy-seven nautical miles south from their base operation barges in Da Nang. They were to remain on station, south of the island, until ordered to close in on the trawler's starboard side. The cutter's task was crucial to the intercept plan. When Skunk Alpha crossed the five-mile line from shore, the speakers would blast the PSYOP surrender message into the night at the infiltrator.

Skipper Norman T. Saunders, US Coast Guard Cutter *Point Orient*, on patrol in I Corps, mid-summer 1967. (Photo credit: Norman T. Saunders)

Prior to departure, an unexpected passenger went aboard the *Point Orient*. Da Nang PAO sent a photographer, D. H. Weber. Lieutenant Reiling, Weber, and a WPB crewman began securing the large, Army-green, dual-unit speakers to the mast, located on the signal bridge, adjacent to and aft of the pilothouse. The men positioned them facing to port. Lieutenant Reiling wrote the surrender message prior to boarding the cutter. He took the tape recorder below deck and had his Vietnamese Navy counterpart record the message in Vietnamese repeatedly for a continuous playback loop.

The weather conditions were ideal: clear skies, light wind with no chop on the rolling waves, and South Texas hot. The *Point Orient*'s best speed of thirteen knots allowed the WPB to ride the six-to-eight-foot swells with ease. The South Vietnamese PSYOP officer showed gray-in-the-gills signs even before leaving the harbor and spent most of the trip, south along the coast, below deck.

At 1602 hours, the *Wilhoite* notified CSC of Skunk Alpha's status. Radar held the steel-hull at 150 degrees and fourteen miles away. She was on a base course of 295 degrees with a speed of eleven knots, ninety nautical miles southeast of Mui Batangan.

Commander Stephan received awaiting trawler confirmation news. After analyzing the photos taken by VP-1 aircrafts YB-10 and YB-7, intelligence sources in Saigon identified the steel-hull as a North Vietnamese gunrunner.

The stage was set.

Commander Stephan and GMG2 Knaup made last-minute preparations and boarded the *Gallup* on schedule at 1700 hours. Fifteen minutes later, the gunboat left the Market Time dock. Passing the point, Lieutenant Commander Bill Spane, skipper of the *Gallup*, advised all on board to stand fast and prepare for max speed. The helmsman eased forward on the throttle marked Turbine.

The bow on the 165-foot patrol gunboat rose like the front end of a dragster as it responded to the J-79 turbo jet engine, the same power plant as in F-4 Phantom II fighter planes. The engine whined as 14,000 horsepower spun the *Gallup*'s twin screws into action. It was designed to reach a maximum speed of forty knots in one minute and fifteen seconds. Its reverse-pitch screws allowed it to attain a complete stop in 330 feet— two ship lengths.

The *Gallup* took a bit more than an hour to catch up with the *Point Orient*. A lookout on the signal bridge informed Lieutenant Saunders.

"Skipper, the *Gallup* is on our stern, approaching fast."

Lieutenant Reiling, standing next to the sailor, turned to Saunders.

"Lieutenant, raise contact with the *Gallup*. Have her pass to port at 500 yards and drop speed to fifteen knots. Tell them to stand by for speaker sound check."

The PSYOP audio blasted to port for five minutes.

"Sierra, Xray. Read you, Lima Charlie."

"Thanks for the help, Sierra. Out."

The message was loud and clear at fifteen knots as well as when the *Gallup* returned to turbine speed, leaving the *Point Orient* in its wake as it continued course to rendezvous with the *Wilhoite*.

At 2030 hours, the *Gallup* went beyond the range of the twelve-mile beam sweep of the Cù Lao Ré Island lighthouse. This powerful beacon served as the main navigational aid in I Corps. The *Wilhoite* changed course to rendezvous with the *Gallup* twenty-two miles east-southeast of the island.

Commander Stephan and GMG2 Eddie Knaup boarded the *Gallup*'s 26-foot motor whale boat and proceeded toward the *Wilhoite*'s port quarter. On the bridge, the messenger of the watch posted the following entry: "2053 hours—CTU 115.1.9 embarked this ship."

Upon boarding, Commander Stephan became the Senior Officer Present Afloat (SOPA) as well as the Officer in Tactical Command (OTC). A junior officer escorted CDR Stephan to CIC, where Lieutenant Commander Hayes waited.

Mr. Bergin kept PCF-79 off the tip of Mui Batangan, guarding the entrance to Sông Sa Kỳ and keeping one mile seaward of Hong Bong Than, a tiny but hazardous flat-rock outcrop located two miles from the peninsula. It was a given that night watches would not be set. Going to battle stations half asleep placed a crew at a disadvantage.

Boats Carver sat on a metal stool by the port pilothouse door, studying the combat chart. I stood in the starboard side area, keeping my eyes focused on the radar screen with anticipation. The sweep on the contact return glass display was hypnotizing. The well-defined Batangan Peninsula appeared as a bright sherbet-orange mass projecting out from the otherwise straight Quảng Ngãi coastline. Close to shore, I maintained the tightest range setting of one and a half mile maximum distance. On the quarter-hour marks, I toggled to the twenty-four-mile maximum range setting, searching for the trawler. The unmarked rock hazard behind us appeared as an irregular blip.

The first-quarter moon kissed the western horizon, bathing our midnight gray Swift Boat. The white sandy beach in the distance remained visible. Within hours, we'd be shrouded in total darkness.

The radio crackled with a call from an unfamiliar unit.

"Same Drink units Delta November, Sierra, and Xray, this is Impair, stand by to authenticate."

"Skipper, who was that?"

"Don't know, Boats. Never heard of Impair."

Mr. Bergin grabbed the Prick 10 handset. Using unofficial OIC call signs, he raised comms with an adjacent patrol boat.

"Royal Flush, this is Mortimer Sierra, over."

"Go ahead, Mort."

"Did you copy last? Who's this Impair guy?"

"Break. Break. This is Impair. COMSEC. COMSEC. Impair, out."

"Oh, hell. Communication Security violation. Something's up."

Mr. Bergin, realizing Impair was monitoring our secondary radio communications, deduced he had to be in the area but, more important, he held an operational control position.

"Boats, take the wheel. Keep us seaward and away from flat rock."

"Aye." Carver climbed onto the elevated helmsman's chair.

Mr. Bergin stepped down into the cabin to retrieve his brown leather satchel. He returned and placed it on the chart table, sifting through the papers. He found the Op Orders.

"Same Drink Delta November, this is Impair. Over."

Mr. Bergin reached up and grabbed the mic. "Impair, this is Delta November."

"Roger. Authenticate. Over."

"Impair, authentication follows."

Mr. Bergin quickly turned pages and found the authentication response for the day and notified Impair.

"Affirmative, Delta November. Stand by for secure message."

"Delta November standing by. Out."

We knew the Same Drink Zulu call sign belonged to the USS *Wilhoite*, and the *Point Orient* used Same Drink Sierra. We were unaware the USS *Gallup* answered to Same Drink Xray. Soon after Sierra and Xray authenticated, we received an encrypted message advising all units to switch to a radio frequency of 3236 KCS immediately.

I raced down into the main cabin and spun the four black AN/URC-58 radio dials to the frequency ordered by Impair and returned to my station by the radar in the pilothouse.

"Radio frequency changed, Skipper."

"Thanks, Bean."

"Impair, this is Delta November. Radio check, over."

"Delta November, Impair. Roger. Stand by."

Sierra and Xray followed with their radio checks. On Mr. Bergin's order, I went back down into the cabin and sat by the radio with a pad and pencil, ready to record the long message. I began deciphering it at once. My palms grew moist as I continued breaking down the message. Our Swift Boat became part of an intercept mission. *She's heading our way. Oh, Lord! There's gonna be shit flying soon.*

Mr. Bergin hollered from the pilothouse, "Finished yet, Bean?"

"Almost done, Skipper. Checking it over right now."

I raced back into the pilothouse. "Trawler's coming into our area, Skipper."

"Read the message, Bean," Mr. Bergin directed.

"It's long, so I'll sum up. Looks like we're part of a trawler blocking force, along with the *Point Orient*, *Wilhoite*, and *Xray*, whoever that is. We're now part of Task Unit 115.1.9 and Impair is the on-scene commander or OTC. Sky Hook is our collective call sign."

Carver twirled the right side of the curled-up tip of his mustache. "So, who is Impair?"

"It makes sense, Boats. You know Article is CTG 115.1, our I Corps Market Time boss, Commander Stephan in Da Nang. Well, Impair must be his afloat call sign."

He glanced back at me. "Is that the entire message, Bean?"

"Negative, sir. We've been assigned positions. We're to take a port quarter slot to the trawler with the *Gallup* behind us. The *Point Orient* and *Wilhoite* will take similar stations on the starboard. Specific details follow."

"Good work, Bean. Get back to the radar and let me know if it picks up any contacts."

"Aye, Skipper."

Contact blips on the *Wilhoite*'s radar included the *Gallup*, the minesweeper USS *Pledge* (MSO-492) to the south, and the adversary, Skunk Alpha. In addition, and ahead of the formation, an LST appeared to be transiting north, perhaps to Chu Lai or Da Nang. Presumably, the trawler's captain determined the well-lit vessel ahead of him was a transiting cargo ship, and thus stayed on course and did not head back out to sea.

As nightfall arrived, the USS *Walker* (DD-517) approached the Batangan Peninsula from the south, preparing for a gunfire support mission. She anchored 4,000 yards south-southeast of the Sông Sa Kỳ river mouth. Knowing the trawler's projected landfall was the Batangan area, Mr. Bergin believed the crew aboard the trawler would reconsider their attempt once they saw the blasts from the *Walker*'s five-inch gun barrels.

We ran a fast course toward the gun-line ship. Riding the southeasterly waves, her bow pointing inland, we came alongside the *Walker*'s starboard side. Mr. Bergin yelled up at the bridge, warning them they were within striking distance of long-range enemy mortar fire and to move south of Batangan. He said nothing about a trawler headed our way. The *Walker* ignored his recommendation. Mr. Bergin wanted them to move far away from the area. He alerted CSC in Da Nang. Soon after, the *Walker* pulled anchor and moved south of the Sông Trà Khúc river mouth, clear of the Batangan area.

Beginning at 2130 hours and continuing for an hour, Skunk Alpha adjusted her course and speed, but in a westerly direction. She reacted to the passing LST, decreasing her speed to eight knots. Determining the large ship was on its way to Da Nang, the trawler returned to ten knots. Her course changes placed her farther south of Cù Lao Ré Island than her DRT projected. It steadied on a westerly course headed straight for the coastline south of Mui Batangan.

Commander Stephan received a message from Captain Di Cori in Saigon containing the last piece of the puzzle. Intelligence sources reported a "reception committee" on the north bank of the Sông Sa Kỳ, ready to unload the trawler's cargo. The river split the interior of the peninsula. Destination confirmed, Commander Stephan finalized the selection of the Swift Boat that would fill the vacant slot on the port quarter of the attack formation. Our boat, PCF-79, was in line for the job. The starboard quarter position belonged to the *Point Orient*.

"Sky Hook, Same Drink Zulu, over."

"Sierra, go ahead."

"Delta November. Roger. Over."

"Xray. Go ahead."

"Sky Hook, Skunk Alpha's 2200-hour position report follows: grid coordinates Charlie Sierra 62 66; course 294 degrees; speed ten knots."

Mr. Bergin's convictions grew stronger. Certain she would be coming our way, he mustered the crew inside the cabin.

"It's been confirmed, we've got a trawler heading this way. You can bet they're heavily armed and a firefight is guaranteed. Listen up, should I take a hit, Boats, you take command and keep the attack going. Porky, you take over if both Boats and I are down. We're not throwing in the towel. Remember our division motto, men: No Quarter. Stand by to man your battle stations on my order. Gunner, Bean, Boats, have your sound-powered phones at the ready. Prepare for action, men."

Impair's message specifying station assignments left no options for Skunk Alpha. The trawler would find itself cornered: either move, left or right, she faced defeat.

Training in Coronado didn't include simulated nighttime firefights with other vessels using dummy machine gun rounds. Any patriotic valor I'd dreamed of back then escaped me now in the approach of the upcoming battle. My stomach fluttered with apprehension, filling me with fear. I just hoped my face stayed blank, not showing how much I didn't want to die.

Flak jackets, helmets, M16s, .50 caliber canisters, and mortar rounds were at the ready. The covers over the twin .50s and aftermount remained in place, protecting them from ocean spray as our boat splashed into each oncoming wave. The sea became choppy. We were running darkened ship, only the blue glare from the night lights splashed across our faces. My eyes stayed focused on the radarscope. I checked the twenty-four-mile scan, but no contacts appeared in the vicinity of Cù Lao Ré Island.

In the three short months in-country, we had yet to experience one-on-one combat action. We knew from training how deadly the fire from our machine guns could be. The sight of returned gunfire was left totally to our imagination. Before daybreak I would no longer have to rely on speculation.

The bright amber glow of the radar sweep returned me to reality. I released myself to God's protection, as my mother taught me to do each time I left the house. Reaching into my shirt pocket, I pulled out the plastic figurine of St. Anthony holding the infant Jesus. I remembered my parents giving it to me at the airport when I left for Vietnam. They entrusted me to his protection while I was away at war. Knowing my mother's prayers for my safety would continue steadily until my return left me feeling reassured.

The waiting continued.

At 2215 hours, the radio once again came alive.

"Sky Hook, Impair. Stand by for encrypted transmission."

All units checked in with "Roger" or "Copy. Out." Message received, I grabbed the deciphering plate and began decoding it. When I finished, I rushed into the pilothouse.

"Skipper, I've got details on the task unit's positions."

"Let's hear them, Bean."

"Here it is. Station assignments on Impair's order only. Trawler's port quarter positions—Delta November at 2,500 yards; Xray at 5,000 yards and twenty degrees abaft the port beam; trawler's starboard quarter positions—Sierra at 2,500 yards; Zulu at 5,000 yards and twenty degrees abaft the starboard beam. Delta November and Sierra, prepare to illuminate the target on my signal. Do not fire without permission. VT fuses are authorized."

"She's not going to be able to escape," Boats remarked.

Mr. Bergin concurred, clenching his fist. "The trawler goes left, we got her. Right, the cutter will be there."

I tapped Mr. Bergin on the shoulder. "What's a VT fuse, sir?"

"Variable Time, Bean. They're mortar-detonation settings, usually used for air burst effect on enemy ground troops. We'll be in too close to use them."

The *Gallup*, *Wilhoite*, and Skunk Alpha were approximately twenty miles south of Cù Lao Ré Island on a westbound heading, twenty-five miles from shore. On orders from Commander Stephan, the *Point Orient* set a southwest course at best speed toward the Batangan Peninsula. The move would place the cutter within range of the trawler as it neared the coast, at which time Lieutenant Saunders would move his vessel aft the trawler's beam at three miles until further notice.

At 2300 hours, the *Wilhoite* placed Skunk Alpha's position at combat chart grid coordinates CS 29 76, maintaining a course of 240 degrees at nine knots. Her destination was thirty-two miles west. During the next half hour, she steadied on a westerly course, inching her way toward Mui Batangan.

Fifteen minutes later, Skunk Alpha crossed into the territorial waters of the Republic of Vietnam. The trawler stayed her course, indicating it was her intent to make a daring run for the mouth of the Sông Sa Kỳ.

Mr. Bergin, Boats, and I heard the following message:

"Sky Hook, this is Impair. Execute order per 2215-hour message. Out."

It was forty minutes before midnight. Mr. Bergin turned to Carver. "Set GQ, Boats."

"Aye, Skipper. General quarters! General quarters!" Carver yelled as he stepped through the main cabin and out onto the fantail.

Final preparations for offensive action were underway. Middleton, already in the guntub, lifted the cover of the twin fifties and handed it down to me. I hauled the big vinyl bulk into the bow sleeping compartment below. Porky and Boats removed the cover from Mount 52 on the fantail. Mac took it into the cabin, then went back out on the after deck. Lieutenant Heidinger stood by the port door in the pilothouse. The Fox, our Vietnamese Navy liaison, took up a position by the after-steering station.

Ten minutes later, another position report came in.

"Sky Hook, Impair. Skunk Alpha grid coordinates Bravo Sierra 99 79, course 265 degrees, speed ten knots."

"Bean," Mr. Bergin called, his voice up an octave.

"Yes, sir."

"Give 'em a Roger."

I reached for the mic and raised comms with Commander Stephan.

"Impair, this is Same Drink Delta November, over."

"Go ahead, Delta November."

"Copy, Skunk Alpha position report. BREAK. This unit manned and ready, over."

"Roger, out."

Per Commander Stephan's encrypted message, the four task unit vessels headed into position. The destroyer moved toward a point 2.8 miles astern of Skunk Alpha's starboard quarter. The *Gallup* took up a mirrored station on the enemy vessel's port side. Mr. Bergin moved the 79 Boat 1.4 miles off Skunk Alpha's port quarter, while the *Point Orient* closed to their designated slot, like ours but starboard of the trawler.

I flipped the range finder knob to the twelve-mile setting. Peering into the radar bonnet, four contacts appeared on the scope. The largest return blip was the *Wilhoite*. I was looking for a partial V-shaped formation heading toward Batangan, but it was too soon, since the units had not yet reached their assigned positions.

Activities on the *Wilhoite* intensified as her crew sped to their battle stations after GQ was sounded at 2334 hours. Commander Spane, his crew on the *Gallup* armed and ready, raced to reach the trawler's port position. The moon setting behind the western horizon, all units stood prepared for the next phase of the operation, the PSYOP surrender message. It would be carried out in total darkness.

At 2340 hours, Skunk Alpha was at grid coordinates BS 96 79, course 265 degrees and speed of ten knots, 9.4 miles from Batangan. Her heading, if continued, would place her nearly two miles south of Sông Sa Kỳ, halfway between the peninsula and the Sông Trà Khúc, the entrance to Quảng Ngãi. We were still 1,000 yards from our designated station.

Commander Stephan received another message from Captain Di Cori. It suggested all units prepare to take the Batangan area under suppressive fire in the event the trawler beached in that area. CSC Da Nang recommended fire support from the USS *Walker*.

Lieutenant Farrell, Coastal Division 16 Commander in Chu Lai, countered. He recommended assault helicopter units from Task Force Oregon be placed on alert to provide illumination. Ground troops called these nighttime flares "daylight." The plan also called for a small fire team to take enemy cargo-unloading handlers on shore under fire if necessary. Commander Stephan granted permission.

Minutes after midnight, Lieutenant Farrell made the call. The request worked its way down the Task Force Oregon command chain. The message reached the 71st Assault Helicopter Company's (AHC) operations center. The Company Commander, Major William Arink, alerted his men for a full combat assault.

Loudspeakers rang out in the Army compound. "Attention in the Company area. All flight crews report to the flight line immediately."

An all flight crews call meant ten aircraft would be airborne within ten minutes. The Blue Dragons, 5th Battalion of the Second Brigade Republic of Korea Marines, would be picked up from their field operations base south of Chu Lai and used in the combat assault at Batangan. Firebird and Rattler teams dashed to the Snake Pit, the flight line. Major George Jackson, the company's executive officer, received coordinates and radio frequency information at the operations tent, including a "customer" call sign.

SP4 Ron Seabolt, a Firebird gunship crew chief, was first to reach the birds and began releasing the tie-down hooks to the helicopter main rotors of the airships in the revetment area. He also gave the blades a quarter turn, making them ready for engine start.

Not long after the night call went out, all but one Slick (UH-1D) and two Gunships (UH-1C) were ordered to stand down until further notice. The mission changed to a light-fire team operation. Major Jackson, call sign Rattler 5, held the Command and Control (CC) position on the mission as well as being the aircraft commander (AC) of a UH-1D Flareship. WO-1 Conrad Howard occupied the "Peter Pilot" (P) slot. Behind the flight deck was PFC Tom Knapp, manning the M60 machine gun.

WO-1 Dave Ellingsworth, call sign Firebird 93 (nine three), was the AC and held the light-fire team lead position; WO-1 Ken Weigand the P. Flying the gunship wingman slot was Captain Joe Daugherty, call sign Firebird 94. His P was WO-1 Ager Davis. A crew chief and door gunner filled the enlisted man slots on each airship.

"Chu Lai tower, this is Rattler Lead with a flight of three for a south departure." Major Jackson waited for the response.

"Rattler Lead, you are cleared for a south departure. Altimeter two-nine-five, winds calm."

Major Jackson acknowledged, "Chu Lai tower, Roger. Out."

Staying below the fixed-wing aircraft airspace, the three Hueys headed south over land along the coast. Batangan was a short 20-minute flight from Chu Lai.

Skunk Alpha position reports came in at increasing intervals. Sensing an approaching firefight, I placed my right hand over my shirt pocket, feeling my St. Anthony statue. *Keep me safe, keep me safe.* At zero hundred hours, July 15, the *Wilhoite* reported Skunk Alpha at combat chart grid coordinates BS 90 79, course 270 degrees and speed of ten knots. I plotted the coordinates, finding it ironic to see the trawler remain on a latitude grid of 79, coinciding with our boat number. It seemed appropriate.

Mr. Bergin continued piloting PCF-79 toward our station. Return blips on radar took on a V-shaped formation—headed by Skunk Alpha—resembling a winter flock

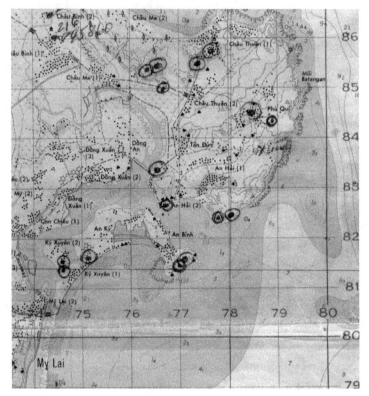

Combat chart South China Sea Vietnam Mỹ Lai, used by Swift Boat PCF-79 in its mission to capture North Vietnamese resupply trawler. (Photo credit: Raúl Herrera)

of migrating birds heading south. This gunrunning bird headed west, toward the Sông Sa Kỳ river mouth. Fast. As we closed the contact, the shoreline seas grew to a choppy six feet, with white caps visible all around us.

"Bean, holler at Gunner to put on his sound-powered phones, then head back to the fantail and tell Boats."

"Yes, sir," I replied and poked my head into the guntub, pulling on Middleton's bell-bottoms. "Headphones, Gunner."

Mac was below in the cabin. I had him pass the word to Boats. Mr. Bergin grabbed the pilothouse headset and put them on.

"Boats, Gunner—how copy?"

"It's taking them awhile to get set, sir. I'll have Mac let us know when they're ready and keep checking with Gunner."

The voice-operated unit consisted of cushioned earpieces secured to a headband. A neck strap supported a black metal chest plate on which a circular junction box held a sound-powered transmitter. Depressing a chrome button on top allowed the user to talk. A cable connected the junction box with a jack plug. Adding to the cumbersome gear, a heavy, oversize metal battle helmet fit over the device. It looked like a modified witch's caldron.

The trawler made no attempt to turn back, since its captain was presumably convinced that he had succeeded in breaking through our picket line of coastal defense.

Skunk Alpha's 0010 hours position report put her at grid coordinates BS 86 79, course 270 degrees, speed ten knots, two-tenths of a mile inside the five-mile line drawn from Mui Batangan.

"Same Drink Sierra, this is Impair, over."

The *Point Orient*'s skipper, Lieutenant Saunders, responded immediately.

"Impair, this is Sierra."

"This is Impair. Commence broadcast, over."

"Roger Impair. Broadcast follows."

"Sky Hook, this is Impair. Stand by for aggressive action on my command. Out."

The speakers on the *Point Orient* came alive, and the message blared into the darkness from the cutter's port side. The message in Vietnamese went out:

"You must stop and don't shoot. You are surrounded! We knew you were coming here. We have been waiting for you for three days. You must quickly wake up to the fact and surrender. The government will be merciful."

For five minutes Lieutenant Reiling transmitted the recorded message. It drew no response. Once skeptical of the mission, the Vietnamese PSYOP Navy officer grew ecstatic about the developments, grabbing the mic, ordering the trawler's captain to stop and surrender. The trawler continued to ignore the personal plea, pressing toward the Sông Sa Kỳ.

Sixteen minutes after midnight Commander Stephan's voice broke the momentary silence: "This is Impair. Delta November, Sierra, proceed with illumination rounds. Over."

I replied, "Delta November, Roger. Out."

"Sierra, Roger. Out."

Arriving on station, I heard the WPB's illumination mortar round blast in the distance. Seconds later, I peered out the starboard pilothouse door, looking into the pitch-black sky above. Another louder pop and a parachute opened, igniting a flare. The blinding white candle flame danced in the distance, too far to shed light on anything below—in particular, an evading enemy trawler. My mouth became dry, and my heart began to race. At any moment, the trawler would open fire on us.

Mr. Bergin pressed the chrome button on the sound-powered phone transmitter.

"Boats, pop two illumination rounds 90 degrees to starboard, full elevation, at my command."

Within moments, Carver announced the mortar round was ready.

Mr. Bergin positioned our boat's starboard side toward the river mouth, making the boat roll on the crest of each wave.

"Mount 52, fire when ready," Mr. Bergin ordered.

Through the small rectangular window on the pilothouse back bulkhead, I saw Porky drop the first mortar round in the barrel. The hull shuddered from the blast.

Through the starboard pilothouse door, only eerie dark shadows were visible in the distance, and none resembled the trawler or the WPB. A glaring flare flickered across the black sky, drifting with the southeast wind as it descended, illuminating the chute and the white irregular smoke trail above it.

The *Wilhoite* provided Skunk Alpha's last position report at 0020 hours. Grid coordinates BS 84 79, course 270 degrees and speed of ten knots—four short miles from her destination. Maintaining this course, she would pass 1,300 yards south of Hon Bong Than, a small but extremely dangerous navigational hazard—a rock outcrop barely projecting out of the water, two and a quarter miles east of the river mouth. As we moved in its direction, I tried locating it on radar. Seas grew turbulent closer to Mui Batangan, making it difficult to distinguish between the contact and white cap blips on radar, including Hon Bong Than.

Mr. Bergin glanced into the radar and then checked the compass.

"Bean, find the trawler on radar and point it out to me."

"Yes, sir," I replied and pressed my forehead against the black rubber radar bonnet. The screen became cluttered with false echoes. Bright orange returns resembled tiny raindrops on a puddle. Identifying the boldest blip was impossible.

All efforts to convince the trawler to stop failed. Impair ordered the *Point Orient* and our Swift Boat to fire warning shots across her bow with our twin .50s. We were too much astern of Skunk Alpha to ensure our shots went only across her bow, but Gunner did his best as he opened fire from the guntub. Bursts of red tracers from both boats formed an X ahead of Skunk Alpha's bow. The captain of enemy vessel number 459 remained determined to penetrate the peninsula, leaving two pursuing craft behind. Engaging her aggressors in combat would impede her progress. She didn't make any attempt to alter her course or intent.

After several minutes of warning shots, the flares drifted with the wind, making it impossible to gain visual contact of the trawler. I couldn't determine Skunk Alpha's location on radar. No one reported the trawler's position. She blended in with all the surface return clutter.

"I can't find her. We lost her, sir," I told Mr. Bergin.

"Did you adjust for clutter?"

"Yes, sir. We're picking up surface chop."

"Look for movement, Bean."

"Will do, Skipper."

Ten minutes later the trawler, apparently responding to radio homing signals from deep within the Sông Sa Kỳ, turned right to course 310 degrees, heading straight for the river mouth.

The chase hastened.

While en route to the Batangan Peninsula, Major Jackson (Rattler 5) advised Firebird 93 and 94 that the mission involved an evading trawler heading toward the Sông Sa Kỳ at Mui Batangan. Following his illumination, the two-gunship fire team would follow with attack runs on his order. The light-fire team arrived in the area forty minutes past midnight.

"Impair, this is Rattler 5. Over."

"Rattler 5, this is Impair. Over."

"Roger, what's the nature of your target? We're prepared to launch flares or assist in firefight. Over."

"This is Impair, strictly my illumination rounds now. Over."

"Roger, we're about one klick to the north at this time." One kilometer placed the helicopters directly above Mui Batangan, on the north bank of Sông Sa Kỳ.

"This is Impair, Roger. This is the target area. Under suspicion is a steel-hulled trawler. There are one Coast Guard cutter and one Swift Boat just astern of it, two larger craft farther out to sea."

"Affirmative. We'll fly overhead and pop daylight for you."

In the pilothouse, Mr. Bergin asked, "Bean, is that large return blip moving?"

While he continued course toward the river mouth at full throttle, I concentrated on the amber radar sweep. A larger blip appeared to be changing position on each sweep.

"Yes, sir. It's the trawler."

"Are you sure, Bean?"

"Affirmative. It's our target, sir."

Mr. Bergin reached over his head for the mic. "Impair, this is Delta November. I hold myself at 1,300 yards from target and closing. Over."

"Impair. Roger. Out."

Our heading placed us between the trawler and the gunboat Same Drink Xray. "Impair, this is Xray. Unable to comply with friendly units in the line of fire. Over." "Impair. Roger. Out."

At 0043 hours, Mr. Bergin ordered Boats to fire two more flares.

Aboard the *Point Orient*, Lieutenant Saunders informed Ken Morris, his XO, "That's Delta November, they just fired two illumination rounds." He followed with, "Oh, there he is!"

Skunk Alpha emerged from the darkness like Jules Verne's feared sea-monster submarine, the *Nautilus*.

"Holy shit, Skipper. There it is," I screamed. Skunk Alpha was visible straight out our front pilothouse window.

Mr. Bergin's voice rose an octave. "This is Delta November. At this time, I hold one contact, moving quick toward river mouth."

Lieutenant Saunders turned to Morris. "Who is that ahead of us there?" Over the *Point Orient*'s pilothouse speaker, they heard the continued communication exchange between Mr. Bergin and Impair.

"This is Impair. Over."

"This is Delta November. I've got one fast-moving contact, 1,300 yards from me, approximately 900 yards from river mouth."

Lieutenant Saunders broke in, "Delta November, this is Sierra. Affirmative, that's your target. Let's go get 'em."

"This is Delta November. I'm on my way!"

Major Jackson moved into position, 2,500 feet above the Sông Sa Kỳ river mouth. He toggled to onboard comms. "Prepare to drop a flare."

Prior to leaving the Snake Pit in Chu Lai, PFC Tom Knapp set the two-stage timers on all the flares to five- and ten-second increments. A yard-long braided wire, attached to one end of the magnesium flare, was snap-linked to the floor inside the cargo area. The stack of prepared flares rested on the floor by the open door.

"Drop flare, Gunner, drop flare," Major Jackson ordered.

Knapp tossed it out of the door. The cable attached to the end cap of the flare snapped taut, allowing the flare to slip away and drop freely into the night. Five seconds later, a loud pop sounded, and the parachute deployed. A louder bang occurred five seconds after, igniting the flare.

Major Jackson circled left around the flare, waiting for it to enter its final stages of illumination.

"Drop another, Gunner," he ordered Knapp.

Another flare dropped, delivering more daylight below.

On the *Point Orient*, Lieutenant Saunders observed that the flares were off the mark. "That's a negative. Have the flare ships move to the west, approximately one thousand yards."

"This is Rattler 5. Roger, one thousand yards to the east. Over."

"To the west, to the west!" Saunders replied.

Like anxious hounds on a fox hunt, our seaborne units were about to have the sly skunk cornered. Lieutenant Saunders exclaimed, "That fucking guy is trying to get away!" To his crew, he called out, "Three two zero, dead ahead. Dead ahead, Mount 51."

"Impair, Delta November. My contact is 700 yards off river mouth. Over."

Mr. Bergin clicked the button to the sound-powered phone. "Gunner, lock and load your .50s. Break. Boats, set mortar to trigger-fire mode and get Porky to load an HE round in the barrel. Stand by to fire to starboard."

I poked my head into Mount 51 and tapped Gunner's leg. He looked down as I slapped the ammo canister ring around the guntub. His thumbs-up signaled he was okay on .50 caliber ammo.

"Impair, this is Xray. Unable to fire with friendly unit in the line of fire. Over."

"Impair. Roger. Out."

"Impair, this is Sierra. If you have your flare ship illuminate where he is now, along the shoreline, it will be beautiful. Over."

"This is Rattler 5. Monitoring you on radio."

"This is Sierra. Roger. If you can drop them right along the shore, outline this guy for us, it would be beautiful. Over."

"Rattler 5. Roger. Out."

After we fired two more rounds of illumination, Ratter 5 broke in urgently.

"Impair, this is Ratter 5! How about turning off your artillery fire at this time?"

"This is Impair, Wilco. Same Drink Sierra and Delta November, this is Impair. Fire no further illumination rounds. Over."

"This is Sierra, Roger. Out."

Mr. Bergin shifted in the helmsman seat. "Bean, eyes on the radar and fathometer, keep us clear of the rocks. We're going in."

"Will do, Skipper." My Timex showed forty-five minutes past midnight.

He peered into the radar for a second, then reached for the mic.

"Impair, this is Delta November. Over."

"This is Impair. Over."

"Delta November. He's headed up the river, request permission to go in and get him. Over."

"This is Impair. PER GRA."

"Delta November, say again. Over."

"Permission granted. Over."

"This is Delta November. At this time, this unit preparing to open fire. Over."

"Delta November is going in there and get him," Lieutenant Saunders acknowledged. His men on the *Point Orient* stood ready to attack Skunk Alpha should it decide to turn north once our attack commenced.

Meanwhile, Major Jackson's second pair of flares fell behind Skunk Alpha, creating a dark trawler silhouette. What a sight to behold. Clearly, it was not a Navy ship. The raised pilothouse occupied the entire aft section, making the rest of the vessel look more like a giant shipping tanker. Racing toward the river mouth at ten knots, Skunk Alpha ignored the illumination on her.

The effective firing range of the M2 Browning .50 caliber machine gun is 2,000 yards. We were closing fast at 1,000 yards.

"Commence firing, Gunner. Open fire. Let 'em have it," Mr. Bergin ordered.

The clatter of the twin-fifties above and behind me was deafening. The pilothouse shook. Hot brass casings rained down off our backs and clinked fast notes on the aluminum deck. Through the front right window, I saw a scarlet tracer round trail cut into the night in short bursts. Gunner trained his weapons to the right, gaining a line on the target. Mr. Bergin turned the helm in the direction of Gunner's tracers. Skunk Alpha lay straight ahead at 500 yards.

Moments later, well within the 1,000-yard maximum mortar effective trigger-fire mode range, Mr. Bergin pulled on the black-ball throttle knobs, placing them in a vertical position, applying full left rudder. The boat slowed to a full stop, placing our starboard side to the trawler's port quarter. He called to Mount 52 on the fantail:

"Boats, fire when ready."

The small rear pilothouse window gave me a clear view of the fantail.

Boats swung the mortar to starboard, raised the back end of the mortar mount, and leveled the barrel. He locked the mount, slightly above horizontal, and took aim. The swells below our keel kept the boat dancing sideways. Keeping an eye through the target finder, he waited until the trawler came into view and fired. The high-explosive round was on its way. Mr. Bergin pushed the throttles forward and turned the wheel hard right, continuing the advance on Skunk Alpha. Middleton kept his dual-barrel .50s on target.

Lieutenant Saunders, on the *Point Orient*, observed the muzzle blast. "He shot that one low."

"Sierra, this is Impair. Are you preparing to open fire, also? Over."

"This is Sierra. Affirmative, fire will follow."

"This is Impair. Roger. Out."

"Delta November. Receiving fire from target. Over."

A heavy machine gun position behind their pilothouse returned fire. Green enemy tracers zigzagged across the night sky toward us.

Battle on.

My attention shifted between the radar, fathometer, and the impressive flickering of red and green deadly fireflies crossing paths in front of me.

Lieutenant Saunders called to his forward over-under gun mount, "On the beam. Our target is in the middle of the river. Don't get mixed up with the Swift."

"Impair, this is Same Drink Echo. We're approximately six miles from action, ready to provide assistance if necessary. Over."

"This is Impair. Negatory at this time."

Lieutenant Morris recommended, "Think we want to cease fire? That Swift is getting in our line of fire there."

"Impair, Rattler 5. Receiving fire from the ship. Receiving fire from the ship."

"Impair, this is Sierra. Receiving fire from the vessel also. Over."

Red tracers cut across our bow from our starboard quarter. Mr. Bergin reacted immediately. "This is Delta November. Cease fire, cease fire!"

"Sierra, this is Impair. Request that you cease fire while Delta November gets into position. Over."

"This is Sierra. Roger."

"They want us to cease fire." Sierra's horn blasted six times. Immediately their machine guns went silent. "OK. Delta November is going in there now," Lieutenant Saunders acknowledged.

Lieutenant Morris added, "That Swift is chewing her up!"

Mr. Bergin raised his voice in calling Mount 52. "Boats, load a Willie Peter [WP] round, I'm coming about."

I peered into the radar bonnet. "Skunk Alpha at one hundred yards, sir."

Small arms fire pinged off our hull. Enemy gunfire was on target. Identical heavy machine gun muzzle flashes were visible from the trawler's mid-section and from behind the pilothouse. Their gunners walked their rounds toward our Swift Boat. Middleton saw this, and let up on the .50s, eliminating us as a target source for them. He resumed fire once out of their line of fire.

Skunk Alpha's amidships anti-aircraft gunners trained their weapons skyward, sending two trails of green tracers in Major Jackson's flare ship direction. Middleton sprayed lead across the ship, from stem to stern. He concentrated on enemy fire coming from the fantail. The enemy gun mount went silent.

Mr. Bergin repeated the broadside maneuver. Porky loaded the WP round, and Boats Carver took aim and fired.

"He hit it! Boats nailed it, Skipper!" I yelled.

"I think that trawler's been hit. Which unit is that?" Lieutenant Saunders asked.

"The trawler," Lieutenant Morris answered.

"Are you sure? He fired a Willie Peter in there, I believe."

Ten minutes before one o'clock in the morning, Skunk Alpha's pilothouse exploded into a blinding chemical white ball of fire. On impact, thousands of white-hot incendiary threads fanned out from the center. At a Fourth of July fireworks event, the display would have received the loudest public cheer. It was a morbid work of art, lasting only seconds. In that short period, the chemical burned at 1,472- to 1,832-degree Fahrenheit, capable of melting aluminum alloy. Bodies in the pilothouse were reduced to bone.

Carver's round hit the aft edge of the port side pilothouse door. The trawler veered north and ran aground on a rocky sandbar, a short distance north of a long, flat-rock outcrop to the right of Sông Sa Kỳ's main channel.

"Delta November, this is Impair. No further mortars. There's aircraft in the air. Over."

Middleton's twin .50s barrage interfered with communications.

"This is Impair. I say again, limit your fire at this time to .50 caliber due to aircraft in the air. Over."

"This is Delta November. Roger, continuing with .50 caliber at seventy-five yards from contact. Over."

Mac poked his head into the pilothouse. "Does Gunner need ammo?"

"Bring up a couple of canisters, just to have them ready, Mac." Mr. Bergin continued, "First, tell Boats to secure the mortar. No more 81 fire, .50 caliber only."

"Aye." Mac headed back into the main cabin.

Abreast of the trawler now, Middleton and Carver continued firing, determined to silence the small arms fire coming from Skunk Alpha's port side. Too close to potential reef danger, Mr. Bergin brought us about on to a seaward heading. Mounts 51 and 52 swung their weapons to port and continued blasting away at the burning trawler.

"Five-one, five-two, five-four, commence firing," Saunders ordered.

"Five-one, five-two, five-four, commence firing," Lieutenant Morris repeated the order to the *Point Orient* machine gun positions.

Three .50 caliber gun mounts on the *Point Orient* began firing at the trawler. Lieutenant Saunders was euphoric. "Did you see the fucker go up when it hit? Let's keep it going, men."

Behind us, the *Gallup* fired 40mm projectiles. On the *Point Orient*, Lieutenant Saunders heard the rapid *pomp-pomp-pomp* of the *Gallup*'s weapon. Above us, Major Jackson dropped more flares, keeping the trawler illuminated. "Firebird 93, this is Rattler 5. Prepare your attack run."

Although the gunships were both UH-1Cs, they carried different armament. Firebird 93 Lead was affectionately called The Hog. It carried two pods of twenty-four 2.75-inch folding fin aerial rockets (FFAR). Ellingsworth preferred fourteen-pound HE warheads in his arsenal. Each rocket had a twenty-meter killing radius. The explosive effect of one rocket was shy of the impact a 105 Howitzer round creates. Two M60s, one on each side of the open cargo area, completed its armament.

Captain Daugherty's UH-1C had mini-guns, one on either side. Each six-barrel Gatling-style weapon was capable of firing 7.62mm of ammunition at a rate of 2,000 rounds per minute. In addition, the aircraft carried two seven-shot rocket pods. Two M60s were manned by the crew chief and the gunner.

Firebird 93 and fire team lead WO-1 Dave Ellingsworth reported: "Firebird 94 making first run. Going in from seaward with a right break."

"Roger," replied Captain Daugherty, the wingman. "Will follow you in."

Nine hundred yards seaward of the trawler and 1,000 feet in the air, Firebird 94 maneuvered into a left echelon position, behind and below Firebird 93 at 200 yards. This allowed Daugherty to take the enemy position, shooting at the lead unit, under fire.

The UH-1C Hueys came in fast. The first two rockets swooshed out of their pods, leaving a sparkling fire trail along their path. The shot was low. They exploded upon hitting the water. Ellingsworth pulled slightly on the cyclic stick, raising the nose, took aim again, and fired two more rockets. These two rounds exploded on the trawler's starboard side hull.

"You hit it! You hit the son of a bitch!" Weigand screamed, repeatedly pounding his fist on Ellingsworth's left leg as he broke right 500 feet off the surface and 600 feet from the trawler.

Daugherty followed with an impressive display of mini-gun firepower, riddling the ship, his rockets also finding their mark, followed by a right break.

"Firebird 93, where are you?" Daugherty asked.

"Staying ahead of the fucking green tracers, 94. Follow them and you'll find me."

Both gunships continued firing runs on the burning trawler, one run after another. During one attack a secondary explosion occurred, but Skunk Alpha remained afloat. At 0101 hours, Lieutenants Saunders and Morris observed the blast from the *Point Orient*'s bridge. It wasn't certain what exploded, perhaps rocket-propelled grenade rounds. The detonation wasn't large enough to indicate cargo in one of the holds was the cause.

While Mr. Bergin maneuvered around the trawler's stern, I helped Gunner reload .50 caliber ammo into the curved canisters in the guntub. During the initial engagement Mac had entered the cabin from the fantail to retrieve more ammo boxes and fallen into the open magazine. He overlooked the fact he earlier left the metal lid off the deck. A small gash on his leg didn't keep him from hauling ammo boxes across the open fantail deck.

Initiating a late nineteenth to mid-twentieth century naval warfare tactic known as Crossing the T, we maneuvered astern of the trawler and onto its starboard side, continuing our attack. The barrels on Middleton's twin .50s glowed red, almost candle-flame yellow. The firefight continued, not as heavy as when we made initial contact, yet sporadic small arms fire still erupted from different locations aboard the trawler. I grabbed an M16, walked out onto the bow in front of the pilothouse, and unloaded two clips at the burning trawler. While reaching for another clip, I felt the bow scrape the reef. I banged on the center Plexiglas window, signaling Mr. Bergin to back away. Our boat was at idle speed and had drifted too close to Batangan. He backed us off the reef, turned us around and headed seaward. Gunner and Boats continued their machine gun fire.

The cutter came close to becoming a casualty of friendly fire at the hands of the *Gallup*. Lieutenant Saunders reacted to three large explosions in the water off their port bow. He'd heard the *pomp-pomp* sounds moments before the rounds hit. He knew it was the *Gallup*'s 40mm gun. "Same Drink Xray, Same Drink Sierra. Put your rounds right over the top of that trawler next time. Over."

Before Xray responded, a larger explosion occurred much closer to the cutter.

"Same Drink Xray, this is Same Drink Sierra. Your rounds are bursting fifty yards in front of us. Over." No response. "Same Drink Xray, do you copy? Over."

"Same Drink Xray. Roger. Over."

"Let's get 'em in," Saunders cautioned.

Overhead, Rattler 5 contacted Impair. "Roger. We've been on station forty minutes. If you don't need any more fire, we're heading back. We've got one Uniform Sierra Alpha (jet) standing by ready to come in if you want."

Saunders exclaimed, "Holy Mother! Back off, back off." The cutter's engines shuddered as they shifted into reverse. Saunders, now livid, reached for the mic. "Impair, Same Drink Sierra. Some goddamn idiot is firing rounds in the water right next to me. Over."

"Impair. All units. Cease fire at this time. Over."

"This is Sierra. Roger. Break. Same Drink Xray, that was your round that went in the water right next to me, one thousand yards short of target. Over."

"Sierra, request you move north. Over."

"This is Sierra. Roger. Request you move your rounds in one thousand yards. Over."

"Xray, this is Impair. Cease fire for approximately ten minutes. Over."

"This is Xray. Roger. Out."

"Delta November, this is Impair. Cease fire for approximately ten minutes. Over."

"This is Delta November. Roger. Out."

Lieutenant Saunders let out a sigh of relief. "Let's have a cigarette. God damn! We got it. We got that son of a bitch!"

Lieutenant Morris responded, "I can go home happy now!"

Commander Stephan (Impair) received an urgent call from a US advisor with the Korean Marine Blue Dragons. They were about to begin an artillery attack on Skunk Alpha and the surrounding area. Since the trawler landed in their TAOR, they immediately laid claim to it and its cargo, taking the expression "possession is nine-tenths of the law" to a higher level.

"Sky Hook, this is Impair. Deploy to seaward 2,500 yards. Repeat. Sky Hook, deploy to seaward 2,500 yards. All units. Over."

"This is Same Drink Sierra. Roger. Out."

I grabbed the mic. "This is Delta November. Roger. Out."

"Impair, this is Xray. Moving to seaward. Over."

"Impair. Roger. Out."

As I reached above my head to secure the mic, Mr. Bergin took it from me.

"Impair. This is Delta November. My bore is clear on contact. Out."

"Impair, this is Rattler 5. Our gunships are out of ammo at this time. We're left with two flares. Heading back to refuel. You want us back on station? Over."

"Roger. This is Impair. I doubt we need you to come back. Over."

"Rattler 5. Roger."

On the *Point Orient*, Lieutenant Saunders authorized his men to remove their flak jackets.

A second small-fire team, the Scorpions from the 161st AHC, with Captain Rod Bither in the lead position, departed Chu Lai at 0115 hours to relieve Major Jackson's small-fire team at Batangan.[1] Arriving on scene, they carefully worked firing runs on the trawler, dodging Republic of Korea (ROK) artillery. During a couple of runs,

Korean shells burst dangerously close below them. Regardless, the two gunships managed to score direct hits on the dying vessel. In addition, they sprayed lead and rocket fire along the north side riverbank, making it impossible for the enemy to approach the stricken cargo ship.

Time passed, and all seaborne units returned to their attack. In addition to raining more .50 caliber machine gun fire on Skunk Alpha, we expended another twenty HE mortar rounds. At 0200 hours, the USS *Walker* moved north toward Batangan to join the attack, providing fire support around the mouth of the river to prevent the Viet Cong from making any organized attempt to off-load the cargo.

The *Point Orient* depleted her remaining ammo and detached from the operation at 0320 hours. Her crew proudly headed back to Da Nang to rearm and fulfill her patrol obligations later that morning. For the past three hours, they had engaged a North Vietnamese resupply vessel, contributing to its capture. At 0330 hours, PCF-20 moved into the operational area from the Delta Mike patrol sector to our north and relived the *Point Orient*.

After our last mortar barrage, we pulled a good distance seaward. Mr. Bergin placed the throttles in the neutral position and gathered the crew once again on the fantail. At 0110 hours the battle ended. I reached for my St. Anthony statue, closed my eyes and gave thanks to God for surviving the battle.

"Anyone injured? Boat damage?"

"My leg is scraped, Skipper," Mac said. "I forgot I removed the ammo locker deck cover in the cabin and fell in. Hurts like hell, but not broken."

"No Purple Heart for a scrape, Mac," Middleton chimed in.

"The engine room took several hits on the starboard side at the water line. They're plugged," Porky reported.

"Can't wait to get back to base to write home about what we did. Are we getting medals, Skipper?" I asked Mr. Bergin.

"Command in Da Nang promised Silver Stars for anyone capturing a trawler in I Corps."

"Dollar to a donut, that shit will never happen," Boats remarked.

"Being alive after that much shit flying over our heads is reward enough for me," Porky proclaimed.

"I saw your barrels turn almost white from the hurt you were putting on them," I told Gunner.

"Hell, I was afraid I'd start having cook-offs, but it didn't happen," he said.

"Did you feel the heat off of Boats' Willie Peter round when it hit?"

"Sure did, Mac," Middleton noted. "Even felt the boat rock from the blast. How close were we?"

"Fifty to seventy-five yards by the radar," Mr. Bergin answered.

"Too damn close," Carver exclaimed. "I swear I could see those fuckers running across the open deck."

"I saw them too, Boats. The view from up there in my guntub was better than sitting front-row center in a movie house back home watching *In Harm's Way*."

Mr. Bergin gave praises all around. "You did an exceptional job, men. Our training paid off. Bravo Zulu—job well done." We shared pats on the back with each other.

"Bean, get back to the helm. Watch the radar and keep us away from ships and a safe distance from shore. Let me know of any important messages."

"Aye, Skipper."

I headed back to the pilothouse. What I had fantasized, while training in Coronado, had become reality. We took down a gunrunning enemy trawler—twenty feet longer than twice the size of our Swift Boat. Gunner put the battling steel hull up against the Sông Sa Kỳ ropes, and Carver landed the Rocky Marciano knock-out "Susie Q" blow to Skunk Alpha's portside jaw—and in a record-setting time of five minutes.

At 0415 hours, we joined the firing line once again to expend the rest of our ammunition. Impair granted permission for us to secure and return to port at 0530 hours. We were replaced by Same Drink Delta (PCF-54).

While Mac and I began clearing the boat of all spent .50 caliber brass casings, I thanked the Lord for keeping our crew safe during the intense firefight. Moreover, I was glad that if there was a self-destruct system in place on the trawler, for whatever reason, it didn't blow up while we were engaged in battle. By 0600 hours, we made the hard-left turn to port into the Chu Lai channel at Rosemary Point.

Mr. Bergin secured our deck broom to the front of the radar mast, above the guntub. As when Dutch Admiral Maarten Troop, in the mid-1600s, had a sailor secure a broom from the ship's mast signifying he had "swept" the British from the seas, Mr. Bergin proclaimed PCF-79 and Crew 74-A made a "clean sweep" of Skunk Alpha.

A celebration committee headed by our Division Commander Lieutenant Farrell greeted us at the Swift Boat dock at 0610 hours. Officers and enlisted men congratulated us and cheered the victory with cold beer. While the storytelling continued on the fantail, I took a moment to check the boat for damage. The enemy had indeed been on target. We sustained three hits: one in the bow, another in the pilothouse, and the third in the engine room.

A Swift Boat crewman observes two South Vietnamese Yabuta Patrol junks approaching a captured North Vietnamese resupply trawler on a sandbar, Sa Kỳ river mouth, Batangan Peninsula, Quảng Ngãi Province, Republic of Vietnam, 15 July 1967. (Photo credit: US Navy)

We finished our cleanup duties and headed for the barracks, exhausted but filled with pride. Gunner and I turned in and slept past lunch but managed to drag ourselves out of our racks in time for evening chow.

After leaving the Batangan area before sunrise, PCF-20 and PCF-54 received permission to carry out firing runs on the grounded vessel, ensuring enemy forces ashore stayed clear of the captured ship. Fires renewed aboard the trawler.

The earlier planned night combat assault on Batangan was called off by mission planners at the 14th Combat Aviation Battalion in Chu Lai. The commanding officer, Lieutenant Commander William Ponder, directed Major John Coates to plan a morning combat assault. During the night, he and Major Derald Smith flew south to coordinate the mission with Major Ted Brunson, USAF ALO/FAC advisor with the ROK's 2nd Marine Brigade.

At daybreak, Major Coates and Lieutenant Commander Ponder were airborne, high above Mui Batangan, directing the air assault. Major Smith stayed behind to continue mission coordination with Major Brunson. By full light, at 0630 hours,

Trawler showing numerous mortar and rocket fire hits on its starboard side. (Photo credit: US Navy)

the *Walker* began hitting designated landing zones on both sides of the river mouth. Shark and Dolphin units from the 174th AHC dispersed to several unfamiliar ROK outposts to pick up troops for the assault.[2]

At 0830 hours, Korean Lieutenant Colonel Yon Okin On, Tactical Deputy for Brigadier General Kim Young Sang (ROK Marine Commanding General), led a marine platoon onto the narrow coral reef and proceeded to lay claim to the smoldering trawler. Lieutenant Col. On deployed to the site to ensure the trawler remained where *they* had captured it. An hour later, ROKs sent to the northern riverbank found a large rubber raft jammed up against the rocky shoreline. They also discovered two severely bullet-riddled bodies nearby.

The Koreans off-loaded rifle-size crates, placed them onto wooden patrol boats from the nearby Coastal Group (CG) 16 base, then transported them onto awaiting choppers on the flat rock. Chinook helos from Chu Lai picked up the weapons and transferred them to the ROK 2nd Brigade headquarters nearby.

Standing proud next to mounds of weapons removed from Skunk Alpha, Colonel Chang Taikil, ROK 2nd Marine Brigade Chief of Staff, addressed a triumphant gathering of Blue Dragons. Charles Black, *Ledger-Enquirer* staff writer of Columbus, Georgia, was there to record the following:

South Vietnamese Navy Command Junk alongside enemy vessel. (Photo credit: US Navy)

You must understand that this is the most significant of all victories, the capture of enemy weapons and ammunition. Think of those who would have been killed if these would have been captured on the battlefield. Here are all these weapons, each more important than killing the men who would use them. The men could be replaced by more Viet Cong, but the weapons cannot be. This is more significant than a battle victory.

Having disembarked the *Wilhoite* at 0700 hours, GMG2 Eddie Knaup, the EOD specialist, and Commander Stephan boarded PCF-20 and proceeded toward the trawler. Stephan was confident that the combined sea and air attack must have prevented the crew from staying around to arm the destructive system.

A hidden reef blocked the Swift from reaching the vessel. Both men transferred to the CG 16 Command Junk. To Stephan's surprise, a handful of ROKs, with rifles at the ready, motioned them to stay away. It took the greater part of the morning before a "Bring her home" message from Market Time Commander, Captain Di Cori, was received. The ROKs backed off.

Skunk Alpha appeared to be caught on her stern, perhaps its rudder or screws. Knowing it would be hazardous walking among all the debris on the trawler's deck,

Commander Stephan left his M14 rifle in the junk, a move he later regretted. The boarding party consisted of four Americans and two Republic of Vietnam Navy personnel. He expected to find empty cargo holds, having seen how expeditiously the ROKs moved about unloading the trawler's cargo. Instead, at first glance, he was glad to see they were full. Knaup went to work immediately, disappearing below deck in search of the self-destruct charge system.

With caution, Commander Stephan advanced toward the bow that rose and fell with each passing wave. Reaching over the bow's gunwale, he removed the starboard number plate, certain he'd find 459 as the SP-2H reconnaissance plane had reported. Instead, it read 418. It appeared the trawler's crew used paint remover to eliminate the 59, repainting it to read 441. The port side plate, later found in the boatswain's locker beneath the pilothouse, read 459 on one side and 418 on the other. It was a known fact the North Vietnamese often changed bow numbers attempting to confuse Market Time surveillance units.

The Naval Support Activity Detachment at Chu Lai sent two Landing Craft Mechanized (LCM 8s), commonly called Mike Boats or Mike 8s, to help salvage the trawler. The craft served as troop or supply and equipment carriers. They arrived at 1300 hours.

Fishing nets identified by Lieutenant Commander Max Branscomb's YB-10 crew lay in a heap between the two holds. A closer look revealed painted wood fish decoys secured to the net. The ROKs removed the three anti-aircraft machine guns, two amidships on either side and the third behind the pilothouse. Expended brass casings lay strewn about the deck at each battle station.

The blaze in the pilothouse during the night had transformed the entire aft section a scorched yellow orange. Blistered drab-olive paint appeared in several areas astern. Square metal cutouts were all that remained where windows once kept the helmsman dry from rain and crashing waves during heavy seas. Everywhere Stephan looked, bullet holes of varying sizes riddled the surface, with numerous larger gaping holes visible along the exposed vertical hull. A probable helicopter rocket hit tore into the starboard exhaust stack.

The intense fire destroyed everything below decks in the living quarters. Skeletal remains of sleeping bunks hung lifeless from chains secured to the ceiling. For unknown reasons, the vibrant silver-painted engine remained unaffected by the intense flames. A half-melted fan dangled from the port bulkhead. Miraculously, the ammo storage locker suffered only burn marks. Its contents were not affected by the fire or immense heat. It contained 12.7 machine gun canisters and 57 mm recoilless rounds.

L–R: US Navy Commander Charles R. Stephan, Commander Northern Surveillance Group CTG-115.1, and Lieutenant Victor G. "Pete" Reiling, First Coastal Zone PSYOPS, on the captured trawler's fantail, Republic of Vietnam, circa July 1967. (Photo credit: US Navy)

Commander Stephan worked his way along the starboard side toward the ladder leading up to the pilothouse. He came to a sudden halt two steps from the top, taken aback at the sight of the charred remains of an unfortunate Skunk Alpha crewman. The nearly unrecognizable body lay on the starboard side deck outside the pilothouse. The massive blast from Carver's mortar round into the port side pilothouse

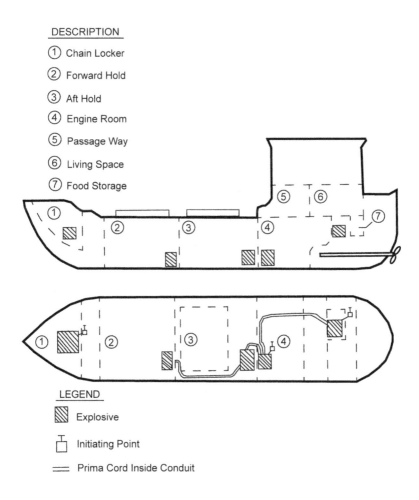

DESCRIPTION

① Chain Locker

② Forward Hold

③ Aft Hold

④ Engine Room

⑤ Passage Way

⑥ Living Space

⑦ Food Storage

LEGEND

▨ Explosive

⌐ Initiating Point

═══ Prima Cord Inside Conduit

TRAWLER SELF-DESTRUCT DIAGRAM
(Reproduced From Original Incident Report)

Reproduction sketch of trawler self-destruct system from official after-action report by GMG2 Eddie Knaup. (Image credit: Gabriel R. Herrera)

ripped open the opposite door with such force that it crushed the crewman standing there, knocking him onto his back, the right knee frozen in the air, his foot flat on the deck. The metal barrel of his automatic weapon lay at his right side. He died fighting.

GMG2 Knaup concentrated his effort in locating the self-destruct charges. He found and methodically commenced disarming five bundled canisters of TNT. Bundled charges were in the anchor chain locker on the bow, one each on forward and aft cargo holds, and a fourth was in the engine compartment. He was puzzled by the fact that the charge in the chain locker was not connected to the forward cargo hold charge. The Primacord was run through conduit and secured on bulkheads throughout the destruct network. Following the Primacord conduit from the bundled charge on the port side of the engine compartment across to the starboard side, then aft to and through a bulkhead, Knaup knew there had to be a fifth charge. The area in question was below the sleeping quarters deck, still too hot to access.

GMG2 Eddie A. Knaup, USN, EODU-2, Team 210; TAD to EODMUPAC Team 12, After Action Report submitted to Chief, Naval Weapons Systems Command–Excerpt, Item 5:

> No conclusion has been reached as to why the destruct charge in compartment 1 was not linked with primacord, to the other charges, and why none of the charges had initiating devices installed. The destruct charges in compartments 1, 4, and 7, had the four wooden pegs in the center can of TNT, either to keep the detonator wells clean or to retain some sort of initiating device against the movement of the vessel. A roll of communication wire, an estimated 15,000 feet, was found on the deck above the destruct charge in compartment 4, and a switch box on the outside of the aft bulkhead of the pilothouse had approximately fifty (50) feet of wire wrapped around it. Just below the switch box, conduit led through the deck into compartment 6 and terminated above the hatch leading into compartment 7 and a destruct charge. The trawler carried electric and non-electric detonators, safety fuse, and parts of mechanical time pencils were found in the burned pilothouse; any of which could have been used to initiate the destruct charges.

The self-destruct system consisted of a total of 2,046 pounds of TNT. The trawler's holds carried 6,880 pounds of C-4 plastic explosives; 1,960 anti-personnel mines; 213 B-40 rockets; 996 82 mm mortars; and 1,700 anti-personnel and concussion grenades. Attempting to visualize the combined explosion of the self-destruct charge and the explosive cargo is unimaginable. We came within seventy-five yards of Skunk Alpha. Our Swift Boat, the *Point Orient*, and the gunships circling above, along with their crews, would have become collateral damage.

It was known that resupply trawlers were rigged with self-destruct systems, all set up with a time-delay mechanism. This allowed the crew ample time to abandon the

EOD Specialist GMG2 Eddie Knaup holding a 57 mm recoiles round aboard captured resupply trawler, Sa Kỳ river mouth, Batangan Peninsula, Quảng Ngãi Province, Republic of Vietnam, 15 July 1967. (Photo credit: US Navy)

vessel and safely make it to shore. The blast from the 81 mm white phosphorous mortar round fired by Bobby Don Carver into the pilothouse must have rendered useless the time-delay mechanism in the pilothouse (if this is where the switch was located).

Fifty-four years later, on October 21, 2021, I was interviewed by Lê Hương Giang of Hanoi Vietnam VTV3 Television Network for a commemorative sixtieth anniversary celebration of the Ho Chi Minh Trail by Sea, the No-Number-Ship Unit of Brigade 125 (their trawler resupply component). A thirteen-minute segment of the elaborate hour and forty-minute stage program was dedicated to the Skunk Alpha incident, surprising to me since they lost that battle.

During the initial interview with Le Huong Giang, I was shocked to learn that three trawler crewmen survived the brutal battle: Captain Vũ Tấn Ích (now ninety-one years of age) and two sailors—an artillery man, Nguyễn Văn Động, and sailor Trần Văn Lịch. According to the interview, the captain was trained in foreign countries. Prior to this mission, he had delivered arms in other successful missions.

During the celebration event, the men were identified as being the only survivors of Ship 198 (Skunk Alpha). I found this odd because when detected near the Quảng

Ngãi coastline by aerial surveillance aircraft YB-10, the bow number was clearly 459. I can only speculate that their reference to No-Number-Ship Unit regarded it as a secret operation.

The thirteen-minute YouTube video of the anniversary program begins with the captain honoring the memory of two crewmen who perished during the battle: Phạm Chuyên Nghiệp and Huỳnh Ngọc Trạch. It was not clear if one of these men was the sailor found on the deck outside the trawler's pilothouse. Further in the video the captain states, "I was the last to disembark the ship. I was in the pilothouse to turn on the self-destruction switch." The artillery man added, "I wished I could have gone back to the ship and sacrifice myself to make sure the ship self-destructed itself." Later he continues, "It hurts us all the boat could not explode. It hurts so much we cry . . . even now. I wish there was a way to make it explode."[3] In my estimation, the 81 mm white phosphorus mortar round that hit the pilothouse destroyed any such device.

On a somber note, the video clip shows the widow of one of the North Vietnamese sailors who died during the fierce battle. She is shown sitting on her small bed, gently stroking the small suitcase left behind by her husband. She didn't learn of his death until 1971.

The boarding party regrouped topside at 1400 hours. They realized the field radio and most of their weapons were left behind on the South Vietnamese Navy Command Junk, giving Commander Stephan cause for concern as dusk approached. He considered destroying the vessel by using the 2,046 pounds of TNT in the event the vessel couldn't be taken off the reef before dark.

At 1500 hours, a flotilla of vessels eased their way toward the trawler, as two LCM 8s rounded the point of Mui Batangan. LCM 8 boat numbers 852 and 798 went right to work. Finding a clear path to the trawler's starboard quarter, crewmen secured lines to the trawler's stern section. The boats pulled at an awkward angle, causing the trawler to dig itself deeper into the reef. They made several more failed attempts during the next hour.

CDR Stephan went back aboard the destroyer at 1632 hours, leaving Knaup to continue disarming the self-destruct charge.[4]

The boat captain of Number 852 passed two towing lines to members of the boarding crew on the trawler. Knaup walked the lines to the bow and secured them. With lines tied to the LCM's port and starboard stern mooring cleats, the boat captain throttled up the two diesel engines. Salt water sprayed off the two lines as they

GMG2 Knaup disarming self-destruct TNT charge aboard resupply vessel. (Photo credit: US Navy)

Trawler sandwiched between two LCM-8 crafts, No. 852 and No. 798, en route north to Chu Lai, 15 July 1967. (Photo credit: L. R. Robinson)

snapped taut. The engines strained as he pushed the throttles forward to their limit. The stern section hit bottom, allowing it to serve as a pivot point. The bow swung to starboard. The trawler turned like a stubborn mule, degree by degree, until it broke free of the sandbar and the jagged reef.

A half-mile off the peninsula, LCM 8 Number 852 came to all engines stop and moved to Skunk Alpha's port side. LCM 8 Number 798 secured itself onto the enemy

Swift Boat PCF-79 passes astern the captured North Vietnamese resupply vessel Skunk Alpha, 15 July 1967. (Photo credit: L. R. Robinson)

ship's starboard side. With the trawler's charred hulk secured between the two LCM 8s, the sandwiched trawler began the slow twenty-nine-mile transit north to Chu Lai.

Heavy smoke billowed out of the two black vent stacks in front of the trawler's pilothouse. Knaup ordered the LCMs to all engines stop. Sailors quickly ran a hose from a Swift Boat, across LCM-798, and onto the trawler. A blast of heat and flames

Captured trawler being towed by LCM-8 craft No. 852 making way north to Chu Lai, 15 July 1967. (Photo credit: L. R. Robinson)

rushed out of the door leading into the first compartment, a passageway beneath the pilothouse, forcing Knaup to step back.

Braving the extreme heat, he put out the flames in the first compartment and entered the sleeping quarters. Knaup called for another fire hose. Nearby was PCF-79. They also ran their fire hose across to sailors on the trawler. Knaup observed an orange glow coming from below deck, the food locker. He peered inside and was surprised to see flames licking at the fifth destruct charge secured to the far bulkhead. The Primacord wrapped around the center charge was smoldering and in danger of igniting. Knaup put them out, preventing a disaster.

Knaup observed that a Primacord conduit ran up along that aft bulkhead, up into the pilothouse, then exited and connected to a switch box on the fantail bulkhead that had approximately fifty feet of communication wire hanging from it. It is my supposition that our gunner, Bob Middleton, in taking the aft gun mount position on the trawler under intense fire from his twin .50s, may have destroyed the self-destruct mechanism, thus allowing us to see another day.

Knaup determined the journey to Chu Lai could resume.

At 1830 hours Lieutenant Junior Grade Bolger, skipper of PCF-99, rendezvoused with the *Wilhoite*. Commander Stephan went aboard and began a daisy-chain trip back to Da Nang. Lieutenant Commander Hays resumed his duty as the *Wilhoite*'s skipper and continued his ship's assigned Market Time patrol.

News of Skunk Alpha's capture raced up the chain of command. By mid-afternoon, congratulatory messages were received. Rear Admiral Kenneth L. Veth, USN, Commander US Naval Forces, Vietnam, sent the following message to Captain Ralph Di Cori, Commander Task Force 115 (Operation Market Time):

> I take great pride in noting the capture of the North Vietnamese trawler by units of TF 115.
>
> Your wisdom in maintaining covert surveillance upon first turning away the trawler was instrumental in the subsequent ambush so ably planned and executed.
>
> The tenacity and patience of you and your units in doggedly shadowing the infiltrator until well within the contiguous zone is in keeping with the intent and spirit of the Market Time mission.
>
> The strict adherence of your units to the rules of engagement, even at the risk of their lives, brings the utmost credit to CTF 115 and his personnel.
>
> Through your shrewd tactical planning, distribution and utilization of air and surface forces—Navy, Coast Guard and free world military forces—you and your units have again proved that the coast of Vietnam is inviolable to steel hull infiltration, and by your actions have undoubtedly saved lives of your comrades in arms.
>
> Well done.
>
> RADM Veth sends

Captain Di Cori sent his congratulatory message to Commander Stephan. It read as follows:

> The destruction of the trawler and the praise received could never have been achieved without the untiring and unstinting efforts of all units concerned.
>
> I am deeply grateful to you all. Now let's go out and get another one.
>
> Captain Di Cori sends

The messages kept arriving. Rear Admiral Veth received a congratulatory message from Admiral John J. Hyland, Commander Seventh Fleet. It read as follows:

> Please pass my well done to USS Wilhoite, Market Time aircraft and other TF 115 units that participated in the successful destruction of the infiltration trawler as reported.

Skunk Alpha moored at Chu Lai Deep Water Pier, 16 July 1967. (Photo credit: L. R. Robinson)

Have been following closely the progress of this surveillance effort and consider it exceedingly well conducted. The persistence and coordination displayed by these forces are indicative of a high state of training and readiness.

Admiral John J. Hyland sends

• • •

I ran up to the Ops Shack and learned the trawler should be arriving within two hours. I dashed back to the barracks.

"Gunner, the trawler is on its way here."

"What for, Bean?"

"The guys at the radio shack told me it's going to get unloaded and patched up."

"I wonder how it'll look in daylight," Gunner said.

"We'll soon find out. We bagged a trawler, Ace! Let's go celebrate at the Straw Elephant before it gets here."

"Let's do it," Gunner replied.

The prize trophy was coming home to Cos Div 16, Chu Lai—Land of No Quarter.

CHAPTER 16
ACCOLADES

Loud banging on our plywood cubicle wall startled Gunner and me out of a deep sleep. It was mid-afternoon, and Porky came by to tell us Mr. Bergin wanted the crew up at his hootch in Officer Country.

By the time we arrived, the officers were busy grilling hot dogs and burgers. All were in a festive mood, celebrating Lord Mort's take-down of Skunk Alpha. Mr. Bergin's moniker was based on his last name. Edgar Bergen, the ventriloquist, created Mortimer Snerd. The Chu Lai OICs dropped the "nerd" and changed it to Sierra. That made him Mortimer Sierra, which was then cut back to just Mort. In leading the attack and capture of Skunk Alpha, they crowned him "Lord Mort." Given the outcome of the battle at Sông Sa Kỳ, his new moniker translated to "King of Death."

We sat together at one of the picnic tables. Mr. Bergin gave fellow OICs details about the trawler engagement while bottles of scotch, whiskey, and beer were passed around. Enlisted men were rarely authorized access to Officer Country. Partaking in a celebration in our honor filled me with pride.

The base CO dropped by to congratulate the Swift Boat officers for capturing an enemy ship. Accompanying him was Lieutenant Roger Staubach, 1963 Heisman Trophy winner. He was the "Beachmaster" of what dock handlers called the Sand Ramp. The Deepwater Pier was part of the LST off-loading facility. Lieutenant Staubach's team of a hundred sailors and Vietnamese daily handled tons of supplies for the Marines and Navy personnel based in the Chu Lai area.

They had come, in advance of the trawler's arrival, to ask where shell damage could be expected on the trawler. Mr. Bergin told them our attack came in off Skunk

Cargo being removed by hand to make room for pump hoses into cargo holds of partially sunk trawler. (Photo credit: L. R. Robinson)

Alpha's port side. He also recommended the machine gun holes along the water line on both sides be plugged or she would sink by morning.

An hour after sunset on July 15, 1967, Skunk Alpha, under tow by two LCM 8s, turned west at Rose Mary Point, Chu Lai, and into the river leading toward the Deepwater Pier. By 2030 hours, she was moored portside to the dock.

Gunner and I were busy penning letters to our parents about the great trawler capture when we heard a horn blast outside our barracks. Mr. Bergin had borrowed a Jeep and stopped by to pick us up. In a scene straight out of *McHale's Navy* television series, our crew of six climbed aboard and sped down the dusty road toward the cargo dock.

Taking a wide curve to the right, we passed the Staubach Field sign on the left. Sandlot games of football took place there every now and again. There were other occasions when Staubach accepted Swift Boat officer invitations to a barbecue and a short football scrimmage in an open sandy patch near the Chapel by the Sea.

We pulled into the dock area. Fifty-gallon drums and mooring lines secured the paved cargo unloading area adjacent to the trawler. A crowd of curious onlookers, officers, and enlisted men as well as Vietnamese sailors gathered to observe the activities. It was too late in the evening to unload the captured booty. A security team patrolled the perimeter, preventing eager war trophy scavengers from boarding the trawler.

When Porky and Boats straddled the rope, they were immediately stopped by an armed military policeman. Mr. Bergin advised the sentry who we were, clearing the way for us to board the trawler.

We stepped down to a horizontal dock wood beam, jumped over the gunwale, and onto Skunk Alpha's deck. Limited night light kept us from checking out below deck compartments. Topside was in shambles. Fishing nets lay randomly scattered over the cargo hold hatches. Noxious fumes filled the air. The smell of charred wood and rubber was prominent.

Gunner found a large screwdriver and stowed it in his back pocket. Mass amounts of spent brass casings were scattered around the base of the machine gun mounts, two amidships and one on the fantail. Proof positive that these were the locations from which we had been receiving heavy automatic weapon fire from nearly twenty-four hours earlier.

An hour later, we were back in the barracks, except for Boats and Porky. They continued with Mr. Bergin to Officer Country. Gunner and I were too fired up to sleep. We continued to write our letters to the folks back home.

As I would later learn, a postal truck pulled up in front of my parents' home one morning with my special-delivery letter. My mother was frightened to open it, so she decided to wait until Dad came home from work. When my father arrived, she told him she hoped it might have news of an early return home. They both sat at the kitchen table while he read it aloud.

Both were shocked to learn of what had taken place. They speculated I must be writing to them from some hospital bed. No one could have possibly come out of such a battle at close range without a scratch. Mom lit a special votive candle and prayed for me and my crew's protection. My relatives were notified and that generated more prayers. They were puzzled that this incident had not made the evening news when it happened.[1]

Back in Officer Country, Skipper, Boats, and Porky kept bending elbows. The OIC of PCF-45, Robert "Bob" Shirley, presented Mr. Bergin with the Communist China flag taken off the trawler. Someone took a picture of Mr. Shirley and Mr. Bergin holding the red flag with one large yellow star with four smaller ones in an arc. Sailors from Coastal Group 16 removed the scorched flag and wanted it given to the officer of the 79 Boat.

During their revelry, one of them came up with the bright idea to go brand the trawler, claiming the trophy as ours. The three headed to the trawler. Boats had the

Chu Lai Deep Water Pier crews preparing to pump water out of trawler cargo holds, 16 July 1967. (Photo credit: L. R. Robinson)

skipper stop by the paint locker, located on the Swift Boat pier. He "borrowed" some yellow zinc chromate paint and a couple of brushes.

At the Deepwater Pier, Boats spotted a paint punt in the water and advised Mr. Bergin. They pulled the tiny flat-bottomed craft between the pier and the trawler's port side. Using the yellow paint, Mr. Bergin painted our division's motto—NO QUARTER. To the right of that he put our boat number, PCF-79. He climbed back up onto the horizontal pier beam and continued drawing. A skull of death was next, below the gunwale. He also added our crew number, 74-A, and a smaller PCF-79. He finished the task by leaving his personal mark on Skunk Alpha, his call sign—MORT.

During the night, water entered the hull through the hundreds of machine gun, rocket, and mortar round holes created during the fierce battle. The water used to put out the blaze by Eddie Knaup added more weight, lowering the draft and allowing holes above the water line to gradually sink beneath the water surface. Skunk Alpha's stern sank alongside the pier as deep as the mooring lines permitted, leaving only the bow elevated and free of flooding. As daylight approached, Chu Lai dock personnel were all hands on deck. They simultaneously removed cargo, pumped out water, and shored the holes above and below the waterline. A crane hoisted her cargo out of the holds. Skunk Alpha's compartments were emptied before noon.

In GMG2 Knaup's after action report, he provided the following:

Table: Trawler Cargo

Item	Quantity
Non-electric detonators	3 boxes
Igniters	6 boxes
Plastic explosives	3,102 lbs.
TNT destruct system	2,046 lbs.
Detonation cord	9 rolls
Electrical detonators	204
.50 caliber machine guns	2
7.62 incendiary bullets	394,563
7.62 ball bullets	311,520
K-44 assault rifles	975
AK-56 assault rifles	159
Rocket launchers (B-40)	25
K-53 assault rifles	9
12.7mm AA weapons	2
Anti-personnel grenades*	1,960
Anti-personnel grenades*	1,250
12.7 mm ammo	5,753
Concussion grenades*	484
B-40 RPG rockets	43
82mm mortar rounds	996
Drum magazine type 63 Chicom machine guns	24

* Anti-personnel grenades is a misnomer. These are actually Chicom fragmentation-type grenades. Cylindrical fragmentation anti-personnel mines and Chicom are copies of the Russian model RKG anti-tank parachute-shaped charge hand grenade.

After lunch, Gunner and I hitched a ride back to the trawler. Ammunition crates were stacked waist high all over the dock. Two Army demolition experts from Task Force Oregon were inspecting rockets and claymore mines. At their feet were grenades, bundles of Primacord, and other explosive devices.

We made our way through the crowd of onlookers along the perimeter. Kodak Instamatic camera clicks recorded a piece of history soldiers would share with their families in years to come. We approached the barricade and jumped over the rope. As we headed toward the trawler, an armed MP yelled at us to halt. Gunner convinced him we were part of the crew that captured the enemy ship. He congratulated us and allowed us to go aboard.

Gunner and I, with our own Kodak Instamatics, took plenty of pictures. The dock crane, lifting a net filled with cargo, served well as a backdrop. I took a picture of stacked blocks of narrow wood crates containing part of the 975 brand-new K-44 rifles.

A large red eagle decal on the trawler's port bow caught my attention. To its left, someone had used white paint and written "HQ 618." The image represented the 71st Assault Helicopter Company Firebird and Rattler gunships that made attack runs on Skunk Alpha, but I was not sure what the HQ 618 represented.[2]

Gunner noticed the yellow branding on the trawler's hull, and we deduced Mr. Bergin, Porky, and Boats were the culprits. I was glad they left our mark on the enemy ship we captured. I squatted next to the yellow painted marking and Bob took my picture. I posed for two more, one by the starboard side smokestack where a mortar or rocket exploded, and the other inside the crew compartment.

I went into the engine room and was surprised by how the motor remained intact. The block was painted silver. In a charred box in the crew compartment, I found a pair of semi-melted Zeiss binoculars. I kept them as a reminder of the fierce Sông Sa Kỳ victory.

Mr. Bergin told us he had learned the charred remains of a trawler crewman were found pinned to the deck by the starboard side pilothouse door. In walking the area, I found a piece of the sailor's skull. Without hesitation, I blew the ashes off the irregular-shaped quarter-size piece, put it in my shirt pocket, and continued inspecting the trawler.

We went back to the dock, and in talking with the officer directing the cargo removal and repairs, we learned the trawler was tailored for its mission. The holds of the ship were sheathed with plywood and insulated with fiberglass. It was equipped with a high-velocity fire main system as well as a high-capacity pumping system. In addition, the engine was muffled for silent running.

The captured North Vietnamese trawler marked with Bergin's, Porky's, and Boats' handiwork. (Photo credit: Dan Daly)

A news reporter dressed in green fatigues approached us for an interview. When the question-and-answer session ended, Bob and I realized we didn't know what newspaper he represented. We wondered if this guy was in fact a war correspondent or part of Intel. We never asked for his credentials.

I would later learn that news of the trawler incident reached the States. The *New York Times*, Sunday, July 16, 1967, edition, covered the story. Sadly, it was squeezed next to a large New York department store's fishnet stocking advertisement in the World News section. Objectively, it seems appropriate, considering the mood of the nation at that time because of US involvement in Vietnam. But, from my point of view, it sucked.

Looking at the mass of destruction, I thanked God that although the exchange of fire at such close range had been so intense, through His protection we managed to come out of the battle alive.

Besides the dead crewman by the pilothouse, I wondered what became of the rest of the crew. Based on the morbid appearance of the charred remains, I could only imagine the worst outcome. By then I was very much engulfed in the numbness of war, where a man's life becomes irrelevant—unless of course it's your own. When we spoke of the enemy, I envisioned only a faceless entity, without mind or spirit. We were eliminating an obstacle incapable of experiencing fear, pain, or happiness. During our firing runs on the enemy vessel, I fired only at an object from which we were receiving heavy machine gun fire as well.

Gunner and I headed back to the barracks, content with all the pictures we'd taken of Skunk Alpha. He turned on his reel-to-reel tape player. Listening to the music, we examined the keepsakes we took off the trawler. In addition to the Zeiss binoculars, I had found small arms ammo paper wrappings, a semi-melted flashlight, and some spent brass casings of various calibers.

I pulled the piece of skull out of my pocket, and as I began punching a hole at one end, it caught Bob's attention.

"What's that, Bean?"

"A piece of the poor fucker's skull."

"Where'd you find it?"

"By the starboard side pilothouse door. The blast from Boats' Willie Peter round must have slammed that door on him and killed him instantly."

"Whatcha gonna do wit' it?" he asked.

"It's my special war trophy, man. I'm stringing it up to wear it around my neck."

"You're nuts, Bean. You shouldn't be doin' dat."

"Hell, why the fuck not? The bastards tried to kill us. You remember. You were there."

"I know, but it's a piece of a dead guy. Can you get into trouble for that?"

"Don't know and I don't give a shit. We won the battle, Bob. It's like keeping the championship game ball. I ain't tellin', so how can I get in trouble?"

"Well, I don't know if it's true or not, but I've heard those Koreans are ruthless. They say they've put coins on the tongues of captured VC and took turns seeing who could knock it off with a bullet from their rifle."

"See, at least I'm not messing with a live one."

Little did I know that mutilation and the taking of body parts as war trophies was prohibited by Article 3 of the Geneva Convention. It specified that "after each engagement the occupant of the field of battle shall take measures to search for the wounded and dead, and to protect them against pillage and maltreatment."

Three-and-a-half short months in-country had altered my moral fiber. Worse than that, I didn't care. I wanted to get back on patrol and take out more of those bastards. A week later, remorse set in. While on patrol one night, I walked out onto the fantail, removed the skull piece from around my neck, offered a prayer, and cast my enemy's remains into the Sa Kỳ river mouth.

Later that evening, Mr. Bergin notified us that we had received orders to prepare our dress white uniforms and make ready for a trip to Da Nang on Tuesday afternoon.

Commander Naval Forces Vietnam Rear Admiral Kenneth L. Veth (left center) and Commander in Chief of the Vietnamese Navy, Captain Trần Văn Chơn (center) inspect the captured North Vietnamese resupply trawler on Deep Water Pier, Chu Lai, 17 July 1967. (Photo credit: B. W. Wendell)

Rear Admiral Veth and Captain Chơn walk the deck of the captured enemy vessel, Chu Lai, Republic of Vietnam, 17 July 1967. (Photo credit: B. W. Wendell)

Rear Admiral Veth and Captain Chơn stand on the captured trawler's fantail examining a cargo item, Chu Lai, Republic of Vietnam, 17 July 1967. (Photo credit: B. W. Wendell)

An awards ceremony was being planned for those involved in Skunk Alpha's capture.

Activity continued at the Deepwater Pier on Monday morning, July 17. Through Vietnamese diplomacy and military urging at the highest level, the ROKs turned over 686 of the weapons the Blue Dragons took off the trawler. Three hundred more were returned to the Vietnamese military the following day.

At midday, as the trawler's hull was being shored, an entourage of high-ranking officials arrived to view the captured arms infiltrator. Rear Admiral Kenneth L. Veth, Commander of Naval Forces Vietnam, was joined by Captain Tran Van Chon, Commander in Chief, Vietnamese Navy at the Deepwater Pier. Cos Div 16 officers and other officials also participated.

The trawler was taken to a position just beyond Rosemary Point in open water, where she was picked up and taken under tow by the Vietnamese Navy's PGM-618 for its transit journey to Da Nang. We were able to watch the activities from the Swift Boat pier as we made ready for our next routine patrol. As if acknowledging our accomplishment, we were given the Delta November patrol area. The scuttlebutt among Swifties was that there were two more trawlers being tracked out at sea in I Corps. We were ready for another one should an attempt be made. We knew combat firsthand and the apprehensive fantasies of a firefight had been eliminated.

On Tuesday afternoon we boarded our Swift and journeyed sixty-four miles north along the coastline to Da Nang. We arrived shortly after dusk, with plenty of time for Gunner and me to make a beeline to the EM Club at Camp Tien Sha. Military transportation was available to almost any location in Da Nang, so we hopped a military bus and five minutes later we were enjoying semi-cool cans of Schlitz beer and watching a USO band perform. All throughout the club groups of men were joined together by their ethnic bond. Soul brothers openly exercised their groove by dancing to the music, their minds certainly not in the present. My compadres in other areas built six-foot-high beer can pyramids, a sign to all who saw that they were the best drinkers alive. Southern boys, not to be left out, hooted their pride to country-western tunes when they were played.

Accidentally, someone was shoved against the table where the beer cans were stacked, and down they came in a crash. At once, bodies flew from one side of the club to the other as the tangled mass of participants swayed uncontrollably within the club. Cheers came from the crowd and were directed at no one group. The shore patrol quickly got things under control, the music began playing again, and my compadres started to rebuild their monument.

The frustrations of war and racial unrest didn't blend too well in Vietnam. Once in combat, however, there was no color barrier that separated the unity between comrades. Bob and I left early, figuring we'd seen enough action over the past week. While in Da Nang we bunked at the APL near the Swift Boat dock.

The following morning, the crew boarded a truck for the drive to Da Nang City Hall. The area was crawling with American, Vietnamese, and Korean military personnel. We were assigned specific locations on the street in front of the raised reviewing stand, which was receiving its final touches. Once our positions were established and a short briefing completed, we were dismissed and ordered to return at 1400 hours in full dress summer whites.

We made a quick trip back to the APL for lunch, dressed, and returned to City Hall for the scheduled awards ceremony. I was awed by the massive turnout, both military and civilian. Bạch Đằng Street ran along the north shore of the Han River. South Vietnamese Rangers and MPs, along with US MPs, cordoned off areas for spectators. Adults accompanied two classes of schoolchildren, all eager to catch a glimpse of their country's leaders.

Our crew was scattered in a group of military personnel at stage left. Mr. Bergin stood in the front row. On his left was GMG2 Eddie Knaup, the EOD specialist who disarmed the trawler's 2,046-pound TNT self-destruct system. Boats Carver took a position on the far left, in the row behind Mr. Bergin. Porky stood directly behind Boats. Mac, Gunner, and I were a couple of rows back. Another group was located stage right.

A cheer, followed by applause, erupted behind us. Our heads turned to see what the commotion was about. Prime Minister Air Vice Marshal Nguyễn Cao Kỳ walked a step behind and to the right of Chief of State three-star General Nguyễn Văn Thiệu. General Dương Văn Minh (Big Minh) followed close behind to Kỳ's right. The trio was encircled by news reporters. This was their first appearance, together, ahead of the upcoming elections, several weeks away. Skunk Alpha served as the perfect backdrop for a presidential campaign photo op.

An honor rifle guard file of South Vietnamese Navy and Army troops snapped to present-arms attention as the dignitaries passed by on their way to the review platform. We were called to attention. That is when I noticed a CBS news team by the stage on the opposite end. Seeing them brought thoughts of the Land of the Big PX to mind—stateside. The CBS crew symbolized home for me. I wondered if my family would catch this on KENS-TV in San Antonio.

Kỳ wore his distinctive black flight suit with his signature lavender silk ascot. He also donned the familiar black ball cap. The brim had silver officer scrambled eggs and a silver edge trim. Two silver stars decorated the front of the cap's crown. Rounding out his unique uniform were the dark aviator sunglasses and soft yellow leather gloves.

Premier Kỳ took a seat on a plum-colored sofa chair. My first impression of him was less than favorable—he looked sinister. Regardless, he was a leader of the Republic of Vietnam. In sharp contrast, Chief of State General Nguyễn Văn Thiệu was in his Army green fatigues. He advanced up the few steps to center stage and took a seat to Kỳ's left on a beige sofa chair.

I had been in-country just a few months, and here I was, among a group whose efforts were being acknowledged by the leaders of a country. Few are the military personnel decorated by heads of state. I wondered if I was the only Mexican American to hold such an honor. I was certain that Mom and Dad would be proud.

At the conclusion of a short round of speeches, Thiệu and Kỳ approached the group, now joined and positioned center stage, and began the medal ceremony. As Premier Kỳ presented medals to the row of men in front of us, I became nervous. The feeling didn't last long. He was pinning the medal on Mac. Gunner was next, then me. I glanced at him out of the corner of my eye as he pinned the medal on Bob. As he stepped in front of me, I snapped to and maintained a sharp salute. I looked straight into his eyes. It surprised me that we both had the same stature: short.

There I was, a pollywog Mexican American seaman, being personally decorated by the leader of a nation with a population of more than seventeen million. He turned

to his aide, removed the Vietnamese Cross of Gallantry medal from a velvet-covered cushion, and pinned it above my left shirt pocket. He returned my salute, shook my hand, and moved on. While he was pinning the medal, I felt isolated from the world. I could not hear a sound. I was overwhelmed by a day I will always remember.

Following Premier Kỳ was Chief of State Thiệu. I saluted him as well and he extended his congratulations and shook my hand, a move I hardly expected. I heard cameras clicking as the ceremony continued. As the presentation of medals was completed, lovely teenage girls dressed in the traditional white *áo dài* filed down each row. A young schoolgirl stood in front of each sailor or soldier. In unison, they draped colorful flowered leis around our necks. Oh, if only Mom, Dad, and all the relatives could see me now. I felt my chest expand.

The Vietnamese Cross of Gallantry medal, one of the nation's highest decorations, was given in recognition of deeds of valor or heroic conduct while in combat. It was given to all the Vietnamese, Korean, and American servicemen involved with the trawler incident. Yet I was disappointed in the limited number of US Navy and Coast Guard personnel present. I wondered if all this pomp and circumstance was set up by Kỳ and Thiệu to gain publicity in advance of the presidential elections, scheduled for September 3.

A large display was set up near the concrete pier leading to the trawler. Weapons of all kinds were stacked chest high. Some were broken down into the smallest pieces and mounted to boards, with each item labeled.

Premier Kỳ and Chief of State Thiệu made their way to the City Hall pier, leading to where the 120-foot vessel was moored. Along the way, the thick crowd pressed in around them, extending their hands. At the same time, reporters pushed mics in their faces, attempting to catch a sound bite.

Two Republic of Vietnam naval officers and five enlisted men stood guard aboard the trawler. A drab yellow 3' x 25' banner stretched along the starboard side stanchion reading:

CONGRATULATIONS AMERICAN, KOREAN, AND VIETNAM MILITARY IN THEIR SA KY VICTORY

Two 12.7mm anti-aircraft machine guns were positioned on the amidships gun turrets. The third machine gun on the fantail was missing. Our crew was allowed to go aboard the gunrunner for the last time.

The charred remains of the enemy trawler had been swept clean of debris. Although patched up, it still showed heavy damage resulting from the surface and aerial bombardment. The captured trawler display served as a loud propaganda message—North Vietnam, you lost this battle!

K-44 and AK-56 rifles taken off captured resupply trawler Skunk Alpha on display at awards ceremony, Da Nang, Republic of Vietnam, 19 July 1967. (Photo credit: Dan B. Odenweller)

Captured AK-56 rifles on display at awards ceremony. Da Nang, Republic of Vietnam, 19 July 1967. (Photo credit: Dan B. Odenweller)

Drum magazine, Type 53 Chicom machine guns on display at awards ceremony, Da Nang, Republic of Vietnam, 19 July 1967. (Photo credit: Dan B. Odenweller)

Mortars, grenades, and explosives on display at awards ceremony, Da Nang, Republic of Vietnam, 19 July 1967. (Photo credit: Dan B. Odenweller)

Portion of arms cache: mixed ammunition and B-40 rocket cases on display at awards ceremony, Da Nang, Republic of Vietnam, 19 July 1967. (Photo credit: Dan B. Odenweller)

AK-56 rifle display at awards ceremony, Da Nang, Republic of Vietnam, 19 July 1967. (Photo credit: Dan B. Odenweller)

Captured trawler Skunk Alpha at anchor on the Hàn River, 19 July 1967. (Photo credit: US Navy)

Commander Stephan summarized the event best in an article he wrote for the United States Naval Institute *Proceedings*:

> One now hears this engagement variously referred to as "that trawler the ROK's captured" or "the Navy's VC trawler" or "that trawler the Hueys beached at Batangan."
>
> The Sa Kỳ River Victory, as it is now referred to by the Vietnamese, is all of those things and more, because that battered hulk represents a victory of the combined Allied arms. The lion's share of the credit, however, belongs to the Operation Market Time Forces, who fulfilled their mission so professionally and admirably.

CHAPTER 17

COASTAL GROUP 16

T he lead US Navy advisor role at the South Vietnamese Naval Junk Base in Quảng Ngãi Province belonged to 29-year-old Lieutenant William Charles Fitzgerald from Montpelier, Vermont. He headed a four-man team, consisting of Lieutenant Junior Grade Anthony Williams, Chief Engineman Harold Guinn, and First Class Boatswain's Mate Leo Pearman.[1]

As senior enlisted men, Guinn and Pearman shared their seamanship experience with the younger South Vietnamese sailors, while the officers advised their counterparts in areas of operational readiness. The US advisory team took turns patrolling the coastline with the Vietnamese sailors aboard Yabuta junks. This type of boat was made of heavy sao wood shipped from Thailand by barge, stripped, then cut into timbers or planks at the South Vietnamese Navy shipyard sawmill in Saigon.

The vessels, originally of Japanese design, measured forty-one feet in length, ten feet wide at the beam, and had a draft of three and one-half feet, barely making a dent in the water. Top speed was roughly eight knots, making it difficult to capture evading Viet Cong on their slim and often motorized sampans.

It took only fourteen days to build a Yabuta. Another two weeks was required to paint the patrol craft and fit her with a gasoline engine, rudder, skeg, shaft, and gun mounts. The final touch was more traditional. It involved painting "eyes" on the Yabuta. For centuries, "eyes of the dragon" have been painted on junks to symbolize good fortune and help guide them through dark and tempestuous seas.[2]

Located on the south side of the Sông Trà Khúc, approximately five miles southwest of the Sông Sa Kỳ river mouth on the Batangan Peninsula, Coastal Group 16

(CG 16) served a vital counterinsurgency role in the southern I Corps Market Time coastal patrol sector. Sông Phú Thọ, a 300-yard-wide estuary, ran south and parallel to the coastline, separating CG 16 from the tiny seashore fishing village of Phố An. To the south and adjacent to the base was another fishing village named Co Luy.

The junk base perimeter resembled an irregular right triangle. The base ran along the sloped western bank of the estuary. Three rows of barbed wire fencing, forty yards apart, stretched along the shore, preventing enemy sappers from gaining access to the base. A rickety wood catwalk pier ran seventy-five yards out from shore, and strands of barbed wire extended the length of the wobbly pier. At low tide, the shallow, sandy shore bottom was exposed forty yards out.

The compound contained numerous tin-roofed, cinderblock, and wood buildings that housed workshops, offices, and sleeping quarters for the Vietnamese sailors and their dependents. Lieutenant Fitzgerald's advisory group occupied a closed-off area at the lower corner of the base. A small sand-bagged bunker was in the middle of the advisor's compound. Tall palm trees lined the shoreline perimeter, giving the tiny area a South Pacific flare.

On a lazy Sunday afternoon, with the sun fading fast behind the western horizon, the banter of Vietnamese sailors and children's laughter at play reached the Americans' compound. When night fell, a tranquil silence blanketed the base. Across the estuary, flickering lantern lights danced from Phố An village. Soon, lights-out found the US advisors hitting the sack, except for one, Lieutenant Fitzgerald. He had the first watch of the night.

At approximately 0300 hours on August 7, 1967, CG 16 came under a heavy mortar and small arms fire attack, initially from across the estuary. Phố An was no longer a friendly Viet Cong–free fishing village. Chief Guinn and BM1 Pearman had no time to get dressed. In their skivvies, they dashed to their battle station and manned the .30 caliber perimeter machine gun. Muzzle flashes from automatic weapons stretched the length of the village's estuary perimeter. The Viet Cong purposely used Phố An to attack the base in hopes the American advisors would hold true to their rules of engagement and not fire into a friendly village.

The ferocious machine gun and mortar fire attack left Chief Guinn no alternative but to return fire. Another heavier adversary mortar and small arms fire attack began from beyond the northwestern base perimeter. CG 16 was under a major attack.

A hot sting on his arm made Guinn exclaim, "Shit, Leo, I've been hit."

"Let me take over, Chief," Pearman suggested.

"No, I'm okay. Just grazed me. Bastards!" Guinn continued pumping lead at the Viet Cong gunners across the estuary.

Both officers were in the bunker assessing the situation.

"Tony, I'm heading out to look for Lieutenant Thong," Lieutenant Fitzgerald announced as he left. "Get the radio and raise comms with Sector. We need help, and FAST!"

"Roger, I'm on it," replied Williams.

Sector was the highest-ranking US military liaison, overseeing the maneuvers of all allied forces in and around Quảng Ngãi.

Enemy mortar rounds fell all around, making it impossible for Fitzgerald to reach the Vietnamese officers' quarters, forcing him to return to his men.

"That was fast. Did you find Thong?" Williams asked.

"Negative, didn't see anyone, anywhere," Fitzgerald responded. "Did you get Sector?"

"I'm about to try now."

From their small-arms locker, Fitzgerald pulled out the M60 along with an ammo box. He set up the machine gun at the rear perimeter where the two enlisted men were. Then he left in search of the Vietnamese officers and hollered at Williams, "I'm heading out, Tony."

This time Fitzgerald observed mortar rounds hitting the open area of the base every ten to fifteen seconds. The Viet Cong gunners were now walking the shells from the dependents' barracks toward the advisor's housing unit. Only a spotter from within the base could be giving the enemy those adjustments, Fitzgerald concluded.

Again, the lieutenant returned with no success. He saw Williams on the horn, attempting to contact Sector as he entered the bunker.

"Void Adam, this is Xray Foxtrot. Over."

No response.

"Flash Traffic. I say again, this is Xray Foxtrot. CG 16 under attack. Request immediate support. Over."

Still, no response.

As enemy fire increased, Guinn's weapon malfunctioned. He and Pearman attempted to get the .30 caliber to work, but to no avail. Guinn moved over to the M60 machine gun and continued suppressing enemy fire. It also failed.

Shining a flashlight beam on the gun's chamber, Pearman exclaimed, "Shit, the damn bolt is broken, Chief!"

Despite the flesh wound, Guinn grabbed an M16 and continued firing across the river. Things were happening at a rapid pace. Lieutenant Williams raised comms with PCF-20 on station in the Same Drink Delta November patrol area at the Sông Trà Khúc river mouth.

On board, the skipper sounded general quarters and headed west at flank speed. They arrived at 0315 hours and immediately began popping daylight over the base. They also sprayed .50 caliber machine gun suppressive fire on enemy positions at Phố An. Lieutenant Williams requested mortar fire be used as well.

"Everyone all right?" Lieutenant Fitzgerald yelled. The team's anxious chatter signaled they were fine.

Guinn took a moment to assist Pearman in firing the 57 mm recoilless rifle, just as Lieutenant Williams was stepping out of the bunker. The back-flash from the gun's discharge partially struck him in the face, injuring his eye. Making matters worse, the 57 mm also failed after several more rounds were fired.

By 0330 hours, an overwhelming enemy force, estimated at 300, broke through the northern mine field barrier and found their way into the Vietnamese Navy base. At the same time, from his position within their separate compound, Lieutenant Fitzgerald called out, "In the bunker, men. Now! Charlie is overrunning the base." The four Navy advisors were the last men standing and the only remaining resistance within the base complex. The survival odds were next to nil and getting worse by the second.

Lieutenant Fitzgerald grabbed the radio handset. "Sector, Sector. Xray Foxtrot Actual." The last word identified the caller as Fitzgerald. He continued, "Drop all you got, my position. Send Spooky. Over." He knew Spooky, the AC-47 Dragon Ship, would need no coordinates. The base was on fire, providing a larger-than-life target.

Artillery never came, but Spooky made contact. Unfortunately, they were twenty minutes away, not enough time to ensure survival. During a lull in incoming mortar rounds, the team left the bunker to man the inner base perimeter and resumed return fire at multiple Viet Cong positions.

The flames from the burning buildings allowed the advisors to see Viet Cong movement. Gut-wrenching screams came from beyond the advisors' compound. Vietnamese sailors, as well as their wives and children, were being killed or critically wounded.

Pearman couldn't believe his eyes and turned to Lieutenant Fitzgerald. "Lieutenant, the VC are all over the compound!"

"It's Charlie, all right. One just raised the Viet Cong flag. Back to the bunker, men!" Lieutenant Fitzgerald ordered.

Prior to entering, Pearman glanced to his right and noticed two VC heading toward their area. They spotted him as well. Pointing at him, one of them shouted "Americans!" and began running toward the bunker.

A mortar round made a direct hit on the advisors' ammo bunker nearby, causing stored mortars and hand grenades to explode as well as bullets to cook off in the heat. It temporarily prevented the enemy's advance on the advisors' position.

Lieutenant Fitzgerald reached for the field radio.

"Void Adam, this is Xray Foxtrot Actual. Over."

"Xray Foxtrot, Void Adam. Go ahead."

"Shell the base. Use Victor Tango artillery my position. Battalion-size enemy force inside perimeter. Evading to Sông Phú Thọ. Out." There was no time to engage in further radio communications. The VT artillery rounds would explode above ground, causing mass destruction and killing standing enemy troops.

"Quiet, men!" Lieutenant Fitzgerald ordered. "The VC might think we're in the river."

Moments later, however, a volley of shouts came from outside their sanctuary. The VC yelled, "Americans!"

Lieutenant Fitzgerald fired his shotgun out the bunker's entrance and hollered at his men. "Head for the river! I'll cover for you. Run!"

"I'll follow behind you. I can't see well," Lieutenant Williams advised.

Guinn went first, weapon at the ready. Exiting the bunker, he came face-to-face with two Viet Cong. The M16, set to automatic, came alive, leveling the two soldiers before they could fire a single shot. Pearman followed Guinn toward the river. They assumed Lieutenant Williams was right behind them. Enemy fire intensified on the bunker as the men attempted to evade toward the river.

Calling out to the two officers and getting no response, Chief Guinn and Pearman dashed along a barrier fence, bullets zinging over their heads and pelting the edge of the river. On reaching the southern end of the junk base, the two men waded to the middle of the river, where they were surprised to find frightened Vietnamese civilians. They swam to a Vietnamese Navy junk and began looking for Lieutenant Williams and picking up the civilians.

Their executive officer had been right behind Pearman as they exited the bunker but opted to climb up and over the back wall, then carefully managed to go over the barbed-wire fence and into the river. He swam out to the pier, where he heard someone calling his name. He didn't answer.

One of the CG 16 junks sped by, nearly hitting him. It rammed a sandbar as a huge explosion erupted in the river, causing him to lose his weapon. Williams spotted a cargo junk, nose up on the sandbar, and swam to it. A small sampan was tied up alongside. With his eyesight still impaired, he heard voices coming from a sand pit on the north end of Phố An, mostly women and children. Lieutenant Williams untied the sampan, clung to it, and tried to swim away. Yet a fisherman reached over and grabbed his arm. Reacting, he reached up and covered the fisherman's mouth and hand motioned in the direction of the river mouth. Reaching the Sông Trà Khúc, he climbed aboard the sampan. For now, he was safe.

At the same time, a number of other units were in the area, including the destroyer USS *Camp* (DER 251), PCFs 15 and 54, as well as a US Air Force AC-47 Dragon Ship. The skipper of the *Camp* became the on-scene commander.

Guinn and Pearman found themselves aboard one of the Swifts and requested the OIC take them back to the base to search for the two officers. The other Swift continued to ferry the wounded Vietnamese to the *Camp*. The AC-47 Dragon Ship was in a circular flight pattern, taking the remaining enemy fire positions under attack. Guinn used the Swift's radio and contacted Sector, advising that a recovery team was headed back to the base. By the time they approached the junk base pier, all gunfire had ended inside the base.

At 0430 hours, the two advisors and an Army sergeant walked onto the base perimeter and jumped the fence behind their living quarters. The fuel storage bladder was in flames and rounds in the ammo bunker continued to explode. Aside from the crackling fires, the group looked around and didn't see or hear anyone. Pearman and the sergeant covered Guinn as he approached the bunker and went in.

Chief Guinn hollered, "I found Mr. Fitzgerald!" He paused a moment. The words struggled to leave his mouth. From within the dark bunker, Guinn's somber voice cried out, "He's dead." Pearman joined Guinn in the bunker. They determined Lieutenant Fitzgerald had died from a small arms round to the back of the head.

They continued their search for Mr. Williams but only found one Vietnamese sailor seriously wounded, his left forearm gone. The team also found two more Vietnamese sailors, a couple of women, and some children, all wounded. A stretcher was located and used to load the sailor with the missing forearm. All wounded were taken to the Swift Boat, for evacuation to the DER.

Guinn and Pearman stayed aboard the Swift. They were heading back to the base to resume the search for Lieutenant Williams when they found him in a sampan at the mouth of the river. They helped him aboard the Swift, where they broke the news about Lieutenant Fitzgerald.

At 0700 hours, two infantry companies of the ARVN Second Division and a company of US troops from Task Force Oregon reached the battered Coastal Group base and launched a counterattack against the Viet Cong units already well beyond the base perimeter. By 0730 hours the allied contingent had regained control of the base.

The Swift Boats provided counter-fire support as well as rescue assistance. They

USS *Fitzgerald* (DDG 62) named in honor of Lieutenant William Charles Fitzgerald, US Naval Advisor, Coastal Group 16, KIA 7 August 1967, Quảng Ngãi Province, Republic of Vietnam. (Photo credit: US Navy)

evacuated approximately forty Vietnamese to the *Camp*, fifteen of whom were subsequently flown by helicopter to the Vietnamese hospital at Quảng Ngãi.

Besides the Coastal Group commander, Lieutenant Junior Grade Nguyễn N. Thong, thirteen South Vietnamese sailors were killed during the attack and thirty-five were wounded. In addition, twenty civilians, most of them sailors' wives and children, were killed or wounded. Of the invaders, eleven were killed, thirty-five detainees escaped, and three were found dead. All but one of the buildings comprising the base complex were destroyed.

By mid-morning, the base was secured by the remaining Coastal Group 16 personnel and augmented by thirty men from Coastal Group 15 and a company-size security unit of Regional Force troops.

The surprise attack, and in particular the ease of enemy infiltration through the northern base perimeter minefield, led to speculation about internal sabotage. In addition, it wasn't difficult to surmise the attack on Coastal Group 16 was in direct retaliation for the interception and capture of Skunk Alpha.

· · ·

Lieutenant William Charles Fitzgerald posthumously received the Navy Cross for his extraordinary heroism and dedication to duty and courage under fire, despite overwhelming odds.

The Surface Warfare Officers School Command, Newport, Rhode Island, dedicated Fitzgerald Hall on August 9, 1980, in honor of Lieutenant Fitzgerald. And, on October 14, 1995, an Arleigh Burke–class destroyer was commissioned as the USS *Fitzgerald* (DDG-62) in his honor.

Via Navy chain of command and with the approval of Commander Naval Forces Vietnam Admiral Kenneth L. Veth, it was recommended that Lieutenant Junior Grade Anthony Chaplain Williams, CPO Norman Harold Guinn, and BM1 Leo Edward Pearman be awarded the Silver Star medal for conspicuous gallantry and intrepidity in action.

CHAPTER 18

SEA STORIES

Swift Boat Crew 74-A rode the triumphant Skunk Alpha trawler intercept victory wave for three weeks. Our jubilation ended when we received news of the Viet Cong attack on Coastal Group 16 on August 7, 1967. We made a stop at the destroyed base days after it was overrun. Moored at their pier, I stood on top of PCF-79's pilothouse and saw the remains of what was once an active South Vietnamese Navy base.

The devastation reminded me of what my buddy, Seaman Terry Vander Molen, told me in port two days after the incident. PCF-15 was on standby at the mouth of the Sông Trà Khúc. When ordered to advance toward the base, the boat's OIC, Lieutenant Junior Grade Dick Jankowsky, ordered Terry to jump ashore and take point as he, along with BM2 Michael Turley, followed close behind. The engineman, EN2 Richard Craig, and the gunner, Seaman Gary Takahashi, remained on the boat, ready to extract their fellow crewmen if needed. The firefight had ended, giving way to the speculation that all on base were either dead or wounded and the Viet Cong were gone. Terry recalled thinking this was where he was going to die.

All three men were armed and ready for any enemy action. Terry got ahead of them, and as he turned a corner in the trail along the bank of the Sông Phú Thọ near the base perimeter, he was startled by what, at first glance, looked like a child mannequin lying up against a tree. It turned out to be a young girl whose skin had been fused together by the explosion of an enemy mortar round.

Terry's remarks made me reflect on how I thought our crew was invincible aboard PCF-79. Standing on top of the pilothouse wasn't improving my odds of surviving the war and getting home safe. Charlie Sniper could have dropped me with one shot. I climbed down to find cover.

A couple of weeks later, we learned through intel that the Viet Cong had a bounty out for the 79 Boat. They learned that it was our boat that prevented their expected arms cargo from arriving. If they retaliated on CG-16 by overrunning the base, what could they possibly do to us? Still, it made me nervous.

The next three months were dangerously mundane, perilous because a lax crew searching a junk or sampan could give a Viet Cong, on the verge of being detained, an opportunity to toss a hand grenade into an open pilothouse door.

On patrol, time progressed like spreading lava. We conducted our patrols according to Operation Market Time requirements and coastal division orders. Boat search activities fluctuated depending on the area we were assigned. At times, we were busy most of the day checking fishing junks peppered throughout our sector, while in stretches of coastline devoid of villages, we'd chase down cargo junks in transit farther offshore, just to break the monotony of moving from one end of our limit to the next, all day long.

During some of those tedious times on patrol, we'd engage in peculiar activities. More than once, Boats Carver placed us in the middle of a sampan fishing fleet off a river mouth, but at a safe distance. Porky would grab a concussion grenade out of the gun locker, wrap an abundant amount of toilet paper around the spoon, alert us, and head out onto the fantail. Mr. Bergin stood at the after controls and gave our engineman the carry-on nod. Holding the encased grenade, he'd pull the pin and toss it into the water. The skipper pushed the throttles forward, lifting the bow up and taking us away at best speed.

The mushy paper peeled away as it plunged beneath the surface, allowing the spoon to separate and ignite the detonator. Seconds later, KABOOM! The fishermen, having not only heard the bang but also felt the vibration of the explosion under the hull of their wood boats, headed straight toward the gusher of water that surfaced. In time, fish rose to the surface, belly up. As we left the scene, the joyful chatter and their smiling faces as they gathered a bountiful catch was all the gratitude we needed. The older fishermen clasped their hands, bowed toward us, then waved.

Unconventional at best, we succeeded in putting a dent in the joint campaign to win their "hearts and minds."

After lunch one day, while on the Same Drink Delta November patrol, a small amtrac unit of the III Marine Amphibious Force (III MAF) in I Corps, attached to the ROK 2nd Marine Brigade Blue Dragons, came out to meet us a short distance from shore, on the south side of Mui Batangan. The assault amphibian vehicle didn't seem seaworthy as it struggled to make way toward us, refreshing the handful of soldiers sitting on top as the flat front end slapped onto each oncoming wave.

On a previous patrol we had joined another PCF in extracting a US Marine from their base camp needing medical attention. A Korean captain ordered him to call in Dust Off for some of his wounded men, but he said he couldn't because he was in the middle of coordinating an air strike, angering the captain. He slammed the butt of a rifle on the Marine's face, breaking his jaw. Blue Dragon officers were not accustomed to having anyone question a direct order.

On board the floating tank were two Marine advisors, Captain Miller and Lieutenant Elmendorf. They came out to invite our skipper to join them ashore for a look at their base camp and partake of a dish of kimchi, the Koreans' side dish staple of fermented vegetables, mostly cabbage, and hot spices. Mr. Bergin left Boats with strict orders not to take the 79 Boat near the beach.

Carver took us out beyond the tip of the Batangan Peninsula and off the mouth of the Sông Trà Khúc. The crew went in different directions aboard the Swift. Boats stayed at the helm, Porky went up to the bow to read a western paperback, Gunner took to the guntub, I settled in the cabin and started a letter home.

About an hour into our time out, I heard Porky yell out toward the fantail to whoever was there to stop shooting over his head. Gunner heard the bullets zing by and told Porky that no one was on the fantail. We were getting sniped at from the beach, from the vicinity of the Co Lay Corral. Boats set GQ. Porky took the helm, Middleton uncovered the twin .50s, and Boats went to the fantail to man the single .50. I stood by the radar in the pilothouse.

We sped toward the river mouth, then took a hard right, putting us parallel to the shore about one hundred yards out. All guns were locked and loaded, but the VC, not interested in getting their asses kicked, didn't fire at us. Boats circled around and we took another run, hoping they'd be foolish enough to pull the trigger. Again, silence from the beach.

Over the Prick 25, Mr. Bergin called on us to move out to a rendezvous point to pick him up. After the fact, we realized we could have all gotten ourselves in a mess of shit with the DivCom in Chu Lai and perhaps all the way up to Da Nang had the enemy stood up to fight and we suffered casualties. Mr. Bergin wasn't happy at all the rest of that day . . . but we were!

At the end of a Same Drink Delta November twenty-four-hour patrol one morning, we made our way to the north side of Mui Batangan to await the arrival of our relief. The seas were unusually choppy that morning, in advance of what appeared to be an isolated summer squall.

Mr. Bergin exchanged pertinent patrol-related information with the relief OIC. Gunner covered the twin. 50s, knowing we'd be heading into heavy seas. About halfway to Chu Lai, Boats took the wheel in the pilothouse and told Seaman McNamara to get him some fresh coffee.

Mac went below into the cabin and in less than a minute he was back in the pilothouse. He told Carver it was too choppy to make a pot of coffee. In addition to the saltiest prefixed language straight from the depths of Davy Jones' locker, Boats made it known it wasn't a request, it was an order. "Quit being stupid," he told him. "Figure it out. I want my cuppa joe, now!"

Mac's face turned heat-stroke red as he stomped back into the cabin. Between moments of loud undecipherable mumbling and banging, he repeated, "Not stupid, not stupid." Carver snickered. Then it happened. The bow of PCF-79 plunged into a cresting five-foot wave, immediately followed by the crash of our shiny chrome Sunbeam electric coffee pot hitting the metal cabin deck. The sight wasn't pretty. Mac's cursing echoed throughout the cabin. He knew it would be his job to clean up the mess. As the engines whined, Mac opened the back hatch and hauled ass onto the fantail. He didn't stop. He used the top of the ammo locker as a springboard, and into the South China Sea he went.

Middleton hollered, "Man overboard!" from his guntub position above the pilothouse. Boats immediately executed the standard man overboard 60-degree Williamson turn to starboard, eventually bringing us back on an opposite heading. At the same time, Mr. Bergin went alongside the port catwalk, grabbing the heavy eight-foot wood boat hook as Carver veered seaward, placing PCF-79 between the heavy seas and Mac. Mr. Bergin took a position on the starboard side fantail two-wire stanchion.

Our crewmate wasn't treading water, he was swimming toward shore. Mr. Bergin tried reaching Mac with the rod, but he didn't make any effort to grab it.

"Where you going, Mac?"

"I'm joining the enemy!" he insisted.

"You don't want to do that," the skipper implored.

Boats took the pole from the skipper and began slapping the large brass end at Mac, while berating him. Curbing Carver's hot-headed reaction, Mr. Bergin ordered Boats to man the after steering and bring the fantail closer, without running the screws over him.

"You've made your point, Mac. It's okay. Now get back onboard," Mr. Bergin insisted.

"No way. I'd rather go fight for the Viet Cong than serve under that fat son of a bitch boatswain's mate!"

Boats' eyes bulged. Mac had the final say.

Eventually, Mac climbed onboard. Lieutenant Bergin stayed with him the rest of the trip back to base. Reaching Chu Lai, he took Mac to the field hospital, trying to convince the doctors he only needed a short rest. Before leaving, he made them promise they wouldn't ship him out.

Days later, Mr. Bergin went looking for Mac. He was gone.

I learned Mac was sent to the hospital ship USS *Sanctuary* off Da Nang harbor for a short period, then on to a hospital in Japan. On August 1, Mr. Bergin wrote a letter to Mac's mother, saying her son had served his crew well and participated in a crucial battle in which a North Vietnamese trawler loaded with supplies for the enemy was captured. Further, he stated that the entire crew, including Mac, was decorated by Vietnam's leader, Premier Nguyễn Cao Kỳ.

I recalled when I met Mac in Da Nang, he told me he volunteered for another year on Swifts. I questioned why he'd done such a dumb-ass thing. He didn't reply, but I wondered if his clenched jaw and distant stare were concealing underlying personal issues. I prayed he'd do well and land firmly on his feet.

It was our crew's turn to be assigned to the Same Drink Echo patrol, the southern-most sector in I Corps. It called for a two-week, two-crew, and one boat (PCF-79) duty rotation aboard a mother ship, the destroyer USS *Newell* (DER-322). Just days after going aboard, my wallet was stolen. The sorry, ignorant soul who took it could not use the currency it may have contained: it was funny money—MPC, Military Payment Certificate—used only in-country. It upset me more that he took my driver license, social security card, and family pictures. Neither the culprit nor the wallet was ever found.

While I was having chow in the mess deck one morning before patrol, the officer of the deck broadcast a stern announcement over the 1MC. "Now hear this. Now hear this. Attention, Phantom Shitter. The darling personal gift you left on the main deck port side is not approved or appreciated. You will be found and sent to court-martial promptly."

I learned that all ships at one time or another have a Phantom Shitter. The clan-destine defecator's vile activity is an unwelcome tradition of sorts aboard ships in the

Navy. Disgusting as it is, the crew laughs and talks about it for the rest of the day, all wondering who the culprit might be. I'm glad the Phantom Shitter never made it aboard PCF-79.

We were getting ready to climb down to our boat and relieve the rotation crew when Carver tried to pull a fast one on me by ordering me to get down to the boatswain's locker and request a pint of wood-bearing grease, prior to getting underway. I didn't fall for it, just like when I didn't bite when he wanted me to fetch five yards of water line. I was beginning to feel a little salty under the gills.

Most of the patrol sector was lined with cliffs and rocky shoreline—little to no fishing junk activity, only cargo junks in transit. About the only distraction in that boring patrol sector was the Sa Huỳnh sniper. On occasion, we'd get shot at by this menacing enemy soldier. Mr. Bergin opted not to fire upon him with our twin .50s or drop white phosphorous mortar rounds on him. He believed if we deep-sixed him, the VC might replace him with someone who could really shoot.

After lunch one cloudless day off Sa Huỳnh, Mr. Bergin walked out onto the fantail with a deep-sea fishing rig in hand. A large, colorful marlin lure dangled off the end of the faded green line. I guessed he borrowed the fishing rig either from an officer aboard ship or from someone back at Chu Lai.

Porky, on the other hand, used a different approach. One day he added mooring line to the end of a four-pronged grappling hook. He and Boats spotted a mammoth manta ray crossing our bow. Porky dashed to the fantail as Carver circled about. From the guntub, Middleton gained sight of the lumbering shadow beneath the surface and provided Carver an intercept heading.

We approached the sea creature off our port side at twenty feet. Porky waited until the ray was behind the boat, then tossed the hook ahead of it. Boats hit the throttles, hoping to hook it on its underside and bring it down. Snake eyes. Porky failed on his one and only attempt.

Mr. Bergin attached an eight-to-ten-inch multicolored bullethead lure to the end of the line. As soon as we began our northbound leg of our patrol, he tossed the lure out behind the boat, letting it trail us about twenty to thirty yards. The lure sliced the surface, creating a small splash as it skimmed the top. He used the fuse setting circular opening device attached to the side of the ammo box as a rod holder. The waiting began.

The crew went about its leisure business in the pilothouse, below deck, or on the bow. By the time someone finally heard his screams to stop engines, it was too late. Mr. Bergin wasn't a bit happy with us.

His screaming order to stop the boat began when he saw a black fin chasing the lure. It didn't take long after that for the ten-foot black marlin to take the bait. Mr.

Bergin never let us forget we were the cause of his failure to land a Chu Lai marlin, a real sea story, one that didn't begin with "This ain't no shit."

A couple of days later, I tried my luck at a big catch. Using a piece of wiener, I dropped the line over the side while we broke for lunch. Not long after, the rod started bobbing and then . . . fish on! We called out to a nearby fishing junk and gave the catch to an old man who was thrilled to take it off my hands.

The constant sights and sounds of war were getting to me. I was tired of seeing the war machine each day—the constant rumbling of 2 1/2-ton trucks (troops called them deuce and a halfs) rolling past our barracks, the popping *whup, whup, whup* sounds of helicopter blades overhead, the prominent smell of diesel engine exhaust, and the base red alert siren blasts in the middle of the night signaling incoming mortar rounds.

I missed home, but April was a long way off.

Over time, the aches of my broken heart caused by Norma's Dear Raúl letter began to fade. Gloria, the Marine sergeant I met in San Diego, helped ease the pain. The once platonic friendship evolved into a long-distance romance. I purchased a small reel-to-reel portable tape recorder and sent it to her. We began exchanging recorded letters. Hearing her sweet voice gave me purpose and focus on the remaining months ahead.

I received other recordings from home as well. My high school classmates, José Cueva and Richard Garcia, sent recordings of hometown bands and barrio targeted radio shows like the Pepsi Peña Show. Between songs, Richard provided bits and pieces of what was going on in SanAnto. I found it odd that his voice carried a remorseful tone. I gathered he didn't want to offend me by sounding cheerful, full of piss and vinegar, while I was among the walking dead in Vietnam. The music was great, and it lifted my spirits. Cueva's mom arranged for Yolanda, a co-worker at Joske's department store and a Sidney Lanier High School pep squad member, to write to me. I enjoyed receiving news from her on how the Lanier Voks were doing in sports.

Mom knew I loved to listen to rock 'n' roll music. One day, I received a "goody box." I knew it had to be *pan dulce*, Mexican pastries. I was wrong. The box contained two reel-to-reel tapes and two records, "Little Bit O' Soul" by the Music Explosion and "Soul Finger" by the Bar-Kays. I gathered someone at a record store must have recommended them to her.

Mom went to KONO radio station and demanded to speak with DJ Don Couser. On Saturdays he hosted a station patio "Swing Time," a homegrown version of American Bandstand. On learning I was in Vietnam, he recorded one of his shows. I was thrilled and played it over and over. The other tape was from my godfather, Roy

Alvarado. He had a *conjunto* band that played weekends at the Cielito Lindo Lounge, a south side neighborhood cantina. Between sets, he'd pipe in with a hearty "Give 'em hell, Roy!" The tape brought tears to my eyes.

The Straw Elephant, the Enlisted Men's (EM) Club for E-3s and E-4s, was our release valve from the daily uncertainties of war. The club, a large plywood structure, was capped by a thatched roof. Second and first-class Petty Officers attended the Acey-Deucey Club, the Chiefs had the CPO Club and officers, the O-Club. Separate clubs helped eliminate fraternizing between ranks.

The club was filled one night. The USO brought in a live show for us. It was an all-girl group from the Philippines called the All Stars. The five girls wore red miniskirts, white sparkle tops, and knee-high white vinyl boots. Serving as backdrop behind the drummer was a larger-than-life painting of Gwen Wong, *Playboy* magazine's April 1967 Playmate—Annette Funicello, step aside. Although I enjoyed how the girls played, I was more interested in fantasizing about the eye candy before me.

On another visit to the EM Club, the shore patrol came in late one night and shut the place down. They had to rescue the burlesque troupe that had been driving us all numbnuts into a frenzy for an hour.

Each of the go-go girls invited one sailor at a time on stage to dance with them. Michael Turley, the bosun on the 15 Boat, jumped up and drew immediate cheers from fellow Swifties. The sweetheart who invited him stopped dancing to enjoy his toe-tapping talents. Turley grooved on to James Brown's Boogaloo, then switched to the Swim, then the Dog. He jumped down with approving rounds of "Fuckin-A's" and slaps on the back from all of us.

The gathering of seamen and third class petty officer Swifties ended the night with a rowdy chant of: "I'm a lover, I'm a fighter, I'm a Swift Boat rider and I give a fuck!"

A long-awaited care package from my mother finally arrived. The box contained a canned selection of Old El Paso Mexican food. As promised, I invited Mr. Bergin and Lieutenant Bruce Wentworth, Cos Div 16 Commander, to a Mexican dinner aboard PCF-79. There wasn't enough to feed the entire crew, but Boats got the opportunity to share in the fixin's as well. I prepared the meal inside our boat, using the hot plate and an electric skillet. The meal consisted of tamales, rice, beans, and corn tortillas. I also made a batch of *papas coloradas*—fried, small-diced potatoes seasoned with salt, pepper, a touch of garlic, and Gebhardt chili powder, giving it the SanAnto Tex-Mex flavor. My mother always told me, "*Mijo*, if it doesn't say Gebhardt, it's not chili powder." The meal was a success.

By the beginning of October, the rainy season was upon us. One afternoon, all boats in the Chu Lai patrol sector were ordered back to port due to high seas. I was happy. It meant we probably weren't going out on patrol in the morning. Yet early the following morning, Porky came by our cubicle, woke me and Gunner up, and told us to head to the boat. We'd been selected to run a weather probe beyond Rosemary Point. The nest of PCFs moored fantail to dock were rising, falling, and bumping into each other in response to the choppy waters in the bay. I had my doubts of even being able to make it out the channel.

Mr. Bergin successfully drove PCF-79 into the white-capped six to eight-foot seas. The entire crew wore life jackets and held on for dear life. I stayed in the cabin, but next to steps leading into the pilothouse. I was relatively stable, but not my stomach. I told Boats I needed to upchuck, and he laughed.

I believe it was Porky who told him I was on the fantail feeding the fish over the side. Afraid I would be thrown overboard, Boats came out and secured me to the stanchion post at the port quarter of the fantail. I knew my face had to have been near in color to the sea-foam green cresting waves. We turned south, passing the officer hootches and radio control shack. The mounting seas were relentless.

Porky came out and helped take me back inside. Mr. Bergin wanted us all in the pilothouse because we were headed back. It was impossible to carry out a patrol. The skipper turned to port and into the mounting seas. They were now reaching fifteen to eighteen feet, with unbelievably short intervals. The six of us were crammed in tighter than a 64-count Crayola box. I was holding onto the radar on the starboard side. The bow of our Swift Boat rode a towering wave and slid sideways down its backside. Hitting bottom, the next wave heaved us upward like a rapidly ascending elevator in a New York City skyscraper. At the top, the wave went out from under us, allowing the oncoming wave to slam into the pilothouse windows, giving us all pucker factors of ten. The 79 Boat shuddered from stem to stern.

Lieutenant Bergin battled the angry sea and won, but the game went into overtime. The last challenge was the most dangerous, the channel entrance. There was only one chance to make the turn—misjudge the approach and a rogue wave could lift the fantail and plunge the bow into the sandy bottom. He spun the helm hard left on the backside of a wave, turning to port and surfed the boat on a following crest, adjusting more than once, letting the rudders keep us in the channel. I breathed a sigh of relief when we rounded the corner by the Straw Elephant and headed toward the Swift Boat pier.

Our crew was assigned an untested OIC for a couple of patrols while Mr. Bergin was on R&R in Australia. During a mid-watch, the OIC called general quarters. He said a radar contact was an enemy trawler. Weather covers on mounts 51 & 52 were removed, manned and ready.

I looked at the radar and shook my head. "That's not a trawler, sir. It's an LST in transit."

"Negative, son. It's a trawler. Prepare to challenge it with flashing light."

Oh, shit, I was in trouble. I wasn't a signalman. Hell, I wasn't a radioman either. I was a draftsman striker. I hesitantly grabbed the bulky hand-held spotlight. We headed toward the contact at full speed. Gunner yelled into the pilothouse from the guntub, "It's an LST."

"Challenge the contact," the OIC ordered.

I positioned myself on the starboard side pilothouse door and began depressing the trigger, "Dit—Dah Dit dit—Dah Dit dit—Dit dit—Dit. Dit—Dah Dit dit—Dah Dit dit—Dit dit—Dit."

Moments later the big ship's signalman responded with an array of fast DAHs and DITs.

"What's he saying?" the young officer asked.

"Hell if I know," I snapped.

"Well, you sent something, and he answered. What did you send?"

"Eddie," escaped my lips in a whisper.

"EDDIE?" he screamed. "Why Eddie?" he demanded.

"I learned it from a buddy seaman in San Diego attending radioman school. His name was Eddie."

Boats caught himself in mid laugh, looked at me, and winked.

Before the discussion continued, the LST lit up like a Christmas tree from stem to stern. Boats secured us from GQ. Gun mounts were covered, and part of the crew hit the sack to get what was left of their sleep time off.

The remaining hours of the patrol couldn't have gone by faster for the young skipper. Lesson learned.

Foul weather kept us in on a day we were scheduled for patrol on Mr. Bergin's return. He learned about my "Eddie" incident and directed Boats to have me practice "flashing light"—Morse code.

I grabbed my portable record player / radio and a few albums and headed to the Swift Boat pier. In Coronado, the radiomen were given a black two-inch-square cardboard practice device. Squeezing the top and bottom exposed a white inner surface through cut slits on the outer part.

I went into the cabin, set up my record player, and began squeezing the DAHs and DITs of the alphabet while listening and singing along to "Las Morenitas" by my hometown band, Sunny and the Sunliners. I let out a typical Tex Mex *grito* just as Carver climbed aboard the fantail. The timing was anything but perfect. He only heard my "shout" along with Mexican music coming from within the cabin.

Boats went livid. "I gave you an order to practice flashing-light and all you're doing is listening to that wetback shit."

"Boats, I—"

"I know what I heard, you little turd. It didn't sound like Morse code. Get your skinny ass in the lazarette and don't come out until you've wiped it clean."

Raising the Morse code practice device to his face didn't have any effect on him. His bizarre stare scared me. He was taking the reprimand to the extreme.

Diesel fume levels were dangerous. The sun beating down on the deck made the bilges a living hell. It was stifling. The longer I stayed below deck, the hotter my father's Mexican blood sped through my veins. *¡Chiquito pero picoso!* is a Mexican expression that implies "small but mighty." Carver finally pushed my limit button. I reached the point of wishing him dead.

I don't know how long he actually kept me down in the bilges, but when he finally said, "Get out. Next time, I'm writing you up," I didn't respond. I wanted nothing to do with the fuck. By the time I climbed out, Boats was gone. After putting my record player out of sight, I hightailed it up to officer country. Mr. Bergin was going to hear about the torture Carver put me through.

An officer must have alerted Mr. Bergin that I was outside his hootch and wanted to talk to him.

"What the hell happened to you, Bean?" he said with a slight chuckle.

"It's not funny, Skipper. That fat bastard bosun put me down the lazarette to clean out the bilges."

He almost choked trying not to burst into laughter. "You must have done something really bad."

"Negative. He told me to practice flashing light."

"Yeah, I told him to get you to do that after I heard about your 'Eddie' message at an LST the other day."

"I was in the cabin listening to my hometown music while practicing with this," I said, showing him my Morse code practice device. "He called it wetback music, sir. That ain't right."

"No. No, it's not, Bean. You did the right thing by trying to clean the bilges and not disobey his orders. Go get out of those diesel-drenched clothes before you burst into spontaneous combustion." He grinned.

"Still not funny."

"I know, I know. I'll have a talk with him, and soon."

As promised, Mr. Bergin did talk to Carver about the incident, but Chunky the Bosun never apologized. Often, the life of a pollywog seaman was a living hell.

CHAPTER 19

THE TONKIN FLYER

T he monsoon conditions occurred across South Vietnam at different times of
the year. The summer, or southwest, monsoon affecting the southern region
of the country, occurred between May and September. Chu Lai was in the
region facing to the northeast. The season of maximum rainfall affecting this area
took place between September and January. Lieutenant Michael Tackney, a boat
driver out of Chu Lai, coined the term "Tonkin Flyer" for these weather phenomena.

By design, the blue-water navy—destroyers, destroyer escorts, and minesweep-
ers—endured heavy seas. Coast Guard cutters, although much smaller, held their own
during these often-dangerous conditions. Out on stubby fifty-foot Swift Boats, the
danger level was high when caught unexpectedly by a monsoon storm.

Unlike engagements with the enemy, which were at times over within minutes,
these harrowing battles at sea with towering waves went on for hours at a time. The
punishment our bodies took, from the pounding of our feet on the deck to the blows
to our heads on the short bulkhead above us in the pilothouse, was merciless. Operation
Market Time units in I Corps suffered numerous losses, both physical and material,
between the last week of October and the end of November in 1966 and 1967.

Cos Div 15, Qui Nhơn, reported a "lost at sea" tragedy on October 25, 1966.
Although not monsoon related, Seaman Gunner's Mate Alvin Lee Levan suffered an
apparent seizure and fell over the side of PCF-87, approximately fifty miles southwest
of Qui Nhơn. Crew members saw him on the surface for only ten seconds and he was
never seen again. An extensive sea and air search for his remains was not successful.[1]

PCF Division 101 established a detachment at the mouth of the Sông Hương, the river leading to Huế, the former capital of Vietnam. This satellite base was located forty-five miles northwest of Da Nang harbor. It helped eliminate transit time for Swift Boats patrolling the northernmost sectors of I Corps and up to the Demilitarized Zone (DMZ).

After dark on October 29, 1966, Lieutenant Junior Grade John Laing's crew of PCF-56 was fighting heavy monsoon surf outside the mouth of the Perfume River, the name derived from the prominent fragrance produced by flowers in orchards upriver from Huế. The 56 Boat hit a rogue wave, violently tossing Boatswain's Mate First Class Kemper Billings over the side. The crew desperately searched for their crewmate, but there was no sign of him. His body was discovered on October 31 at 0730 hours on a nearby beach by a squad of Ruff-Puffs (South Vietnam Regional and Popular Forces).[2]

Two weeks after the Billings tragedy, the Tonkin Flyer tested the courage of Swift Boat sailors operating out of the Da Nang detachment at Huế. Intel was intent on the possibility of a Chinese submarine moving south to attempt delivery of arms and supplies. All PCFs were placed on high alert.

Lieutenant Junior Grade Lou Masterson and his crew were aboard PCF-75, guarding the 1A1 patrol sector's northern boundary, the DMZ. A malfunctioning radar could easily cause a Swift Boat to stray into the territorial waters of North Vietnam. Patrolling the mouth of the Perfume River was PCF-22, with Lieutenant Junior Grade Mitchell Gibbons-Neff as officer in charge. The southern sector was patrolled by Lieutenant Junior Grade David Wilbourne and his crew aboard PCF-77.

The three boats got underway early Monday morning, November 14, 1966. Leaving the base and river channel behind, they proceeded to their areas under normal sea conditions. Late in the evening, PCF-77 proceeded to their southern patrol area to rendezvous with a PCF out of Da Nang who was daisy-chaining Chief Machinery Repairman Willy Scott Baker for assignment at the Swift base in Huế. PCF-13 OIC, Lieutenant Junior Grade James Stephens, recalled Baker, a thirty-eight-year-old sailor, reenlisted in the Navy, requesting Vietnam duty with hopes of helping his "kids" make it home.

After midnight, Lieutenant Masterson reported increasing winds and heavy seas. The other two PCF crews also began experiencing mounting seas. Rough seas angst ran high on a PCF during daylight hours, and it went beyond the fear pucker factor in the dead of night.

Sea conditions deteriorated fast as the first several hours of the new day ticked away. The three officers decided it was senseless to attempt a return to base. Daring a run at the irregular channel entrance would be nothing less than ensuring a meeting with Davy Jones' wardroom at the bottom of the sea. The plan was to make their way toward the channel entrance, arriving shy of daybreak. All crews donned their life jackets. They poked holes in the South China Sea all through the night.

Lieutenant Junior Grade Anthony Taylor described navigating the Perfume River channel as "a white-knuckle run." The approach is straight toward the beach, north of the river mouth. At just the exact moment and in a smooth trough, a full left rudder is executed, swinging the boat to port and placing you broadside to the seas. Difficult in normal surf, perilous during the monsoon. You punch the engines to their limit, hoping to clear the sandbar and run into calmer waters.

Before dusk, only the roar of the crashing waves at the channel entrance could be heard by the crews on the boats waiting a mile out. At first light, the men were shocked by the massive turbulence before them. Their radar screens displayed a clutter of false echoes. There was no way that features defining the channel could be discerned. Odds of success were not in their favor.

Without warning, a rogue wave, estimated at twenty-five to thirty feet, lifted PCF-77's stern, and the RPM needle pegged as the screws, now out of the water, whined. The bow plunged into the trough, and the impact hurled bodies around like rag dolls. The engineman, EN2 Arthur O'Neal, was ejected from the guntub as the boat toppled over.

For an instant, Lieutenant Wilbourne saw only green frothy water through all three pilothouse windows. Just as quickly, he saw daylight and exited the port side hatch. On the next wave, BM2 Alma Junior Twitchell popped out of the same door.

As the boat sank, the skipper saw his seaman gunner, Thomas Doyle Hodson, inside the cabin attempting to slide open the window. Together, they managed to open it and the young sailor escaped. Chief Baker was last seen entering the cabin compartment where the radioman was believed to be trapped by heavy deck plating covering the ammo storage locker.

Three men were missing: Third Class Boatswain's Mate Harry Giles Brock, Radioman Third Class Bruce Allen Timmons, and Chief Baker. PCF-77 disappeared from the surface, keel up.[3]

The four surviving sailors swam toward one another. Lieutenant Wilbourne clung to his men's orange life jacket collars. The distance to shore was at least 1,500 yards, based on the last radar reading. While the swimmers contemplated their next move, the bodies of Brock and Baker surfaced. Helicopters rushed to the scene, rescuing the four survivors and the remains of BM3 Brock and Chief Baker.

PCF-77 sank in only thirteen feet of water. The mangled bow, with a portion of the pilothouse attached, washed ashore 2,500 yards north of the channel entrance.

Bow of Swift Boat PCF-77 washed ashore by monsoon storm, Perfume River, Republic of Vietnam, 15 November 1966. (Photo credit: Lou Masterson)

HCU-1 Salvage Master reported that salvage efforts could not be attempted. Although divers tried to locate the remainder of the craft and searched for Timmons, neither was found.

Sông Thạch Hãn was thirty-six miles up the coast from Huế, eighty miles north of Da Nang. It was commonly known as the Cửa Việt River, because the military associated it with the tiny village by the same name on the north side of the river mouth.

The 1954 Geneva Accords established the 17th Parallel as the division line between the Democratic Republic of Vietnam to the north and the Republic of Vietnam to the south. After unification elections failed to take place in 1956, the Sông Bến Hải became the de facto border. The DMZ straddled this meandering river, three miles on either side.

On July 7, 1967, Coastal Division 14 established a Swift Boat detachment base on the south side of the river. On November 1, Lieutenant Thomas Yankura took over control of the Cửa Việt detachment operations from Cos Div 14 personnel; the base was now under Cos Div 12 command.

The arrival of the monsoon season brought a decline in Operation Market Time activity in I Corps. Least likely to be out in open water were small junks and sampans.

Lieutenant Junior Grade Dan Daly's PCF-76 crew was tight. BM1 William Fielder was his trustworthy second-in-command. The rest of the crew consisted of EN2 Oscar Wells, the engineman; Radarman Second Class Michael Newcomer; John Mueller, a Seaman Fire Control Technician striker (gunner); and Seaman Bobby Buck.

Sunrise on Monday, November 6, 1967, provided nothing less than an ideal chamber of commerce backdrop for a "Come Visit Cửa Việt" vacation flyer. The sky was a comforting deep blue, but the wind not as welcoming. Gusts were stiff at thirty to forty miles per hour, coming from the northeast. Typhoon Emma had crossed the Philippines as a category 5 two days earlier and was reduced to a tropical storm once it passed the large landmass. It then began a northwest track that would narrowly miss Hainan Island's eastern shores. Nonetheless, Cửa Việt felt the residual effects of the passing weather system.

PCF-76 was scheduled for an early patrol that day. Although life jackets were available, Lieutenant Daly believed they were too bulky and would hinder an emergency exit from within the pilothouse or cabin should the boat capsize. The crew broke them out of storage and placed them on the two bunks in the cabin.

BM1 Fielder stood next to Lieutenant Daly behind the radar on the starboard side of the pilothouse. The rest of the crew was below in the cabin, holding on as best they could. The two pilothouse doors as well as rear cabin hatch were latched, as were the side windows, but the heavy metal ammo storage compartment cover on the deck flew airborne each time a wave went out from under the boat and gravity took over, slamming onto the deck with loud bangs.

Crashing into the first two waves, Lieutenant Daly realized the period between waves was perilously short, four to five seconds. It was unsafe to continue. PCF-76 was in danger of capsizing and taking its crew down with it. Lieutenant Daly made a command decision immediately following a near ditching plunge down the back side of the third wave.

Lieutenant Daly called to his men to hold on as he prepared to initiate a hard left on the back of the next wave. He jammed the starboard throttle forward and pulled on the other one, spinning the wheel to port. On the way down the back side of the wave, the 76 Boat began sliding sideways to starboard. Nearing the trough, the boat was swung past the 180-degree mark when the next wave heaved the twenty-three-and-a-half-ton PCF up with such force that it shifted the roll to port. The 76 Boat didn't reach the crest. The roll continued and tipped the boat over, slamming its top onto the surface, the crew tumbling inside like clothes in a dryer.

Lieutenant Daly saw the blue sky turn murky-green in seconds, prior to closing his eyes preparing for hard impact. Water filled the pilothouse. He forced his eyes open and spied surface light coming from a busted door window. He somehow managed to wriggle through it and surfaced.

Hammered by the surf, he sensed darkness above his head. The boat was at the top of a crest, and he was in the following low. Fortunately, the displacement pressure of the falling boat pushed him away into the next wave. The boat was now upside down and moving faster toward shore than he was. His first reaction was to remove his heavy deck shoes. Exhaustion kept him from removing his trousers and shirt.

He reached deep for strength and swam toward the sinking boat. Reaching the stern, he grabbed onto one of the zinc plates and a rudder, pulling himself up to the anti-fouling crimson bottom.

After catching his breath, he scanned all around in search of his crew. He was filled with joy in seeing four of his men, some in life jackets, clinging to the boat's life raft. It apparently had broken loose. Since the intake of water pushed the bow down, the cabin hatch remained above water, for the most part. The crew had moved fast, exiting that door and taking a couple of life jackets. He hollered questions at them, attempting to keep them alert. Deep inside, he feared the worst for his lead petty officer, Fielder. He'd been under for ten minutes or more. Hearing a splash, he turned, looking back toward the propellers. Fielder's head popped up. Nothing shy of a miracle.

Days later, Fielder detailed his saving moments to PCF-80's BM2 Stirlin Harris. He had fallen into the cabin at the same time the ammo locker covers came flying off. Fifty-caliber ammo boxes and mortar canisters came crashing upon him. He was temporarily knocked out, but the cold saltwater brought him back around. He was able to break free from the heavy load, managed to open a side window, and exited the cabin. He made his way under the boat's fantail stanchions and surfaced behind the twin props.

The crew was intact. Daly helped Fielder cling to one of the shafts. He wore only a T-shirt and skivvies. The skipper was glad to see his men holding onto the raft. They would soon be rescued by an approaching Swift. At the same time, he realized they wouldn't be able to bring the boat close enough to his capsized PCF. Any rescue attempt could become disastrous.

Soon, a helicopter approached, a Sikorsky H-34. A horse collar at the end of a hoist cable was lowered. Fielder went first. The life ring was lowered a second time. Lieutenant Daly slipped his hands through the opening, followed by his head. Once his arms draped over the ring, the harness secured under his armpits, the cable began pulling him up. Below, four of his men were being taken aboard by Lieutenant Tom Jones' boat, PCF-80.

The helicopter headed toward shore. Lieutenant Daly crawled toward the cockpit, tapped the pilot on the leg, and hollered the best he could a grateful "Thanks" and held a thumb up. The pilot acknowledged with a nod. The two were taken to the field hospital in Dong Ha, upstream from the Swift base.

When the weather conditions improved, divers determined the craft was broken up and deemed it non-salvageable. The Tonkin Flyer had taken another PCF to the shallow depths at Cửa Việt.[4]

On November 30, 1967, three Swift Boats returned to base at the end of their twenty-four-hour patrol, all at the same time. Seas grew during the predawn hours that Thursday morning, forcing the PCFs to head home at best speed. The PCF-58 was the last boat in the surf, attempting to enter the notorious channel entrance. They passed fishermen and families on sampans also desperately seeking safe passage through the violent surf.

Halfway to the Swift Boat pier, PCF-14 and PCF-55 were heading back toward the river mouth at full speed. The crews signaled the men aboard PCF-58 to follow them. While watching the progress the 58 Boat was making its way through the surf, they witnessed the horror of sampans being tossed end over end into the rumbling surf, the passengers flung in the air and into the water.

Boatswain's Mate Second Class Tony Snesko was at the after steering controls. He turned the PCF-58 around and followed. The rest of his crew prepared life rings and grabbed the boat hook. Reaching the river mouth, Snesko was shocked to see the lead boat, PCF-14, being tossed up and over, landing belly-side up. In addition to the Vietnamese fighting for their lives in the water, six Swift Boat crewmen needed to be rescued as well.

Approaching the capsized vessel was PCF-55, with BM2 Kenneth McDonald at the after steering controls. Snesko couldn't believe he was about to see a replay of what happened moments before to PCF-14. A rogue wave caught McDonald by surprise as he was maneuvering the boat, so his crewmates could pick up survivors in the water. The twenty-foot green wall began to curl, taking the fifty-foot craft on its side and into an eighty-five-degree roll, hurling overboard not only his shipmates but the crew of PCF-14, as well as numerous Vietnamese they had rescued. McDonald managed to hang on and through his skillful work of rudders and engine throttles surfed the wave into the safety of calm river water.

The effort of rescuing two boat crews and dozens of Vietnamese belonged to the crew of PCF-58. One by one they began the urgent task. The fantail quickly became crowded with shivering passengers.

Snesko heard a scream off to his left as he stood behind the wheel on the fantail. It was one of the boat officers, his hand stretched out to the sailor behind the after helm. The PCF was riding into waves that at times made it seem the angry sea wanted to body-slam it on the sea mat. Snesko took one daring chance to leave the wheel momentarily to attempt to bring the officer on board. He succeeded.

A young crewman sat on the deck by the helmsman. Weeping, the sailor told Snesko that he had two children under each arm but lost them after something hit him on the head and made him lose sense momentarily.

Snesko was too busy looking out for the next wave. He had no time to contemplate any other options. He had the conn. At the top of a frothing crest, the determined bosun spun the wheel hard right, pushed the port throttle forward, and pulled back on the starboard. The boat responded, and in the trough the port quarter pushed into the oncoming wave.

The fantail rose and the boat began surfing ahead of the wave. Snesko maintained control of the craft, not allowing the wave to push it sideways and into a compromising position. All on board breathed a sigh of relief as the boat glided into the tranquil waters of the Sông Thạch Hãn.[5]

Orders from Cos Div 12 directed Lieutenant Yankura to secure the detachment and return all craft and personnel to Da Nang. The Tonkin Flyer left its morbid mark in I Corps Swift Boat operations during the 1967 northeast monsoon season. Three PCFs were sunk—PCF-76, PCF-77, and PCF-14; four Swift Boat sailors drowned— BM1 Kemper Billings lost overboard in heavy seas; CPO W. S. Baker, BM3 Harry B. Brock, and RM3 B. A. Timmons drowned when PCF-77 capsized. Swift Boat sailors engaged the Viet Cong in combat and challenged the might of the Tonkin Flyer, never backing down.

WE REMEMBER...

CHAPTER 20

THE ALBATROSS

rriving at the pier, I heard the rumbling of the engines and the gurgling sound the exhaust flaps created. The powerful, constant smell of diesel fume exhaust is something I would always remember. I reached over the stern stanchion and placed a heavy box of groceries on top of the mortar ready box. My cheerful mood went south when I saw two Army types mounting a set of loudspeakers on top of the cabin, port side.

PSYOPS today, I thought. A weathered sergeant and a young PFC were a surprise addition to our crew. It was too late to go back to the commissary for more grub, for we'd be shoving off soon. Leftover fruit from our last patrol would help.

We had never been assigned a permanent crewman to serve as our deckhand after McNamara left us five months prior. A fill-in seaman helped me organize stores while I began radio and radar checks.

A familiar melodic voice echoed from below deck in the snipe locker.

"Hey, Bean. Yer lookin' good, man. Ya been sick?"

"What the hell you doin' in Porky's cave, Hogjaws? He don't let just anybody lay hands on his girls. He authorized you down there?"

"Why, hell yeah, he did. He loves me, you know."

"You bilge rats are all alike, always lookin' for someone to check your oil."

"You're just jealous, Bean, I can tell. I had an eye on you since trainin' back in Coronado. You remember. But Boats said he wanted you for his sea chicken."

I flipped him off and headed toward the cabin. From behind me, I heard him blow a kiss, saying, "I'm still yer idol, ain't I, Bean?" Hogjaws excelled in grab-assing.

I was standing on top of the cabin, checking the lubricant level in the radar housing on the mast, when Mr. Bergin came aboard.

"About done with your equipment checks, Bean?"

"Yes, sir. Radio's fine. Hey, Mr. Bergin, did you already know we were scheduled to run PSYOPS today?"

"Negative. Found out when I picked up patrol orders a while ago. They're from the 244th PSYOP Company."

The PSYOPS team conducted a low-volume sound check. A black wire ran from the green public address speakers through a slightly open portside cabin window and connected to the portable five-inch reel-to-reel tape player.

I was in the pilothouse laying out the Mui Batangan map on the chart table when Carver showed up.

"Your sweetheart Porky wasn't there to wake you up this morning, Boats?" I chided.

"Shut the fuck up, Bean, or I'll shove you down the lazarette again," he warned, lunging toward me. "Come here, you little fu—"

"Engines ready, Skipper," Hogjaws interrupted, poking his head into the pilothouse.

"Get us underway, Boats," Mr. Bergin ordered.

"Bean, you and the kid bring in the mooring lines."

"On my way, Boats," I responded.

Mr. Bergin took the controls aft, while Carver stayed at the helm in the pilothouse. A Swiftie on the pier helped remove the mooring lines from the dock cleats.

"Lines in and secured, Skipper," I called from the fantail.

Mr. Bergin tapped the throttles forward, moving PCF-79 away from the floating dock. I went into the cabin and radioed Article the usual getting underway and patrol destination coded message. Middleton was in his heavily armed "crow's nest" position. In the pilothouse, Boats had the conn and Mr. Bergin sat on a wobbly wood barstool by the chart table.

That Wednesday, December 6, 1967, was a typical northeast monsoon season day: mostly cloudy, humid, rolling seas, except during passing squalls. We rendezvoused with the PCF-57, on the north side of Sông Sa Kỳ. Pulling alongside, the OIC, Lieutenant Junior Grade Arlie Joe Pope, reported they had taken fire from an area north of the Sông Trà Khúc, harassment fire mostly. Other than that, it was all calm along the Mỹ Lai shoreline, our intended PSYOPS location south of Mui Batangan. He and his crew were brand-new to Chu Lai and didn't have but a handful of patrols under their belt.

The scent of my *picadillo* wafted throughout the cabin and the pilothouse. Like nagging children on a long journey, the crew paraded through "Bean's Galley," asking if lunch was ready. The water I used to help cook the diced potatoes in the mix needed another half hour to reduce. The dish wasn't considered a soup, but it didn't have the consistency of chili either.

"Lunch is ready when you are, Mr. Bergin," I announced at last.

"Boats, take us two miles out, opposite the river mouth into CG-16. We'll break for lunch there," Mr. Bergin ordered.

Carver didn't acknowledge verbally. Instead, he pushed the throttles to half speed and pointed the boat in a southeasterly direction and away from shore. Reaching a suitable location, he turned us fantail to the prevailing northeast winds and waves. He brought the throttles to idle position, and we began to drift.

The electric skillet full of Mamá Sarita's *picadillo* was gone in one sitting. I was lucky to have saved a small portion for myself. It made me happy the crew enjoyed a taste of down-home Tex-Mex food.

As Boats was finishing up a sandwich, a wide-spanned bird approached us from the south. It seemed to float in the air, without the need to flap its wings. Its yellowish beak was bulky and it had a face only a mother could love.

"What kinda bird is that?" I asked as it flew low and over us.

"It's an albatross, Bean," Mr. Bergin answered.

"Not good," Boats muttered. "Bad sign."

"Another one of your sea stories?" I razzed, not knowing he was serious.

Boats kept his eyes on the bird as it circled our Swift Boat and landed thirty feet off our port quarter.

"No, Bean," Mr. Bergin said. "In the old seafaring days, sailors feared the sight of these oversized seagulls. They believed an albatross carried the souls of dead sailors and flew the seas in search of more. Some say the fable is tied to Samuel Taylor Coleridge's 'Rime of the Ancient Mariner.'"

An unexpected cool breeze swept over the fantail.

We checked a few fishing boats on our way into shore.

"Sergeant, I'm heading in. You ready to broadcast?" Mr. Bergin asked.

"Affirmative," he responded.

"Schneider, take us in on the north side of Sông Trà Khúc. Stay outside the surf and ride the shoreline at a low RPM."

Hogjaws headed to the pilothouse to man the helm. Without orders, the rest of us manned our battle stations, donning flak jackets and helmets. The PSYOPS team stepped into the cabin to initiate the broadcast. I took up station to one side of the radarscope in the pilothouse on the starboard side. Jim sat in the helmsman's chair to my left.

Using my sound-powered phones, I contacted Carver on the aft-fifty and Middleton above in the guntub.

"Boats, Gunner, how copy? Over."

"I hear you, Bean," Boats responded from the fantail.

"Me too," Gunner checked in. At the same time, I heard his voice coming through the guntub opening behind the helmsman's chair.

Mr. Bergin's GQ station on this PSYOPS mission was sitting on the fantail deck behind a .30 caliber machine gun mounted on a port stanchion post. The sergeant stepped out of the cabin and took station by the mortar box on the starboard side.

Jim began his turn to the north seventy yards from the breaking surf line and decreased speed as he moved us in twenty-five more yards.

"We've got eight feet below us, Jim," I reported, looking at the fathometer.

"Lock 'n' load your fifties, Gunner," Boats said through my headset. Bob pulled on the two wood retracting slide handles, creating a clanking sound, and raising the hair on my neck. Five and a half inch rounds in each chamber were ready to fire at the enemy.

I looked aft through the small rectangular window on the back bulkhead. Carver stood behind his single-fifty, scanning the sand dunes through his binoculars. The oversized helmet he wore fit over the bulky earphones, making him look like a futuristic galactic warrior.

The palms of my hands were moist, from my heart rate reacting to apprehension. Lieutenant Bolger's PCF-99 crew's encounter with the VC at the Co Lay Corral had been bloody, requiring a daring Dust Off extraction. Not knowing if—or worse, when—the bullets would start pinging the boat and shattering windows pushed my pucker factor beyond ten.

Co Lay was made up of three separate hut groupings. Co Lay (3) was closest to the river, (2) was in the middle, and (1) was the farthest north. The first village began at the edge of the river mouth and owned 400 yards of beachfront. Five hundred yards separated the first two areas, while six hundred yards divided (2) and (1). A thousand yards beyond the last settlement was the large village of Mỹ Lai.

The Vietnamese-language Chiêu Hồi recording began as we approached Co Lay (3). A man's voice announced a plea to the Viet Cong and NVA soldiers. The message invited them to lay down their arms and report to a rallying point, a safe welcoming station. Propaganda material established Swift Boats as places where an enemy soldier could seek refuge.

The tape was repeating for the third time as the first village went by. Schneider kept us on course as the water depth fluctuated between eight and twelve feet. Our navigational chart indicated a two-fathom line, 300 yards from shore. With a draft a bit less than two yards, twelve feet was enough water in which to safely operate. It was the shallow depth that concerned me; it meant we were dangerously close to scraping bottom. Every now and again I'd look over the starboard side, checking for signs of cloudy surf. An uncharted sandbar could cause anxiety, especially so close to shore. We'd become an open target for the Viet Cong if we ran aground in the surf line.

"Looks like Charlie ain't home."

"That's fine with me, Bean," Jim replied as we went beyond Co Lay (1). Up ahead, the beach curved to the right, defining the south side of Mui Batangan. We were now 5,000 yards north of Sông Trà Khúc, passing the north end of Mỹ Lai.

Boats' order came through my headphones. "Bean, tell Hogjaws to take us back out."

"Copy. I'll tell him."

We cut across the cove and passed the southern tip of Batangan. The wheel spun quickly, left, right, and once more, signaling Mr. Bergin had the control on the fantail. Gunner crawled down from the guntub and the three of us went aft.

"See any movement on the dunes?" Mr. Bergin asked.

"Nah," Boats answered.

"Me neither," Gunner added, "and I was eye level to the tops of the dunes."

"Yeah. Quieter than a classroom full of mimes," Hogjaws quipped.

"Boats, on the next run, you and Gunner keep a close eye out for bunkers," Skipper ordered.

I noticed Boats gazing skyward in all directions.

"Searching for faces in the clouds or Japanese Zeroes?" I asked. "I know tomorrow's December 7th, but it's a different war, Boats."

"Making sure that albatross is gone, Bean," he said, eyebrows crinkled.

His concern about that gooney bird put me on edge. I didn't question him. I didn't want to know what his answer might be. I wondered if the strain of Native American blood running through his veins had stirred his soul. Was he sensing an omen?

Schneider came out of the engine room, having checked who knows what. Back topside, he lowered the heavy hatch, letting it go inches from the deck, creating a loud crash.

"Engines ready for another run, Schneider?" asked Mr. Bergin.

"They're fine," Jim said, wiping grease off his fingers. "Just checking the throttle linkage."

"Lieutenant, ready for a second run?"

"Let's do it."

"Schneider, take us in again," Mr. Bergin ordered. "Everyone stay alert."

The crew manned battle stations. In the pilothouse, I grabbed the green deck log and posted the following entry:

1330 Hrs. COMMENCING 2ND SHORELINE PSYOPS RUN, NORTH FROM SONG TRÀ KHÚC. COORDINATES BS 74.9 75.5.

"You copy, Boats, Gunner?" I called out through my sound-powered phone.

"Gotcha," Gunner replied.

"I'm here," I heard Boats say.

The tape started up. My pulse rate quickened. I looked into the guntub, tapping Middleton's leg and gave him a thumbs-up. He reciprocated. Carver spied the beach through his binoculars. I leaned out the port hatch, looked aft, and saw Mr. Bergin sitting on the deck behind the .30 caliber machine gun.

"Gunner, sharp eye on the dunes in front of the village," Boats said. "Charlie puts themselves between us and a friendly village, so we won't shoot back."

"All clear so far," Middleton replied.

Nearing Co Lay (2), the broadcast switched to a recently produced *Wandering Souls* propaganda message.[1] The Army's 6th PSYOPS Battalion and Operation Market Time Navy units used this effective Chiêu Hồi recording. It was anchored on the strong Vietnamese cultural belief that the departed would wander in anguish and without direction if they were not laid to rest in their homeland. The notion hit the enemy hard, especially the NVA soldiers since they were far from their native soil in North Vietnam.

Several rounds of frenzied wailing echoed in pain. As we passed by the middle group of huts behind the sand dunes, the message repeated.

I reached into my pant pocket and pulled out the small plastic St. Anthony and Baby Jesus figurine Mom and Dad gave me at the airport in San Antonio when I left for Vietnam. It fit perfect into the left flak jacket pocket, the tiny faces peeking out. Squeezing it gently, I prayed for their protection.

"Boats!" Gunner called out. "Up the beach, three hundred yards, I've got a gook in a black pajama top, wearing a dink hat."

"What's he doing?" Carver asked.

"Just standing there, behind the dune."

"I can't find him. Give me more details," Boats demanded.

"Nah, man. You'll find him and then tell Bergin."

"Tell me where, damn it!"

"I don't like it. It ain't right, man. I'm taking the fucker down."

"Hold your fire, Gunner," Boats insisted.

"He's between the second and third palm tree. But don't tell Skipper. He'll play John Wayne and want us to stop."

"That's our mission," our sixteen-year dedicated bosun replied.

In the main cabin, the PFC increased the loudspeaker's volume, then stepped out of the cabin and joined the sergeant on fantail by the mortar box. The howling voices chilled me. I looked at the radar, checking our position from shore. We were 100 to 150 yards off the beach and the fathometer indicated at least a six-foot clearance below our hull.

"Anyone else with him?" Carver asked.

"Negative. He's alone, just looking our way. I'm cutting him in half if the motherfucker makes a move."

Gunner sounded angry, perhaps fearful of what might happen next. I looked out the center windshield in the pilothouse but couldn't see the guy. Jim kept steering us clear of the surf, maintaining speed.

"Hold your fire, Gunner," Boats repeated. "Let me find him." He raised the binoculars to his face and scanned the shoreline, the palm trees still ahead about seventy-five yards. "I got him. I see him now!"

Carver spun the gun mount forward to the safety stop. He leveled the barrel, rested the binoculars on top of the machine gun cover plate, and looked through them again, spotting the suspicious Vietnamese man behind the dunes.

"What's going on, Bean?" Jim asked.

"There's a gook on the beach up ahead at ten o'clock."

"Where? I'll look for him."

"Hold up, Jim. I don't see Carver."

We were approaching the midpoint between Co Lay (2) and (1). The wailing intensified, or perhaps my anxiety made my ears more sensitive. It was now a chorus of agonizing voices.

For some reason, Carver's talk button stayed stuck in the depressed position. I heard him say, "Skipper, I think there's a bunker right there."

"Fuck!" I heard Gunner shout from the guntub. "He's telling Bergin."

I stepped behind the helmsman's chair to the starboard side of the pilothouse. The radar unit was between me and the front windshield. Glancing through the small vent window on the back bulkhead, I saw the skipper get up off the deck and the .30 caliber machine gun, then move toward the fantail gun mount.

"Where, Boats?"

Carver pointed to the sand dune, fifty yards ahead.

"I don't see anything," Mr. Bergin said.

Boats took the binoculars and laid them on top of the machine gun receiver plate. "Okay, I'm on him, take a look."

Mr. Bergin lowered his head to the binoculars. As he placed them to his eyes, all hell broke loose. The beach erupted in a clatter of automatic weapons fire. The Viet Cong hit us from three positions along the beach: aft, midships, and forward.

I heard a clink near me but couldn't tell where the round hit. Still looking aft, Boats shoved Skipper to the deck and out of harm's way, then rushed behind the .50 and sprayed the shoreline. Mr. Bergin crawled over the deck and pumped .30 caliber rounds into the middle and rear bunker positions.

Above me, Gunner's twin-fifties filled the air with deafening metallic clatter. The pilothouse shook as four-inch brass casings rained down on the deck from Middleton's machine guns.

Schneider's first reaction was to get us the hell away from the beach and out of the line of fire. As he pushed the throttles forward, Mr. Bergin, on his knees, reached up from the fantail deck and slammed the aft steering throttles ahead. The sudden, simultaneous action pumped a surge of JP-5 fuel on the twin 12V71 diesels, shutting both down. We were dead in the water.

While Jim frantically attempted to start the engines, I looked out the front windshield. Like being caught by the bright flash of a camera, I froze. From the bunker off our port bow, a row of bullets kicked up sand, then waterspouts as hot lead raced toward me. As if pushed by an invisible force, I fell back as I heard a loud thud followed by the shattering sound of breaking glass.

"You hit, Bean?" Jim hollered.

"I'm okay, I think."

My reaction threw me up against the bulkhead and down to the deck. I reached for my St. Anthony figurine. It was facing toward me, away from the incoming bullets. Getting up off the deck, I noticed Middleton's guns had gone silent. I thought he'd been hit. Looking up into the guntub, I saw he was anxiously trying to unjam the right gun. The oiled rag he kept over the bullets, protecting them from ocean spray, had been pulled along by the bullet linkage and had gotten stuck in the breach. In disgust, he stopped his attempt and continued firing with only the left gun.

"Flash Traffic, Flash Traffic, Same Drink Delta November," I called over the radio. "Receiving heavy fire from three bunkers at Co Lay. Position BS 75 77. Out."

Another round hit the cabin.

Schneider finally lit up the engines. Pushing the throttles forward, he spun the wheel to starboard, angling us away from the beach, giving both gun mounts the ability to continue suppressive fire as we left the area.

I looked to the fantail and didn't see Carver.

"He's hit! Boats got hit!" screamed Middleton.

Jim heard him. "Take the wheel, Bean. I'm going to the fantail."

He exited the port side and stepped back along the cabin amidst a storm of bullets. He saw Carver's body lying on the starboard side of the fantail, between the gun mount and the engine cover. A pool of blood flowed on the deck from behind his head. His headset wrapped around his neck.

"Stay low," Mr. Bergin yelled as Jim passed behind him.

Schneider went to check Boats and immediately saw an entry wound in his right eye. Boats gasped for air. Jim snapped his head to one side, fighting back emotions. He knelt by his buddy and Swiftmate, slid his hand under Carver's neck, lifting his head. Immediately he felt warm wet matter in his hand. Jim cradled his head in his right arm, so Carver's back rested on his thigh. The attempt to help Carver breathe didn't help. Jim feared the worst. It filled him with rage.

Still under heavy automatic weapons fire, Jim gently lowered Boats to the deck, got up, and began firing the remaining rounds left in the unauthorized 500-round capacity bullet canister, cursing like a true sailor. He hooked up another 100-round box of ammo and emptied it as well in sheer retaliation.

Unconsciously, I abandoned the helm and made my way to the fantail along the starboard side. Mr. Bergin spotted me and yelled, "Stay away, Bean. Get to the pilothouse and take us out to sea. Send Flash Traffic. Call in Dust Off and raise Firefox or Zebra, whatever tin can is out there. Need medical assistance ASAP."

The sight of Bobby Don Carver's body lying in a puddle of blood shocked me. I couldn't move, I couldn't think, I couldn't hear.

"Bean!" screamed Mr. Bergin.

This time I heard him. He repeated his orders and I turned around, lips tight and holding back tears. Breaking down was not an option. I needed to get Boats help, and fast.

There was no visual out the front windshield. I steered the boat while standing on the port side, by the chart table. I leaned over to the radar, checking for any contacts ahead. I needed to be sure our Swift Boat didn't collide with any fishing junks or sampans. For now, the course ahead was clear.

"Flash Traffic, Flash Traffic," I called out on the radio. "Possible KIA on board. Request Dust Off ASAP. Heading east from BS 76 79. Break. Same Drink Zebra, request immediate rendezvous. Need emergency medical assistance. Repeat, possible KIA onboard. Over."

Article and Zebra responded with a "Roger, Out." Adjoining patrol area Swifts reported they were heading our way.

I double-checked the radar. All clear. Enraged, I grabbed the M79 grenade launcher and loaded a round. I brazenly left the wheel on autopilot, walked alongside the cabin toward the fantail. I saw Jim holding Boats in his arms, his shirt soaked in blood.

I pulled the trigger, launching a grenade toward the beach. The blast startled Jim and Mr. Bergin.

"Bean. Get back to the pilothouse, now!" Mr. Bergin ordered.

If it would have helped, I would have walked on water to get at the sumbitches that shot Bobby Don. I loaded another round and fired. *"Aquí tienen, hijos de su chingada madre. ¡Pinches cabrones!"*

"Back to the helm, Bean," Jim told me. "You don't need to see this."

Clear of danger, Mr. Bergin returned to the pilothouse to continue the rendezvous with the destroyer in our area. Middleton climbed out of the guntub, walked on top of the cabin, and made his way to the fantail.

"I think Boats is dead, Gunner."

"It don't look good for him," he told me, his face flushed.

I climbed to the top of the pilothouse and sat up against the guntub.

On the fantail, Gunner grew irate. He blamed Mr. Bergin for Bobby Don's death. But Boats had carried out the orders of the mission. His duty was to advise our OIC, Mr. Bergin. Carver had informed him not about a man on the sand dune but rather about a bunker. Gunner didn't know that.

Nonetheless, in his fit of rage, he screamed harsh accusations. Jim heard Gunner and knew he meant Mr. Bergin. He reached up and held Middleton back.

"It's over, Gunner. It wasn't Mr. Bergin's fault. We got hit from three positions. No one else got hit, so it was a lucky shot. Any one of us could have been plugged, just like Bean. He almost got hit. The damn round tore through the bottom frames of the front windshield, shattering the glass, and the fuckin' slug dropped right by the compass. It was headed straight for Bean."

Jim's words calmed Gunner down. He went back and sat on the mortar box, staring at the Co Lay Corral.

The action left me numb. Aside from a heavy heart, I had no feeling. I sat staring straight out toward the horizon. I didn't want to look back toward the fantail. I felt lost. My eyes caught sight of a destroyer as it approached us from off our port bow. Mr. Bergin knew I was on top of the pilothouse.

"Bean, get down and prepare the bow mooring line," he said in a somber voice.

We approached the deck-gray vessel from its starboard quarter. Insensible, I didn't take note of the ship number. Mr. Bergin set the throttles to neutral a safe distance from the ship, giving him time to head to the steering station on the fantail.

Coming alongside the ship, I flung our mooring line up to a sailor standing near a ladder leading up to the fantail deck. Our deckhand on the stern quarter likewise tossed his line up to an awaiting sailor. A Jacob's ladder was already in place over the side of the destroyer. A senior corpsman and medic came down quickly. The ship's executive officer (XO) also came aboard.

Middleton and our deckhand helped lower the Stokes stretcher to our deck, moving it closer to the medical team. The wire lift basket offered the wounded comfort and a sense of security while they were being transported.

The starboard rails on the destroyer was overloaded with crewmen, cameras in hand. Seeing the picture takers above on the ship, Schneider hollered, "Respect our fallen crewman, you bastards."

Middleton reacted next. "I'm gonna shoot the next asshole that takes a picture."

"I'll shoot the next sailor who dishonors my dying LPO. Put those damn cameras away," Mr. Bergin told the picture takers.

The XO understood and cleared the deck.

I couldn't make myself go near Boats. I feared losing control of my emotions. I stayed in the cabin, observing what I could from inside the rear hatch, a parched mouth and a knot in my throat, making it difficult to swallow.

The medical team checked Boats for a pulse and placed a large white square gauze pad on the exit wound in the back of his head, which immediately turned to crimson. They placed a smaller one over his right eye, then bandaged his head. Jim and Mr. Bergin helped the ship's medical team lift Carver and eased him into the Stokes litter. The medics secured our mortally wounded crewmate with two straps.

Seeing his body being carried, arms dangling in the air, took me beyond the edge of restraint. My heart could take no more; I burst into tears. My nemesis, my mentor, my brother was dying. I had to do something to help him. There was only one thing I knew that could make him feel better: a hot cup of coffee. He loved his coffee. Delirious, I grabbed his disgusting crusty mug and the shiny chrome electric percolator and stepped out onto the fantail and approached the stretcher.

"Here, let me give him some coffee. I know he'll get better. I know he will." Tears streamed down my cheeks as I sobbed uncontrollably.

Middleton reached from behind and pulled me away. I began screaming in denial and anger. I slipped and realized I was stepping on the blood-stained deck. It angered me even more. With all the force I could muster, I flung the coffee pot, slamming it against the starboard side cabin engine vent. Gunner tried to comfort me, but I didn't want to be consoled. It was Boats who needed attention, not me.

The four men lifted the wire basket, carried it over to the port side, and raised it above their heads where sailors aboard the ship reached down and grabbed the stretcher.

Responding to my urgent flash traffic Dust Off[2] request was Major Patrick Henry Brady, second-in-command of the 54th Medical Detachment (Helicopter Ambulance) in Chu Lai. He hovered his helicopter astern of the destroyer, waiting for the helicopter detail on the ship's fantail to signal they were ready. For his heroic action the following month, Major Brady would later be awarded the Medal of Honor.

Transfer made, we brought in the mooring lines, pushed away from the destroyer, and set course for Chu Lai. Our fantail was strewn with spent .50 caliber machine gun brass casings, along with Bobby Don Carver's blood. Schneider's and Mr. Bergin's uniforms were soaked scarlet.

Climbing the cabin ladder on the starboard side, I heard Mr. Bergin's voice. Grabbing Middleton's arm, he said, "I'm sorry about what happened, Gunner." The crew went about their business in silence after that. He gave no orders. We proceeded to Chu Lai.

Less than fifteen minutes after we left the destroyer, I heard the *whup, whup, whup* of the Dust Off chopper approaching from astern. It sped over us, flying low and tilting its blades right and left, as if Boats was bidding us farewell. They were on their way to the Second Surgical Hospital at Chu Lai.

From my sitting position above the pilothouse I heard the radio come alive through the guntub. "Same Drink Delta November, this is Dust Off 5 5. Over."

"Copy, five-five," Mr. Bergin replied.

"Roger. Adrenaline brought pulse back but didn't last. Regret we've lost him. Over."

"Roger. Out," Mr. Bergin said softly.

Our somber return to base continued. I wanted to remain separated from the rest of the crew and not speak to anyone, but Mr. Bergin asked Jim to take the wheel and he joined me atop the pilothouse. He sat to my right on a lower section of the pilothouse roof.

"How are you doing, Bean?" Mr. Bergin asked.

I lowered my head between my knees and didn't answer. He continued to talk; I only heard a muffled voice. I felt uncomfortable having to listen. I didn't want to be reminded about what had just occurred. His persistence in getting me to talk stirred my festering emotional pot once again.

I finally broke.

"Why not me? Why not me?" I screamed over and over, rocking back and forth.

Mr. Bergin was no longer talking. I turned to him and was shocked by what I saw. He sat staring out at the horizon, eyes tearing up and white spittle oozing out from the corner of his mouth. Perhaps my plea was something he also felt. I knew that as an OIC, the responsibility for the boat and crew rested squarely on his shoulders. Easy for guilt to set in under the tragic circumstances.

He tapped my knee several times and returned to the pilothouse. In time, we turned west at Rosemary Point and eased our way to the pier. A large crowd of fellow Swifties, officers and enlisted, were there to receive us. Lieutenant Pope and his crew came aboard and offered their condolences. They were wide-eyed, knowing it could have been any of them, having been patrolling the same area the day before. Mr. Pope's crew and others on hand said they'd take care of the cleanup. Each of us stepped off the 79 Boat and headed in different directions.

Our division commander, Lieutenant Wentworth, went to Graves Registration, located south of the Second Surgical Hospital, to identify Carver's remains, in advance of our arrival.

I took a long aimless walk, following the dusty red clay road. Later that night, I drank excessively. I don't recall hitting the sack. The liquor served as anesthesia. It helped me avoid total recall and forced me into a deep sleep.

That same evening, Mr. Pope accompanied Mr. Bergin to Graves Registration. Bobby Don's remains had to be personally identified. It was a task no boat officer wanted to endure. Mr. Pope remembers well that our skipper was distraught and depressed. Mr. Bergin expressed his sense of responsibility for the decisions that led to the tragic outcome.

Lieutenant Pope stood by Mr. Bergin, hand on his shoulder, as Graves personnel exposed Boats' remains with utmost respect and dignity. Identification complete, they both headed back to their officers' quarters, in silence. In time, Mr. Bergin shared with fellow OICs the events and aftermath of the incident to educate and caution them for similar circumstances. It was a tough learning experience for Lieutenant Pope.

On Friday, a fellow Swiftie asked, "Are you okay now, Bean?"

"Still can't get it together," I replied.

"No, I mean from last night?"

"Last night? What are you talking about, man?"

"I was on mid-watch on the pier. I found you sitting on the 79 Boat mortar ready box in your skivvies, staring at the bay."

"Oh, that," I recalled. "Just a nightmare. It'll get better, I hope." I was embarrassed to share the trauma of feeling Carver's cold, dead body on top of me as I lay in my bunk the night before.

"Well, hang tough, amigo. I'm here if you want to talk."

"Thanks, dude."

On Saturday, a memorial service was held at the Chapel by the Sea, next to the officers' quarters. The in-port Swift Boat community attended as well as many Navy base personnel who knew Carver. Porky made it back from the Philippines in time for the service. Mr. Bergin, Jim, Gunner, Porky, and I sat together near the front. A commemorative program was handed out for BM1 Bobby Don Carver, USN, 1935–1967.

An organ prelude was followed by the hymn "Abide with Me." One of our Swifties gave the Old Testament reading. After the chaplain's testimonial, a boat officer presented the New Testament reading. The chaplain then shared memorial prayers. The organ player led us into the Navy hymn, "Eternal Father." The chaplain concluded his part of the service with the blessing.

The chaplain invited us to spend a moment in silent prayer for the repose of Carver's soul. We bowed our heads in prayer and remembrance. Warm tears trickled down my cheeks.

I reflected on how he had been a pain in the ass to me, ticking me off from the time we first met in Coronado when he slapped the "Bean" moniker on me. I recalled how he kept harassing me, wanting me to be his "sea chicken," or when he tried to kick me over the side by telling me to lean over from the starboard pilothouse door to check for the boat's fenders. I also remembered how much I hated him for sending me down into the lazarette to clean the bilges, and how he taught me to do fancy rope work on the support column in the cabin. He was responsible for my growing up some and drying the moisture from behind my ears. I would forever miss him.

Taps followed, ending the service.

The temperature was in the high 50s in Richmond, California, when a military team approached the front door of 224 Collins Street. They delivered an unexpected Western Union telegram to Betty Ellen Carver, Boats' wife, now widow. The sender was the Chief of Naval Operations.

BM2 Bobby Don "Boats" Carver holding AK-56 rifle at the awards ceremony, Da Nang, Republic of Vietnam, 19 July 1967. (Photo credit: Ronald M. Rinehart)

I DEEPLY REGRET TO CONFIRM ON BEHALF OF THE UNITED STATES NAVY THAT YOUR HUSBAND, BM1 BOBBY DON CARVER, USN WAS KILLED IN ACTION ON 6 DECEMBER 1967 AT QUANG NGAI PROVINCE, SOUTH VIETNAM. THIS OCCURRED WHILE

ON COMBAT PATROL ON PCF 79. THE BOAT YOUR HUSBAND WAS ATTACHED TO WAS AMBUSHED BY AUTOMATIC WEAPONS FIRE.

YOUR HUSBAND DIED WHILE SERVING HIS COUNTRY. I EXTEND TO YOU MY SYMPATHY IN YOUR GREAT LOSS. A LETTER FROM HIS COMMANDING OFFICER SETTING FORTH THE CIRCUMSTANCES OF DEATH WILL FOLLOW. I WISH TO ASSURE YOU OF EVERY POSSIBLE ASSISTANCE.

The telegram went on to provide Mrs. Carver with additional burial related details.[3]

A similar telegram was delivered to Bobby Don Carver Jr. in care of his mother, Gladys Lee Carver, of Simpson, Louisiana. Boats' eldest son was thirteen years old when his father died. Upon receiving the news, the family gathered at the home of Robert Clarence and Maudie Leona Bennett Carver, Boats' parents. His two sisters, Patty Rae and Virginia, were there to console their parents as well.

Mr. Bergin had Porky go through Boats' belongings, directing him to avoid including anything racy or questionable. Mr. Bergin wrote a personal letter to Boats' widow. He never expected this outcome, the same way a parent never anticipates having to bury their child. It was not only difficult to find the words, but painful.

Dear Mrs. Carver,

I know that this letter will find you in the deepest grief. I and the rest of the crew cannot believe our loss. Everyone in Coastal Division Twelve and indeed all the Swift Boats in Vietnam have been affected by this tragedy of war.

What I have to say is not meant to be in consolation for Boats' life, it is only to tell you the circumstances of his death.

He was, in addition to being my second in command, also the gunner on the aftermount. PCF-79 was ambushed by three automatic weapon positions near the hamlet My Lai. Boats' suppressing fire kept two of these positions from firing after their initial burst. If he had sought cover, most probably the whole crew and boat would have been lost. I was at Boats' side when he was hit; he died immediately and suffered no pain.

Mrs. Carver, there is something else that I feel you should know. I don't know if Boats ever told you about stopping a North Vietnamese trawler. His action accounted for 3,600 automatic weapons and tons of mines and explosives from reaching the Viet Cong. I realize that these were only weapons, but how many other Americans would have died if they had reached their destination? Premier Ky presented Boats with the Cross of Gallantry for his action.

Medals are only a small tangible token of a government's appreciation. But our thanks and thoughts are the greater tokens, and they will remain with us always.

PCF-79 will fly her flag at half-mast as long as I command her and all of us will grieve the loss of your husband.

Enclosed with this letter are Boats' more personal effects.

If there are any difficulties or arrangements that I may help with, please write.

My deepest condolences,

Ed Bergin, LT (JG) USN

The box containing our lead petty officer's personal belongings was shipped to the states. Mr. Bergin's letter was placed inside.[4]

On December 13, Lieutenant Ian M. Bailey, Commander Coastal Division Twelve, wrote a letter to Betty Ellen Carver, advising her of her husband's death and commenting on Boats' dedication to service. In part it read:

As a member of the crew, Don was serving in the capacity of lead petty officer of PCF-79 and second in command. He never faltered in the performance of his duties. His experience and leadership were instrumental in guiding less experienced men under his charge. The men of Coastal Division TWELVE are proud of Don's outstanding performances of duty and his high degree of professionalism in maintaining the highest level of naval tradition.[5]

• • •

The Navy offered Mrs. Carver the option to have her husband's remains transported with an escort to any place she designated and at no expense. She chose to have his remains taken back to his hometown in Louisiana. The government also offered financial assistance toward funeral and interment expenses.

Bobby Don's remains took eight days to reach Leesville, Louisiana. It was decided not to have him buried in a national cemetery. Hixson Funeral Home handled the arrangements. A vigil was held at his parents' home. Reverend A. D. Kirby ministered the 10 a.m. burial service that took place at Welcome Cemetery, Simpson, Louisiana, on December 18, twelve days after his death.

BM1 Bobby Don Carver military grave marker at Welcome Cemetery, Simpson, Louisiana. (Photo credit: Raúl Herrera)

Fair winds and following seas

Boats Carver

HE DIED SERVING HIS COUNTRY IN VIETNAM

WE REMEMBER

CHAPTER 21

ALL ASHORE

Though day after Carver's memorial service, I penned a short letter to my father. It began with, "I'm doing okay, thanks to God." I let him know how much fun I was having making copies of taped music, bragging about the fourteen reels I had already recorded. I told him how excited I was about buying a stereo on my return home. I asked Dad to tell the relatives hello for me. I ended with, "Until my next letter, do take care and may God bless. Your #1 Son, Roy."

The letter mentioned absolutely nothing about Carver's death, how close I came to being killed four days earlier, or the fear I had in going out on the next patrol. I couldn't bear telling them the truth and bringing them anguish. As it was, I learned from Martha, my oldest sister, that my parents wanted nothing to do with any festivities while I was in Vietnam. They wanted the family to hold off on any celebrations until my return. If invited to a party, they wouldn't attend.

The remaining days of December brought a sparkle of joy. José Cueva, my best friend at Holy Cross, sent a tabletop-size aluminum Christmas tree. I paid no nevermind to the personal warning note José pinned to a branch on the tree — "DON'T hang lights on the tree!" Now, what's a Christmas tree without lights, right? Gunner and I strung lights on the tree anyway.

Several days later after a patrol, I found another box waiting on my bunk, this one square but large. It was from Mom. I ripped it open immediately. Inside were six shoebox-size packages, each wrapped in cheerful Christmas paper. She had sent the entire crew a gift. My bright smile slipped away when I saw Carver's tag on one present. The boxes added that special touch to our glimmering tree, a bittersweet sight.

On Christmas, I gave each of our crew their gifts. The boxes contained note pads, envelopes, pens, caramel candies, sweat socks, and a can of Planters cashews. Inside Cueva's gift box was a bright red sweatshirt with the logo of the San Antonio semi-pro football team, the Toros. I put it on, took a picture, then stowed it in a safe place. Wearing it out on patrol would only serve to tease Charlie, like Manolete waving his *muleta* at a menacing bull.

Carver's box remained under the tree until the end of the year.

Lady Luck was in our favor toward the end of the month. We were off patrol when the Bob Hope Christmas show came to Chu Lai. I thumbed a ride south to the Americal Division 5,000-seat amphitheater the Seabees built adjacent to the Second Surgical Hospital.[1]

It was a great show. Les Brown's Band of Renown accompanied stars like Elaine Dunn, Barbara McNair, Earl Wilson, Phil Crosby, and Peruvian model Madeline Hartog, Miss World 1967. But it was bombshell Raquel Welch who stole the hearts of all the troops that day.

I learned, days later, that at the Saigon show, General Westmoreland introduced Vice-President Nguyễn Cao Kỳ. In somber tone Kỳ addressed the soldiers present: "I would like to take this opportunity to express to all my fellow fighters, on behalf of my people of my country, our gratitude. We know how big your sacrifice. We know how big your dedication. I am sure the generation of Vietnamese today, and those to come, will remember you. Merry Christmas and Happy New Year to all of you."

"It's official, Bean," Gunner announced. "We're SHORT, one hundred days and a wake-up, man. Then we'll be on our way home."

"No shit, Bob?"

"Yup. Here's your Short Timer's chart."

It was Friday, December 29. Fourteen weeks later, we'd be going to sleep in the air-conditioned APL at Da Nang and wake up the next morning to board a freedom bird back to The World, the Land of the Big PX, the United States of America. SanAnto. I was ready.

There were numerous variations of these countdown calendars available, all unofficial and sexually explicit, of course. Those with artistic talent drew pencil sketches of naked girls in various titillating positions, their bodies marked in paint-by-number style. They were also called FIGMO charts. Fuck It. Got My Orders. One picture had the Good Witch of the States bending over the prone naked body of an anxious sailor, her magic wand about to touch the tip of his attentive member, where the number one was located.

My FIGMO Girl sat on the floor. The profile view showed her resting her butt on the back of her bent legs, arms stretched behind her, making her full bosom rise. Her right hand contained the number one hundred, the ONE occupied the tip of her perky breast. I grabbed a pencil and shaded the first block.

One Hundred Days and a Wake-Up.

Swift Boat Crew 74-A was split up at the start of January. Mr. Bergin's scheduled separation from the Navy was set for February. He began training new OICs and their crews. Gunner and I stayed with the 79 Boat, while Porky was transferred to Lieutenant Junior Grade John E. English's crew on PCF-20.

The 79 Boat had a new crew. Lieutenant Junior Grade Walter Doblecki became the OIC. The LPO responsibility fell on BM2 Elvin Hurley. As our lead petty officer, he made certain the boat was always ready for patrol. The engines were in the able hands of a second-class engineman, Robert Guptill. My duties as radio / radarman were turned over to Daniel Overcast, a second-class radarman. I became the boat's deckhand, and Middleton maintained his position as gunner.

Although we missed our old crew, we got along well with our new shipmates. When we happened to get the Same Drink Delta November patrol off Mui Batangan, I made certain everyone knew the Co Lay Corral was not an ideal area to cruise at minimum speed. With four months left on my tour, I didn't want my luck tested by going anywhere near the Mỹ Lai shoreline. Patrolling on the 79 Boat felt awkward. Being anywhere near the fantail always reminded me of that tragic day when Carver was killed. I hardly slept on those patrols, for the ugly memories kept repeating in my mind.

I penned a letter to Gloria, letting her know I'd be leaving Vietnam on April 7. Our mini tape-recorded voice messages were filled with physical want and expectations. I asked if she had leave available on the books so we could meet in San Antonio upon my arrival.

In a follow-up letter, she told me she'd be able to meet me in San Antonio in April. I daydreamed of what my homecoming would be like. I shaded more days off my FIGMO chart.

One chilly morning, a couple of days after the Tet Offensive, word spread through the barracks that two Swifts were stationary at the channel entrance by Rosemary Point. Gunner and I went out to see what the commotion was about.

Standing on top of the bunker inside the barbed-wire perimeter along the rocky channel shoreline, I saw someone wearing dark brown corduroy cutoffs doing calisthenics, mostly jumping jacks, on the boat's fantail. It was an officer. With a life jacket on, he jumped into the water off the ammo box. The boat throttled forward, slowly leaving the swimmer behind.

The Swift's bow rose as the engines pushed the boat forward. Behind, the swimmer came up on skis. The PCF sped toward the hard-left turn and headed in the direction of the deep-water pier. Halfway there, the Swift came to all engines stop, causing the skier to sink into the bay. The crew pulled in the line, then helped the officer climb aboard the craft. By that time, Bob and I were on the Swift pier along with a handful of curious onlookers. To our surprise, the skier turned out to be none other than Lord Mort, Mr. Bergin. He decided to come in off his last patrol in style.

Days later, we were on the Same Drink Charlie patrol and were requested to proceed south to Rosemary Point. We were called in to daisy-chain our old skipper north toward Da Nang. Mr. Bergin was heading home. On our way south for the rendezvous, I went down to the bunks in the bow, beneath the pilothouse. I stayed there until after he transferred onto the PCF out of Da Nang.

I don't know what drove me to do that. Could have been resentment for being left behind, not wanting to face a sad farewell, simple indifference, or belief it was a cop-out on his part. Bottom line, I didn't want to say goodbye. At the end of the month, Mr. Bergin mustered out of the Navy in Newport, Rhode Island.

In early February 1968, I received a surprise reply letter from Mr. Irv Weinman, Director of Public Relations for Hemisfair 1968 in San Antonio. I had written to them weeks earlier after receiving paper clippings telling the story of how the city church bells rang and fire station sirens sounded all over town the moment the top-house of the Tower of the Americas reached its final resting place. Its roof-top elevation was 622 feet above ground. For taking such an interest from far way in Vietnam, my family was given reservations to the tower restaurant on my return from the war.

Our patrols continued. Each day I filled in another space in my Short Timer's chart. On Saturday, February 17, I shaded the number 50, located on FIGMO

Girl's left forearm. I wanted time left in-country to move faster. On the other hand, what I'd read in the *Pacific Stars and Stripes* didn't paint a pretty picture. Turmoil was the word of the day, every day, in the States. The Vietnam War led the controversy.

I passed the E-4 draftsman exam for the second time and was waiting to be moved up a grade to third-class draftsman; however, my score wasn't high enough and I remained an E-3 Draftsman Striker. Still a pollywog sailor. I should have taken Mr. Bergin's field promotion offer of Third Class Radioman.

My frustration didn't last long. FIGMO became a reality. I Got My Orders! I was headed to the Naval Submarine Base in Groton, Connecticut, after my one-month leave was over. It turned out just like Gunner predicted.

Forty days and a wake-up.

Intending to save face after the failed plan to bring South Vietnam and its allied forces to its knees during the Tet Offensive, North Vietnam made one last daring attempt to smuggle arms and supplies to its demoralized forces. Market Time aerial surveillance aircraft detected four suspicious steel-hulled trawlers near the coastline on February 28 and 29. Two trawlers were observed in II Corps, one in I Corps, and the fourth in III Corps.

An Xuyen Province Trawler

On February 28, at 1830 hours, a two-day surveillance of a suspect trawler began, approximately 150 miles east-southeast of Vũng Tàu. Swift Boat Coastal Division 11, An Thới, patrolled those waters along the coast. The vessel, with bow plates of 498, was on a southeasterly heading. The next day at 2100 hours, the ship turned course to 310 degrees, heading toward shore, at which time the USCG *Winona* (WHEC-65) commenced covert surveillance. The enemy ship crossed the twelve-mile contiguous zone at 0120 hours on March 1.

Four Swift Boat crews were on the *Winona*, operating off PCF-72 and PCF-92. OICs Lieutenant Junior Grade Dale Barnes and Lieutenant Junior Grade Ron Schookner and their respective crews were on patrol at their designated stations off the Cà Mau Peninsula. Lieutenant Junior Grade Bob Finley and Lieutenant Junior Grade Bernard Wolff, with their crews, were aboard the *Winona*. On orders from the Coast Guard skipper, the Swift Boat officers were directed to remain in the wardroom, crews in their quarters.

After the trawler ignored challenges, the *Winona* first opened with .50 caliber machine guns, followed by steady fire from its 5"/38 gun. The trawler responded with accurate aim from their 12.7mm machine gun mounted on its foc'sle. Lieutenant Wolff paced the wardroom. He heard the starboard .50 caliber machine fire go silent after numerous hammering of enemy rounds hitting the exterior bulkhead, sending the gunner below deck for cover and leaving the weapon unmanned.

The crew handling the 81 mm mortar and illumination rounds lost the fuse wrench over the side. Without illumination rounds, the fire control officer, having no visual on the trawler, suspended suppressive fire. Lieutenant Fineley's gunner, GMG3 William C. Lockerman, suspected the *Winona*'s .50 caliber machine gun went silent due to the possibility that the gunner was wounded. He went topside and saw only an unmanned weapon.

He immediately lock-n-loaded the weapon and began hosing the trawler's 12.7mm gun with unrelenting suppressive fire. This gave the fire control officer a target, and once again the *Winona*'s 5"/38 gun came alive. One round found its mark, resulting in a large explosive fireball. The trawler sank in open water, seven miles from shore and approximately forty-three-miles northeast of the tip of the Cà Mau Peninsula.[2]

Khánh Hòa Province Trawler

Ninety-one miles east-northeast of Nha Trang, in the Cos Div 14, Cam Ranh Bay, patrol sector, an aerial surveillance aircraft spotted a steel-hulled vessel at 1714 hours on February 29. The suspicious contact was kept under surveillance by aircraft as well as Coast Guard and Vietnamese Market Time units as it kept a southerly course. Twenty-eight miles northeast of Nha Trang the ship turned toward shore and made a run for the beach.

The seaborne units took the enemy trawler under fire at 0200 hours on March 1. An AC-47 gunship joined in the attack. When the steel-hull beached eleven miles up the coast from Nha Trang, in the Hòn Hèo Secret Zone, South Vietnamese Fleet Command ships PCE-12 and PGM-617 took the beach area under attack, preventing the vessel from being off-loaded. At 0230 hours, a 2,000-foot fireball lit the sky. The trawler's holds contained 745 82 mm mortars, eighty-one cases of RPG-2 ammo, twenty cases of C-4 plastique, and mass amounts of small arms rifles and ammo. Salvage operations took twelve days.[3]

Bình Định Province Trawler

Two hours before midnight on February 29, Market Time surveillance aircraft radar picked up another suspicious contact 120 miles northeast of Qui Nhơn in II Corps. It inched its way closer to the beach during the next several hours. Its destination appeared to be the Lò Diên beach area, forty-two miles north of the Cos Div 15 Swift Boat base.

Fifteen minutes past midnight on March 1, while being shadowed by Navy and Coast Guard vessels, the trawler made an abrupt change in course thirty miles from shore. It was headed back out to sea. Per orders from CTF-115, aerial and blue-water ships continued clandestine observation of the vessel until it neared the mainland of Communist China.[4]

Quảng Ngãi Province Trawler

VP-1 Market Time aircraft were kept busy at the end of the month. In mid-afternoon on February 29, the last of four suspected North Vietnamese trawlers was detected 103 miles east of Mui Batangan. An aerial patrol unit found the suspicious radar contact on a due west heading, immediately raising the red alert flag at the I Corps Coastal Surveillance Center in Da Nang.

Lieutenant Bruce Wentworth, OIC of the Chu Lai Coastal Division 12 Detachment, sent the in-port crews of PCF-18 and PCF-20 to the area at best speed. Skippering the two PCFs were Lieutenant Junior Grade James McConnell and Lieutenant Junior Grade John English, respectively. Early speculation pointed to the trawler giving the Sông Sa Kỳ river mouth a second try, the same destination the July 15 trawler (Skunk Alpha) had the previous year.

All during the day, Market Time units, including the USCGC *Androscoggin* (WHEC-68), USCGC *Point Welcome* (WPB 82329), and USCGC *Point Grey* (WPB 82324) received position reports on the suspected infiltrator. Lieutenant Wentworth established communications with the Americal Division Tactical Operations Center (TOC). He advised them on the potential of two trawlers attempting landfall in the southern I Corps area with a tentative ETA of 2300 hours.

On orders from Da Nang, Lieutenant Wentworth requested TOC have two gunships and two flare ships placed on standby alert. By 1950 hours the III Marine Amphibious Force became involved. Major Finn placed the 198th and 11th Brigade, G3 and G2 artillery on standby. He also assigned identification numbers to each of the two trawlers, 29F1 for the southernmost trawler and 29F2 for the Batangan contact.

At 2207 hours, Lieutenant Wentworth provided an update to TOC. He advised them that only one trawler was expected to attempt landfall in southern I Corps and in the Batangan area. Two trawlers were being tracked in II Corps.

The G3 artillery position alerted the 11th Brigade to prepare a ground reaction force of one company for possible use if the trawler landed at the Batangan Peninsula. The 11th contacted TOC that B-4-3 at Landing Zone Uptight was best suited for troop insertion. The 101st Airborne Division helicopters would be used for the deployment.

A half hour before midnight, the trawler was located at fourteen degrees 56' north, 109 degrees 27' east, heading 235 degrees at ten knots. An hour later, the enemy vessel's course projected a landfall two to three miles north of Đức Phổ. Lieutenant Wentworth still considered Mui Batangan a high possibility. Major MacKnight, 11th Brigade, alerted gunships and a flare ship.

Minutes past midnight, March 1, 1968, the Coastal Surveillance Center in Da Nang reported that Mỹ Lai combat chart coordinates BS 820 465 was the probable location where the trawler would beach. At 0114 hours, the vessel lost its suspicious contact status when it crossed the twelve-mile territorial limits of the Republic of Vietnam, twenty-two miles southeast of Mui Batangan.

Similar to the Skunk Alpha incident, five US seaborne assets sat in wait. After the trawler refused to respond to its challenges, the *Androscoggin* fired 5"/38 warning shots ahead of the ship. No immediate reaction occurred. At the same time, the 101st Airborne Division scrambled two gunships, directing them to join the flare ship already on their way south.

Three miles from shore, Seaman Terry Vander Molen took aim and fired illumination rounds over the target vessel from his 81 mm mortar station on the fantail of PCF-18. It provided a visual for all units to open fire on the evading trawler, which engaged in a counterattack. Aboard PCF-20, EN1 Ronald Rinehart on the aft .50 caliber machine gun and Seaman Michael Basham on the twin .50s unloaded direct fire at the trawler as the flare ship above dropped illumination rounds exposing the enemy ship. Gary Hartman, the boat's radarman, observed a hail of incoming enemy tracer rounds off their port side, as an unending flow of burning hot .50 caliber brass casings rained down into the pilothouse.

Seaborne units reported, at 0133 hours, the trawler was either burning or laying a smoke screen. Eight minutes later, the flare ship pilot advised the on-scene commander that he was running low on starburst shells and had called for another unit to assist. The two attack helicopters hovering nearby were ordered to take the trawler under fire. Fifteen minutes before two in the morning, they reported receiving fire from the trawler.

The steel-hulled infiltrator beached twenty-five-miles south of the Batangan Peninsula at 0214 hours. Six minutes later the crew onboard the trawler attempted to detonate its self-destruct charges with limited success. However, at 0235 hours, the North Vietnamese crew succeeded in blowing themselves up along with all the ship's cargo. The debris stretched out the length of five and a half football fields.

The mangled remains of the enemy infiltrator were reported to be at grid coordinates BS 882 346 and fifty feet offshore. No crewmen were seen abandoning the vessel prior to the explosion.

EN1 Ronald "Porky" Rinehart, our engineman on the 79 Boat, had been sent to PCF-20. Porky duplicated Carver's action on the night of the Skunk Alpha trawler capture by firing an 81 mm mortar round into the trawler's pilothouse before it beached. Chu Lai Swifties knighted him "Two-Trawler Porky" after this incident.

The four infiltrators thwarted on March 1, 1968, brought the total number of such incidents since February 1965 to thirteen. No confirmed reports of successful trawler infiltrations were ever reported. It sent a loud message to North Vietnam.

The picket line of defense created by diligent units of Operation Market Time remained impenetrable.[5]

Thirty-seven days and a wake-up. I shaded the number on FIGMO Girl's left calf. On Friday, March 8, I packed my footlocker for shipping back to San Antonio. If only I could put myself in that trunk and surprise my folks when it was delivered onto their gray wood porch back home. I was like a second-string quarterback on the verge of being tapped by the coach to be put in the final game. *Now, coach? Now, coach?*

A block above FIGMO Girl's right knee marked the spot for twenty-one days and a wake-up. Seven patrols to go and its A, B—C'ya, **Mike Foxtrots!**

I'd been checking the flight manifest posted in our lounge every day, hoping to see my name up there. Once the last week in March began, my restlessness made me check the board twice a day. On Tuesday of that week, I couldn't wait to come in off patrol, finish my boat cleanup duties, and *di di mau* it up to the barracks at best speed.

I stopped by the cubicle, tossed my ditty bag on my bunk, and went up to the lounge. There it was.

DMSN Raúl Herrera; Departure Date 7 April; Time 1000 hours; Da Nang.

I checked the list and saw Gunner's and Porky's names as well. Happier than a kid on Christmas morning, I sped downstairs with the news. Gunner went up to check for himself.

Hot diggity, it was confirmed. I was heading home! Eleven days and a wake-up. I happily shaded a spot on FIGMO Girl's left ribcage. Three more patrols.

My mind was preoccupied with going-home thoughts. Although ecstatic about my departure from Vietnam, wanting to get the last patrol and the possibility of danger behind me, I felt like I was on third base and heading for home plate in slow motion. Then the last patrol day arrived, Sunday, March 31, 1968. I wondered how many more memorable March 31 days lay ahead in my future. For now, this one was the best.

During the 0200 to 0600 hours watch, I sat in the guntub, rocking and rolling to the sea's motion as the boat plowed ahead at minimum speed. The stars were brilliant in the cloudless ebony sky above. In my solitude, I thanked God for having allowed me not to suffer any physical battle injuries. The Purple Heart was a medal I prayed never to receive.

Twilight began with a soft blue hue and grew first from a blush of vermilion into the sun's fiery orange smile. Clouds beyond the eastern horizon touched the light, filling the sky with scattered scarlet rays. It was the most beautiful sunrise I'd seen in the past twelve months. Or was it that I had paid it no nevermind all this time? God was smiling on me, and it felt grand.

After Gunner and I completed our post-patrol cleanup duties, we bid farewell to Mr. Doblecki and the crew.

"Our work here is done, Gunner," I told him as we climbed over PCF-79's rear stanchion for the last time, a bittersweet moment. I wondered if she would take new crews into harm's way and what the outcome might be.

I wished her the best.

On Saturday morning, April 6, the remaining three Swift Boat sailors of Crew 74-A—me, Gunner, and Porky—were set to hitch a ride by truck to the airfield south of our Navy base. Joining us was our sister PCF training group, Crew 73-A. We were all dressed in clean dungaree bell-bottoms, pressed chambray shirts, shined boondockers, and the iconic white "Cracker Jack" cover, or as often called, the Dixie Cup.

I shaded the last block on my Short Timer's calendar. The number 1 was located at the tip of FIGMO Girl's perky tit. No more days remained . . . just a wake-up that would take place in Da Nang.

"I'm heading home, fuckers," I shouted, stuffing the chart in the manila envelope along with my DD 214 and orders.

Goodbye, Chu Lai. Farewell, Vietnam.

It was Wake-Up Day, Sunday, April 7, 1968. We arrived at the air base an hour before our scheduled departure at 1000 hours. At the check-in center, a handful of clerks took our belongings, while airline employees reviewed our flight documents. The next time I'd have a seabag over my shoulder would be in California, United States of America. It all felt like a dream, a good dream, and I was living it. Gunner spotted Porky and waved him to us.

"Hey, Porky. Seen Hogjaws?"

"Nah, Bean. Schneider's gone," he said in a somber tone.

"Killed?" Gunner asked.

"Nah, he took a .30 caliber round in his hip up in Huế last month. Last I heard, Dust Off choppered him to the hospital ship *Sanctuary*."

It was hard to believe I was aboard a Continental Airlines 707, the Proud Bird with the Golden Tail. I joined the more than 200 happy travelers. No more hurry up and wait. The cabin was rumbling with chatter, laughter, and cheers. Gunner and I got adjacent seats because we checked in together. Luck was with me as I snagged a window seat toward the back of the plane.

"On our way home, Gunner."

"Fn'A, Bean! Don't get any better 'n-dis."

The noise level diminished as the plane approached its final turn. As at the beginning of Mass, the cabin grew silent. Around me, men stared out windows. Some just sat there, eyes closed, presumably in deep thought.

As I looked out my window, recollections of the past twelve months crawled through my head: the dreadful fear on my first Swift Boat patrol; Norma's Dear Raúl letter; being sent to Chu Lai, leaving behind air-conditioned APL accommodations in Da Nang; the pucker factor as we prepared to engage a North Vietnamese resupply trawler; being decorated by Premier Nguyễn Cao Kỳ and Chief of State Nguyễn Văn Thiệu; and the trauma of witnessing the death of Bobby Don Carver during a firefight along the Mỹ Lai shoreline.

The four engines revved to a high pitch. The pilot released the brakes, and the thrust pushed me back. Da Nang air base sped by. The plane's nose wheels lifted off the ground. Seconds later we were airborne in a steep climb, leaving behind the end of the runway. A thunderous cheer erupted in the cabin. Dollar to a doughnut, there wasn't a handful of dry eyes on board. I squeezed droplets from mine, then wiped them with my fingers.

Going home. . . . Going home, minus one.

After a grueling flight, we landed at Norton AFB in Bakersfield, California. Vietnam was now well beyond the western horizon and that was fine by me.

"We're back in the land of the Big PX, Gunner."

"It's about time," he grumbled.

"I hope I can get change somewhere inside. Got to make a call to my cousin."

"You've got a while yet before we're let loose, Bean. There's still customs we gotta go through."

"It's a good thing I gave the Chicom stick grenade to that Chicano weather probe-plane crewman. He's going to ship it home for me," I told Gunner.

"Bean, you're easy, man. You'll never see that trawler trophy again. Anyway, I heard customs is a scam. They'll pass us through a room and tell us they will step out for several minutes, giving us time to empty out any contraband or suffer legal action."

"Anyone been caught?" I asked.

"A scam, Bean. A scam. They check only the first two layers of your seabag, then push you out. The assholes divvy up the booty, then sell them off base. At least that's the scuttlebutt I've heard."

We made it off the plane to awaiting buses, real buses. After retrieving our seabags, Gunner and I followed directional arrows to the checkout station. I was surprised to find no evidence of a shakedown room. Instead, our orders were stamped, and we were released. Just like that, with a monotone, "You're free to go." We were back home!

We reached the base gate expecting to fight off hippie protestors. We were ready for combat with not-so-friendly fellow Americans. It never occurred, although we did see a crowd of placard-carrying protestors, some chanting obscenities at us.

"Well, Bob, looks like it's Splitsville for us. My cousin told me to find Del Rosa Drive, west from the base gate, and call them."

"Okay, man. Don't forget to call me when you get to the subbase in Groton."

"I will, Bob," I said, shaking hands with my Swift Boat shipmate. "Count on it."

It was a short two blocks' walk to Del Rosa. I found a phone booth at the corner of Realto Ave. My cousin said to stay put. It would take them an hour to travel the sixty miles from Downey. I found a shade tree nearby and lowered my seabag to the ground. It was a startling change in scenery: no Hueys, deuce-and-a-halfs, Dust Off choppers flying overhead, or soldiers wearing combat gear and carrying rifles and ammo belts.

Down the street, a short distance away, I spotted a BAR sign. Of legal age now, I decided to go in for a cool brew. Walking in, I made my way to the bar and dropped my seabag.

"I'll have a Coors," I told the barkeep.

"Can't do that," the stout man answered with a look of disdain.

Presuming I looked underage, I pulled out my military ID.

"I don't care if you're thirty," he said in a stronger tone. "You just got in from Vietnam, didn't you?"

"I sure did, and I'm glad to be back home."

"Well, you can march your ass right back out that door. We don't serve Vietnam troops here."

His response shocked me. I didn't move, thinking I heard wrong.

"What you waiting for, sailor? Out."

I felt rage come over me, turning my face red with anger. But what good would it do for me to argue with the idiot? I felt like an outcast. I was a decorated war veteran. I'd seen combat, cheated death, and now I was being denied service for having fought for my country. There was no need for alcohol; my head was spinning with outrage.

"Fuck you kindly, sir!" I shouted from the doorway and walked out.

I saw Ray's '64 white Chevy Impala approach. It was great reuniting with Cookie. As expected, after a big hug from her, she made the sign of the cross on my forehead and welcomed me home. Ray tossed my seabag into the trunk. They brought their lovely baby girl, Yvonne, just shy of her third birthday, with them. I sat in the back seat playing with her on the ride to their home.

After a nice lunch, I wasn't ready for anything but sleep. Exhausted, I hit the sack, missed supper, and slept through the night. The next morning, after a late breakfast, they took me to visit Hollywood Boulevard and the Sunset Strip. I was in awe as we walked, in total culture shock. The teenage scene had undergone a drastic change in the twelve months I was gone.

The Strip was a concentration of the hippie scene. It was a live version of the Beatles' "Sgt. Pepper's Lonely Hearts Club Band" album. Psychedelic colors abounded. I even saw one guy dressed in a turquoise, ankle-length tunic, wearing round rose-tinted glasses, holding a rigid dog leash, and walking an invisible dog. I decided the hippie movement would have to exist without one more *loco en la cabeza* fool in their freaky ranks.

That afternoon, still exhausted, I took a nap. I woke up after dark and was told by my cousin that I had slept through an earthquake that measured 6.5 on the Richter scale. Ray went in the room to check on me and said I was sound asleep while the bed shook. Although the quake took place in the Borrego Mountain range, 120 miles to the south, the Downey area merely experienced hard tremors.

The following day, April 9, 1968, my cousin took me to the Los Angeles International Airport for my return flight to SanAnto. My excitement peaked once again. I bid farewell to Cookie and Ray. Although it was a short visit, I was grateful to have family waiting for me on my arrival back in the states.

Once airborne, the flight took shy of three hours. My stomach danced the jitterbug. I should have drawn up another Short Timer's chart for 180 minutes. Numerous scenarios of my arrival ran through my head, making me fidget often en route home. There'd be no way I could keep my eyes from tearing. I prayed my mother would not faint from the excitement. It occurred to me I had failed to inform my family I had a new girlfriend, and she'd be waiting for me as well.

I kept checking my Timex flex-band wristwatch every minute it seemed. Two hours passed. I felt a reduction in airspeed, followed by a sense of downward movement.

"This is your captain speaking. We're commencing our descent into San Antonio. We should be on the ground within the hour. Enjoy the rest of your flight. It's been a pleasure serving you."

My nerves were loaded with anxiety. The plane's wheels were deployed. The sound of the landing gears engaging startled me. Looking out the window, I saw spring's vibrant green fields below. The sight filled me with warmth.

Gracias, Diosito for bringing me home safely, I prayed silently.

I grabbed the tiny St. Anthony statue from my uniform breast pocket and held it tight, thanking him for being my faithful companion in Vietnam. It saddened me to see the infant Jesus' left arm was missing. It had broken off during the ambush on the day Bobby Don Carver was killed.

In minutes, the wheels contacted the runway. Breathing a sigh of relief, I felt my eyes moisten. I did my best to straighten out my dress white uniform, adjusting the two rows of military ribbons below my left shoulder. Looking out the window, I took time to roll the top edge of my white Navy hat. Being inspection-ready for my family . . . and Gloria . . . was a must.

The plane pulled up to the elevated passenger ramp and stopped. The clicking sounds of safety belts unbuckling spread throughout the cabin, while passengers along the aisle stood reaching for their carry-on baggage. I remained seated, nose pressed against the window, eager to see *mi familia* through the tinted terminal windows. I only saw shadows. As the passengers to the rear of the plane finally started moving forward, I got up, feeling weak in the knees.

Before exiting the plane, I straightened my black silk neckerchief, double-checked that my wallet was secure, and walked out. Ahead, I could see the open terminal area but only managed to notice the tops of heads and hands up in the air waving to arriving passengers. I couldn't find my family.

"*¡Allí está!*" I heard a lady's voice shout.

"Yes, it's Chapo. I see him!" another lady yelled.

"¡*Mijo, mijo, mijo!*" I heard Mom cry out.

Off to my right, at the back of the crowd, a bunch of hands waved high in the air. I pushed in that direction. And then I saw Mom and Dad. She rushed toward me, sobbing uncontrollably, Dad following close behind, as were the rest of the folks who came to welcome me home. I hugged Mom and Dad for the longest time, while the family waited patiently for their turn.

Mom, amid tears, made the sign of the cross on my forehead, heart, across to the other side and down to mid-chest, forming a larger cross symbol. I kissed them both and told them how much I missed and loved them as I showed them the St. Anthony statue. Mom grabbed my hand and brought the figurine to her lips and kissed it.

The family moved in, and the scene turned into a giant Texas-size hug.

But where's Gloria? I wondered. She said she'd be waiting for me. With me between Mom and Dad, we all began heading away from the passenger waiting area.

My eyes caught view of a beautiful brunette leaning against the wall ahead of us. The smile was undeniably Gloria's, as was the rest of her shapely figure. We ran toward each other and smashed into a tight embrace and a lip lock that wouldn't quit. The family burst into a loud cheer and applause. I grabbed Gloria's hand and turned to my parents.

"Mom, Dad, this is Gloria."

"Hello. Good to meet you," Mom said, not knowing what else to say, but with a puzzled look on her face.

"I'm glad to meet you as well, Mr. and Mrs. Herrera. Your son has told me a lot about you and the family," Gloria said.

"Thank you for coming to welcome Roy home, miss," I heard my father tell her.

"Roy?" Gloria asked, eyebrows crinkled.

"Yeah, I'll explain later. And this is *mi familia*."

In unison, sisters, aunts, uncles, and cousins, raised their hands, saying, "Hi!"

"Welcome home, son," Dad said, patting my back.

"*Bienvenido a casa, mijo,*" Mom said, squeezing my arm.

I grabbed Gloria's hand and together we led the way toward baggage claim.

• • •

The journey home was complete. Through God's grace, I came through on the promise I made to my parents. I'd been to hell and back. I was alive and well.

EPILOGUE

O n April 7, 1968, Seaman Raúl Herrera boarded a Continental Airlines plane in Da Nang, Republic of Vietnam, for his return flight to the continental United States—"The World," as homeward bound soldiers, airmen, Marines, and sailors called it. Like the Swifties before and after him who made their way home, he took his own set of memories, as well as a game plan for getting on with his life after war. Behind him, in Vietnam, the battles raged on and on.

None of us realized or appreciated the small craft combatant history we were building, or the brotherhood that would be created once we started to reconnect many years later. The Swift Boat legacy began when General William Westmoreland, Commander Military Assistance Command, Vietnam, called a conference to investigate how a joint US Navy–Vietnamese Navy offshore picket line of defense could be set up. Securing the coast from North Vietnamese resupply vessels was the Operation Market Time mission.

The first shallow-water Market Time vessels used were converted eighty-two-foot Coast Guard cutters. In the summer of 1965, they joined a handful of blue water ships, mainly destroyers and surveillance aircraft, already patrolling the 1,200-mile coast of South Vietnam.

Following the arrival of the first two Swift Boats, PCF-3 and PCF-4, on October 30, 1965, five bases were set up in suitable ports: PCF Division 101, An Thới; 102 in Da Nang; 103 in Cat Lo; 104 at Cam Ranh Bay; and 105 at Qui Nhơn. On January 1, 1967, they were designated as Coastal Divisions 11, 12, 13, 14, and 15. A detachment of Da Nang in Chu Lai was established as Coastal Division 16 on June 16, 1967, and returned to detachment status on November 1, 1967. A best estimate indicates that

600 officers and 3,000 enlisted men rode Swift Boats. Add to that, hundreds more served in maintenance and division staff capacities.

Division mottos captured the Swiftie esprit de corps. In ascending numerical order: Numbah One Watch Dog; For Freedom We Fight; Vigilance; Any Time Any Place; We Can Hack It; and Coastal Division 16's No Quarter.

Under the Task Force 115 (Operation Market Time) banner, from October 30, 1965, to December 1, 1970, fifty Swift Boat sailor fatalities occurred from a variety of causes—combat, storms, illnesses, and accidents. We refer to these gallant sailors as our Swift Boat Honor Crew, those Still on Patrol.

The first personnel and craft loss occurred on February 14, 1966, when PCF-4 and her crew fell victim to a Viet Cong trap. As they pulled alongside the enemy's flag tied to a pole driven into the soft mud in shallow water, a submerged massive mine blast took the lives of four crewmen and critically wounded two more. The gaping hole in the boat's starboard bow caused it to sink. Although recovered, PCF-4, after being taken to Subic Bay in the Philippines, was deemed not repairable.

Four members of our Swift Boat Honor Crew remain missing in action. One fell overboard (either from a seizure or sniper fire) off the central coast of South Vietnam in October 1966; another was lost when his boat was flipped end over end while trying to enter the Huế River the next month; and another was lost during a controversial aerial attack near the DMZ in June 1968. The last MIA Swiftie was blown over the side after the boat's 81 mm mortar exploded in July 1969.

We lost seven Swift Boats in Vietnam: PCF-4 by a submerged mine detonation; PCF-41 by mine and shore bombardment; PCFs 14, 76, and 77 were sunk in heavy seas in Northern I Corps; PCF-19 sunk by aircraft fire; and PCF-43 was hit by B-40 rockets, beached, and destroyed when the onboard cargo of explosives and PCF mortar rounds detonated.

Swift Boats—these tiny aluminum-hulled Men o' War—like the men that rode them, were resilient. PCF-97 was one example. In June 1967, while on patrol off the Cà Mau Peninsula, the southernmost tip of Vietnam, it was hit by a recoilless rifle round and sank in thirty-five feet of water. It was recovered, taken aboard the USS *Oak Hill* (LSD 7) to the Philippines for repairs. PCF-97 was back in service at Cam Ranh Bay on December 29, 1967. It can be said that the mighty 97 Boat was never lost, she simply had a six-month makeover in Subic Bay. Many other PCFs suffered major damage and lived to fight another day.

On November 12, 1970, PCF-97, along with PCFs 45, 87, and 692, entered the Eo Lon Canal south of Ben Tre in the mid-Mekong Delta to insert Kit Carson Scouts. US Navy Black Ponies provided fixed-wing air support. Two Scouts were killed and two Swifties were wounded. This was the last incident in the Vietnam War in which Swift Boat sailors were wounded in action.

By the time President Nixon's Vietnamization strategy was announced in November 1969, Rear Admiral Elmo Zumwalt had been Commander of Naval Forces in Vietnam for fourteen months. The process of training Vietnamese Navy personnel, officers and enlisted, began in earnest. The first turnover of all Swift Boat assets took place on November 5, 1969, at Qui Nhơn when the US Navy's Coastal Division 15 was disestablished and placed in the hands of the South Vietnamese Navy.

Coastal Division 12 in Da Nang closed its doors on February 28, 1970; Cam Ranh Bay, Coastal Division 14, followed on April 1, 1970. Coastal Division 11, An Thới, dissolved at Cat Lo on October 1, 1970. The last Swift Boat turnover ceremony took place at Cat Lo, Coastal Division 13 disestablishment on December 1, 1970.

PCF-79 was among the US Swift Boats turned over to the South Vietnamese Navy during the ceremony held in Da Nang. A total of seven PCF crews served on this Swift from August 1966 to February 1970. With a South Vietnamese Navy crew, it continued patrolling the waters in I Corps, fighting the enemy as PCF-3881.

The US-manned Swift Boat lamp was turned off.

The last four American Swifties perished while serving as advisors to South Vietnamese Navy Swift Boat crews. In addition to the fifty American Swifties Still on Patrol, other brave US and Republic of Vietnam military personnel died while serving on Swift Boats. One such hero was South Vietnamese Navy Petty Officer Bui Quang Thi. He died in the aerial attack on PCF-19 near the DMZ in June 1968 and is missing in action.

Years after the war in Vietnam ended, a select group of Swifties remained on active duty in the US Navy and other branches of the Armed Services. They brought their unique combat experience and skill sets to the dangerous, fast-changing world the US faced. Swifties rose through the enlisted and officer ranks. QM2 Merrel William Yocum is our senior Career Enlisted. He retired in 2005 as the Brigadier General Deputy Commander (Support) of the 28th Infantry Division, Pennsylvania Army National Guard.

Career-officer Swifties also rose through the ranks. Lieutenant Junior Grade Harold Webster Gehman Jr., our senior career officer, skippered PCF-27 out of Chu Lai. He retired in 2000 as a four-star admiral. He served as NATO's Supreme

Allied Commander, Atlantic, Commander-in-Chief of the United States Joint Forces Command, one of the United States Unified Combatant Commands, and Vice Chief of Naval Operations. In 2003, Admiral Gehman served as the Chairman of the Board investigating the February 1, 2003, NASA space shuttle *Columbia* STS-107 accident.

Lieutenant Junior Grade Norman T. Saunders, USCG, Commanding Officer, USCGC *Point Orient* (WPB 82319), played a key role in the capture of Skunk Alpha. He retired in 1999 as a Rear Admiral (Upper Half) Commanding the 7th Coast Guard District.

Swifties continued to serve their country after the Vietnam War in hot spots like Panama, Grenada, Somalia, Desert Storm and Desert Freedom, Kosovo, Afghanistan, and Iraq. Vietnam shaped them for future invaluable and dedicated service to our nation.

Many of us returned to "The World" from Vietnam as civilians. Most tried to put harrowing recollections of combat behind us. We built careers, raised families, and contributed to our communities. It took years to realize that many of us brought back disturbing memories of war, stowed away deep in the seabags of our psyche. Like termites, they ate away at our being, destroying relationships along the way. We needed healing.

We felt isolated and incomplete.

Then the internet search engines came along. We connected with other Swifties and searched for crewmates. We shared sea stories. This helped soothe the soul. The brotherhood began to sprout. The Swift Boat Sailors Association was officially formed in 1995 when Swifties across the United States converged on Washington, DC, for the dedication of Swift Boat PCF-1 into the hands of the Naval Historical Center at the Washington, DC, Navy Yard.

We held reunions and built websites. The depths of our bonds forged in combat became more apparent, and they were strengthened as we reconnected after many years. Some chose to avoid such memories and friendships. We have honored and respected those wishes. But we feel most fortunate to have the opportunity to better understand our time in Vietnam and how it affected the rest of our lives.

On May 21, 2005, the Vietnam Unit Memorial Monument was dedicated at the US Naval Amphibious Base, Coronado, California. It was there that we trained from the summer of 1965 to 1969. The names of the 2,564 Navy and Coast Guard sailors who died in Vietnam are inscribed on this wall of honor. The static display includes three Vietnam-era combat craft—PCF-104, representing Task Force 115; a PBR, representing Task Force 116; and CCB 18, a command-and-control Monitor, representing Task Force 117. It should be noted that none of the combat craft sent to Vietnam were ever returned to the United States. The craft on display served as training platforms in California during the Vietnam War.

When US Swift Boat operations in Vietnam ended, the PCF Training infrastructure in Vallejo, California, was out of a job. The Navy donated two training boats, PCFs 813 and 816, to the newly independent country of Malta. The boats were used, primarily in coast guard–type roles, for almost forty years. In 2012, PCF-816 was returned to the United States under the auspices of the Swift Boat Sailors Association and the San Diego Maritime Museum. After an extensive overhaul by Swift Boat sailor volunteers—deemed the Dirty Boat Guys—PCF-816 began offering passenger runs on San Diego Bay in 2014.

In the summer of 2016, PCF-816 made a "show the flag" run along the coast of Southern California. Its northbound leg ports included: Oceanside, Newport Beach, San Pedro, Port Huếneme, and Santa Barbara. The southbound leg ports were Oxnard, Marina Del Rey, Long Beach, and Dana Point.

Swift Boat PCF-79—Crew 74-A

Lieutenant Junior Grade Edward J. Bergin (aka Lord Mort) returned to Florida and joined the Navy Reserve in 1968. He rose to the rank of captain, retiring in 1986 after twenty-two years of service. He spent five years at IBM, transitioned into commercial real estate, and eventually moved to Tampa, forming his own company. He ultimately set up Walter Development Company, partnering with Jim Walter. He and Mary Lupien were married in 1987 and currently live in Safety Harbor, Florida.

BM1 Bobby Don "Boats" Carver was killed in action on December 6, 1967, Quảng Ngãi Province, Republic of Vietnam. At the Swift Boat Sailors Association reunion held in New Orleans, Louisiana, Admiral Elmo R. Zumwalt Jr. presented the Bronze Star medal posthumously to Bobby Don Carver for his action in pushing PCF-79 skipper, Edward J. Bergin, out of harm's way as heavy machine gun fire from three bunkers on the beach strafed our boat. His son, Bobby Don Carver Jr., accepted the award. "Boats" is buried in Welcome Cemetery, Simpson, Louisiana.

EN1 Ronald "Porky" Rinehart settled in the Texas Gulf Coast, near Houston. He continued working in the marine engine field, married Yoli, his Philippine sweetheart, and had two daughters. Chu Lai Swift mates will remember him as "Two-Trawler Killer Porky" for his involvement in the capture of two enemy cargo ships during his tour on Swift Boats in Vietnam. He suffered from COPD but could not overcome his addiction to Lucky Strikes. Porky passed away on April 1, 2010, at the age of seventy-one.

TM3 Robert "Gunner" Middleton went home to Lake Garda in Burlington, Connecticut. He attended Computer Processing Institute in East Hartford for one year. He married Sandy Cherven in August 1969 and had two daughters. He furthered his computer science studies, enabling him to enjoy a twenty-eight-year career that began as a computer programmer and later excelling as a systems analyst for numerous corporations. Bob and Sandy have been RV travelers since 1997.

EN2 Jim "Hogjaws" Schneider returned to Custer, South Dakota, after being discharged from the Navy in November 1968. He worked a variety of craftsman jobs and married Monica Guisinger in May 1969 and had two children. He moved to Rapid City when offered a job with their fire department and retired as captain after twenty-two years of exemplary service. He accepted a four-year volunteer job with VFW Post 1273, bringing the canteen back into the black. He also served as a director of the Swift Boat Sailors Association for numerous years. Jim and Monica live in Rapid City, South Dakota.

SN Timothy "Mac" McNamara, after receiving treatment in Japan, was ordered to the Naval Hospital Oakland for medical rest. During this period, he helped process servicemen out of active duty at Treasure Island, between San Francisco and Oakland. After he was released from the Navy, he returned to Vallejo, California. He married, had four boys, and worked as a postal clerk. On May 23, 1970, Mac rescued two youngsters from a burning vehicle at the Vallejo Marina. The city of Vallejo awarded Mac a Certificate of Commendation and in addition to receiving the Superior Accomplishment Award, the postmaster presented Mac a check for $200.

Unfortunately, the first marriage failed, bringing the financial burden of child support on him. A second marriage ended in divorce, adding a heavy IRS tax burden. After child support deductions, his take-home pay from the post office often left him with $40 per month. He became homeless and lived out of his car, alcohol his only comfort. Alone, Mac struggled with severe PTSD until an angel, Jeanette Arias, crossed paths with him in October 1985. She helped put him back on his feet. Tim retired in 1992 after twenty-three years of service with the USPS. The couple married in March 2001. In January 2013 they moved to Vacaville, California. After surgery for a bone infection, Mac's condition deteriorated. Diagnosis did not identify bladder cancer, a result of Agent Orange. Mac died on June 27, 2018.

DMSN Raúl "Bean" Herrera finished his four-year tour of duty in the Navy at the US Naval Submarine Base, Groton, Connecticut, in 1969. He moved back to San Antonio to work and begin his studies in engineering, earning an associate degree in engineering technology. He has five children from his first marriage. Raúl served as Board Director of the Swift Boat Sailors Association from 1995 to 2013, the last four years as president.

Raúl's involvement with the Houston writing community began in the early '80s. He is a member of the Houston Writers Guild, the Nonfiction Authors Association, and the Military Writers Society of America. As a free-lance writer, his articles have appeared in *Nuestras Vidas*, an English-written magazine featuring stories of people from Houston's Latino community. Articles relating to Swift Boats and the capture of Skunk Alpha have been published in the former *Houston Post, Vietnam Magazine, Sea Classics Magazine*, and *The New York Times*.

Raúl's appended story of Skunk Alpha has been published in three books: *They Answered the Call: Latinos in the Vietnam War*, by Gil Dominguez, *War in the Shallows: U.S. Navy Coastal and Riverine Warfare in Vietnam, 1965–1968*, by John Darrell Sherwood, and *White Water, Red Hot Lead: On Board US Navy Swift Boats* by Dan Daly. Raúl participated in oral history projects sponsored by the US Navy Memorial, Navy Log; the Texas Capitol Vietnam Veterans Monument, Living Monument Veteran Stories series; the Fiftieth Anniversary of the US Government's Vietnam War Commemoration Campaign; and *Voces* Oral History Program, University of Texas.

Raúl worked in the civil engineering field from 1969 to 2010. In the last twenty-one years in Houston, he worked for Dannenbaum Engineering Corporation as a computer design technician in the Land Development Department. In May 2004, he married his third wife, Luz Analida Sabogal Bedoya, from Colombia. They live in Richmond, Texas.

. . .

Memorable stories from our former comrades are still coming to light. Books like *Capturing Skunk Alpha* help strengthen the Swift Boat brotherhood and serve as a salute to the valor of these extraordinary and gallant sailors. The Swift Boat saga will forever be remembered with pride.

BRAVO ZULU, SWIFTIES.

ROBERT "BOB" BOLGER

PCF-99 SKIPPER

AUTHOR'S NOTE

A vast number of Vietnam War books originated from an author's desire to share a personal story of fear, valor, and survival. In some instances, plans to write a book in this genre began while the veteran was on the battlefield or recovering from wounds. *Capturing Skunk Alpha* was never a preconceived idea. The driving force behind this book was a commitment to brotherhood and evolved from years of emotional torment over the loss of one of our crewmen.

I slipped back into society with ease on my return from Vietnam, after spending the last year of naval service at the submarine base in Groton, Connecticut. In fall, 1969, José Cueva, my best friend in high school, arranged to have a job on a survey crew waiting for me in San Antonio. I considered myself fortunate; I had a good job and was happily married. Our first child was born in May 1971, and a second girl arrived (prematurely) a year later, in June 1972. Although my newlywed life and work occupied most of my daily mental exercise, memories of war often stirred inside me.

Every now and again around town, I saw what I presumed to be Vietnam vets. Most let their hair grow long and had beards. They hung on to what for them was real; they dressed in combat greens, bush-hats, and jungle boots. I learned many were homeless. I gathered their time in the field fighting the Viet Cong went far beyond what I experienced. They were the psychologically wounded warriors.

I too was scarred but didn't yet realize it. Demons born in battle stowed away in my persona prior to leaving Vietnam. They began their destructive work on my psyche for the first time one day at a gas station. A news bulletin on the car radio triggered an unexpected morbid reaction in me.

The day was May 8, 1972. President Richard M. Nixon addressed the nation, defending his decision to escalate the air and sea offensive against North Vietnam. On April 16, to shut down the resupply of arms to their military forces doing battle in South Vietnam, Nixon ordered the renewed bombing of Hanoi and the mining of Haiphong Harbor.

In South Vietnam, the responsibility of curtailing the infiltration of ammunition and supplies belonged to Operation Market Time seaborne units all along the 1,200-mile coastline, Swift Boats forming the last line of defense.

I cheered Nixon's directive; it involved the US Navy. My mind drifted off to the action taking place in Haiphong Harbor and Hanoi. It pleased me assuming the bombs hitting Hanoi were destroying the North Vietnamese war machine, human life included. It was a small payback for what the enemy did to us that December day in 1967, when the Viet Cong ambushed our Swift Boat along the Mỹ Lai shoreline, killing our lead petty officer, Bobby Don Carver.

I grew anxious, wanting to hear the estimated death count rise. Although safely back home, I still had an enemy. My war was not over. I fantasized sitting behind a machine gun raining terror on the North Vietnamese. Adrenaline filled my body. The loud clank of the gas pump handle startled me out of the scene I envisioned.

I kept those dark desires and feelings locked away.

I couldn't confide to my wife how I felt, for we had opposing views on the United States' involvement in the war. Tensions grew each time the subject was debated. The ideological differences led to more unrest at home. The arguments intensified, regardless of the reason.

Seeing Walter Cronkite on the evening news announce the latest weekly US casualty count added to my torment. The stowaway demons began controlling my thoughts and actions. I started losing my gregarious nature, making marital matters worse.

At the height of arguments, I'd scream, "I wish I had died in Vietnam instead of Carver! Why not me, why not me?" Suggestions I erase the war from my memory only served to enrage me further. A festering urge to get behind Gunner's twin .50s and destroy everything in my line of sight frightened me.

Anger invaded my world. My smile vanished.

The sounds of helicopters or the smell of diesel engine fumes gave me chills and whirled my thoughts to Vietnam. I wanted to be left alone. I longed for the sounds of battle and the smell coming from hundreds of spent machine gun casings that hung over our boat after a firefight. I grew unhappy and depressed.

"Why not me . . . why not me?"

The Vietnam flashbacks spurred haunting episodes. I developed a severe irrational fear of taking showers. Days passed between baths; washing my hair became a daunting task. At times, I sprinkled my head with baby powder, attempting to hide the greasy appearance. I dreaded going into the bathroom.

An eerie feeling engulfed me once I locked the door. Working up the courage to close my eyes while shampooing my hair strained every muscle in me. The instant I shut them, the hair on my arms and on the back of my neck stood on end. I sensed the presence of our deceased boatswain's mate. I took shelter in the corner of the shower, certain he stood in front of me, and opening my eyes, I would see his bloody face.

I shared this troubling secret with no one.

In June 1979, on the Greek island of Limnos, I sat on a beach admiring the deep blue waters of the Aegean Sea. Nearby was the small village of Varos. My thoughts turned to Vietnam and to our coastal surveillance patrols. Coincidentally, a fishing boat, weathered sails and all, appeared on my left and moved into view. I thought I was daydreaming of the wooden Vietnamese junks dotting our patrol area daily. I began reliving the tragic day in December 1967 when the Viet Cong ambushed us, and Bobby Don took a machine gun round through his right eye. *Boats, are you reaching out to me from the beyond? Why?* Perhaps the episodes in the shower were real and not a figment of my imagination . . . *but why? What do you want from me?*

I thought of the family he left behind, Bobby Don Jr. and a young son, Kevin. I wondered what the government told the family about his death. Because of his bravery on the open deck of PCF-79, and through his skillful accuracy on the 81 mm mortar, he single-handedly brought down a 120-foot steel-hulled enemy trawler. Through his action, the lives of hundreds of free world forces were saved. Furthermore, had he not done that, the trawler's crew might have had the time to detonate the 2,046-pound TNT self-destruct charge and blow us out of the water as well.

Perhaps Carver wanted me to write the saga of PCF-79 and tell the story of gallant Swift Boat sailors who took the fight to the enemy while serving in Operation Market Time. I made up my mind then and there. I decided to write this book in Bobby Don's memory and as a tribute to the fifty Swift Boat sailors who gave their all in that war and the many more who brought Vietnam back with them buried in their souls.

I merged letters my mother kept with a chronology of the war between April 1967 and May 1968. I wrote to Congressman Henry B. González, and through his assistance and the Freedom of Information Act, loads of declassified confidential and some secret documents began arriving. I roughed out a chapter outline and began writing this story.

The haunting episodes in the shower mysteriously ended.

One night, the phone rang. An unfamiliar voice asked, "Is this Raúl Herrera?" I responded in the affirmative. The man said, "This is Admiral Kenneth L. Veth, calling you from California. I understand you've been trying to reach me about a book you are writing on Operation Market Time."

I couldn't believe it, COMNAVFORV was on the line . . . calling ME! The Commander Naval Forces Vietnam called to offer his support and any information that might be of use for me in writing the Swift Boat story.

Fast forward four decades.

The *Capturing Skunk Alpha* journey that began in the late '70s encountered countless setbacks, the last being a six-month delay brought about when Hurricane Harvey hit Houston. Each delay, however, generated a renewed hope and drive.

Keeping the story true was easy; I lived the scenes I am in. Respecting privacy, some names have been changed, others omitted, and some invented. Choosing to occasionally weave Spanish into the writing helped define and maintain the point of view. Actual events portrayed are reality based. Literary license allowed the characters to come alive through fictional dialogue. Interviews enabled the creation of presumed conversation.

Regarding the foul language in the book—and perhaps it is a myth—Eleanor Roosevelt said it best: "Sailors have the cleanest bodies and the filthiest minds." Cursing was common in Vietnam, by all troops. It seemed that every other word we used was F-this, F-that, or F'n-A. I was told by a Swiftie that during a family dinner, soon after his return from Vietnam, he asked his mother to "pass the fucking butter." When I questioned him on what happened next, he told me, "She passed the fucking butter."

Research was extensive, perhaps overkill at times. A need for accuracy demanded it. Declassified government documents and reports were an invaluable asset. I relied heavily on the US Naval Forces Vietnam Monthly Historical Supplements. Numerous trips to the National Archives in College Park, Maryland, yielded the deck logs of ships involved in all the stories, except one. The identity of the destroyer we rendezvoused with for the transfer of our mortally wounded crewmate regrettably remains a mystery.

As for the Skunk Alpha trawler incident, a copy of a recording made aboard the Coast Guard Cutter *Point Orient* provided the actual radio communication between all units: land, aerial, and seaborne. The Naval Institute's *Proceedings* published the article titled "Trawler!" written by Charles R. Stephan, Commander of the Northern Surveillance Group.[1] He was the planner and on-scene commander of the Skunk Alpha intercept operation (IMPAIR). The information contained in that piece was invaluable to the story.

On October 21, 2021, I was interviewed by Le Huong Giang of Hanoi Vietnam VTV3 Television Network. The country was celebrating its sixtieth anniversary of the Ho Chi Minh Trail by Sea. It was during this interview that I learned that the trawler's captain set the time-delayed self-destruct mechanism in motion. Shortly after the crew abandoned ship, Carver's 81 mm white phosphorous mortar round hit the pilothouse, destroying the explosive charge ignition device.

An interview with the USS *Wilhoite*'s radarman confirmed his ship's deck log entries. The tattered remains of our PCF-79's Mỹ Lai combat chart served well in determining relative positions of all units and distances between each other, including the trawler and the Sông Sa Kỳ river mouth at Mui Batangan. Adding to the accuracy was my own handwritten PCF-79 logbook entries of that triumphant night.

Word count limitations prevented an in-depth account of the last major North Vietnamese four-trawler infiltration attempt of March 1, 1968—regrets to all Operation Market Time units involved. Countless Swift Boat stories of bravery under fire in the Mekong Delta remain untold, additional places where Swifties also fought alongside naval units in Operation Game Warden Task Force 116 and Mobile Riverine Force Task Force 117, and Helicopter Attack Squadron (Light) HA(L)-3, the all-volunteer US Navy helicopter unit whose job it was to support Naval Special Warfare operations and Task Force 117 missions in the delta.

It wasn't until 1980 that the American Psychiatric Association's *Diagnostic and Statistical Manual of Mental Disorders* added Post Traumatic Stress Disorder (PTSD) with specific symptoms to its list of psychiatric disorders. Treatment for PTSD at VA medical centers wasn't immediate. It didn't matter; I remained convinced I was okay and didn't need to seek psychological care.

In 2010, fellow Swift Boat sailor veteran Warren Jenny learned I had been struggling emotionally for many years. Through his persistence and encouragement, I came to accept that I was suffering from PTSD. He and his daughter, Leah, stayed with me every step of the way and guided me through the multitude of Veterans Administration forms. The process took weeks, but all the physical and psychological exams eventually confirmed several conditions I had been suffering for so long. Working on this literary labor of love supplements the VA medical care I'm receiving—it's been a catharsis.

· · ·

Capturing Skunk Alpha is a true account of young brave Swift Boat sailors who fought an unconventional war along the 1,200-mile coastline of the Republic of Vietnam.
    BRAVO ZULU.

NOTES

Chapter 1

1. Map showing the entrance to Chu Lai base at Vũng An Hòa. The Swift Boat dock faced the Trường Giang River at Chu Lai. http://www.a-1-6. org/1-6th%20site./1st%20bn%206th%20inf%20web%20site%20off%20 line/TraBongNE250.jpg.

Chapter 2

1. PFC Roy C. Berrones' grave marker is located at Fort Sam Houston National Cemetery. He was assigned to the 318th Infantry Regiment in World War II and killed in action (KIA) on October 8, 1944.
2. 10 US Code § 502 Oath of Enlistment, https://uscode.house. gov/view.xhtml?req=granuleid:USC-prelim-title10-secti on502&num=0&edition=prelim#.
3. Independence would at long last be attained in Mexico as *El Grito de Dolores*: Mexico's battle cry for independence, *Encyclopaedia Britannica*, https://www.britannica.com/event/Grito-de-Dolores.

Chapter 3

1. Chuck Gunderson, "The Beatles Live! At Balboa Stadium 1965," *Journal of San Diego History*, https://sandiegohistory.org/journal/2009/january/

index-htm-8/.

2. Naval Training Center, San Diego, California; names and references gleaned from the yearbook *The Anchor: United States Naval Training Center, 1965, Recruit Company 498.*

3. "Up With People History," *Mackinac Island* (blog), http://mackinacisland. blogspot.com/2010/07/smile-till-it-hurts-history-of-up-with.html.

4. National Archives, Vietnam War Casualty Statistics, DCAS Vietnam Conflict Extract File record counts by incident or death date, casualties through end of 1965, https://www.archives.gov/research/military/vietnam-war/casualty-statistics#hostile.

Chapter 4

1. President John F. Kennedy's Joint Session of Congress speech regarding unconventional warfare, May 25, 1961; John F. Kennedy Presidential Library Historic Speeches, https://www.jfklibrary.org/learn/about-jfk/historic-speeches/address-to-joint-session-of-congress-may-25-1961.

2. Vice Admiral Wallace M. Beakley, "US Navy SEAL Teams from Establishment through Operation Urgent Fury: 1962–1983," *Defense Media Network*, http://www.defensemedianetwork.com/stories/u-s-navy-seal-teams-from-establishment-through-operation-urgent-fury-1962-1983/.

3. Christopher E. Goscha, "The Maritime Nature of the War for Vietnam (1945–75): A Geo-Historical Reflection" (Paper presented at 4th Triennial Vietnam Symposium, Texas Tech University, Vietnam Center, Lubbock, Texas, April 13–16, 2002), https://www.vietnam.ttu.edu/events/2002_Symposium/2002Papers_files/goscha.php.

4. Michael C. McCurry, "Riverine Force–A Vital Navy Capability for the Joint Force Commander" (research paper), February 13, 2006, https://apps.dtic.mil/sti/citations/ADA463522.

5. Bucklew Report Basic Conclusions, February 15, 1964, Operational Archives, Naval Historical Center, 2–5, boxes 230–32, Vietnam Command.

6. James S. Bowers, personal interview via email correspondence; World History Project on the Internet at https://worldhistoryproject. org/1965/2/16/vung-ro-bay-incident; R. L. Schreadley, *Vietnam–The Naval Story*, ed. Frank Uhlig Jr. (Annapolis, MD: Naval Institute Press, 1986), 281–83); R. L. Schreadley, *From The Rivers to the Sea* (Annapolis,

MD: Naval Institute Press, 1986), 78–82; John Darrell Sherwood, *War in the Shallows* (Washington, DC: Naval History and Heritage Command, Department of the Navy), 31–34; Goscha, "The Maritime Nature of the War," 16–17.

7. R. L. Shreadley, "The Naval War in Vietnam, 1950–1970," *US Naval Institute*, https://www.usni.org/magazines/proceedings/1971/may/naval-war-vietnam-1950–1970.

Chapter 5

1. "Patrol Craft Fast," https://www.wikiwand.com/en/Patrol_Craft_Fast.
2. Sherwood, *War in the Shallows*, 43.
3. Alex Larzelere, *The Coast Guard at War, Vietnam 1965–1975* (Annapolis, MD: Naval Institute Press, 1997), 39.
4. Schreadley, "The Naval War in Vietnam."
5. Shreadley, *From the Rivers to the Sea*.
6. Shreadley, *From the Rivers to the Sea*, 83.
7. "Patrol Craft Fast," https://www.wikiwand.com/en/Patrol_Craft_Fast.
8. Larzelere, *The Coast Guard at War*, 9–21.
9. Goscha, "The Maritime Nature of the War," 17.
10. Uhlig, *Vietnam–The Naval Story*, 283.
11. Ibid.
12. Ibid., 287.
13. "$4 Million Contract Given Sewart Seacraft by Navy. Construction Contract for Navy Swift Boats." *Franklin Banner–Tribune*, August 24, 1965.
14. Sherwood, *War in the Shallows*, 67; interview abstract conducted by Dr. John Darrell Sherwood, Naval Historical Center, June 19, 2008; Arthur P. Ismay, personal correspondence.
15. Edward J. Marolda, "The Years of Combat, 1965–1968," in *By Sea, Air, and Land–An Illustrated History of the US Navy and the War in Southeast Asia* (Washington, DC: Naval Historical Center, 1994), 63–65.
16. "Monthly Historical Summary," Naval Forces Vietnam, May 1966, 1–9, https://www.history.navy.mil/.
17. "Monthly Historical Summary," Naval Forces Vietnam, June 1966, https://www.history.navy.mil/; Stephen T. Ulmer, *Point League* skipper, personal correspondence.

Chapter 6

1. Fleet Airborne Electronics Training Unit, Pacific Detachment Whidbey Island, Oak Harbor, Washington. SERE Training during week of 6 February 1967, Survival, Evasion, Resistance and Escape, author copy.

Chapter 7

1. *Times Picayune*, update on the construction of the Swift Boats by Sewart Seacraft of Berwick, Louisiana. "LA-Built Boats are in Vietnam," February 2, 1966.
2. Paul Hurard, "Viet Cong Commandos Sank an American Aircraft Carrier," *War is Boring*, https://medium.com/war-is-boring/viet-cong-commandos-sank-an-american-aircraft-carrier-7f243ede06b3, also in *Navsource Naval History: Photographic History of the US Nav*, http://www.navsource.org/archives/03/011.htm.
3. "Monthly Historical Supplement," US Naval Forces Vietnam, January 1967, 29–31.

Chapter 8

1. Personal correspondence; eyewitness account by Fort Marion crewman RM3 Harry Leroy Blankenship Jr.; *Coastal Squadron One Swift Boat Crew Directory*, http://swiftboats.net/ PCF Group 1–9.
2. Larzelere, *The Coast Guard at War*, 48.
3. Ibid., 52.
4. Charles D. Lloyd and Robert Russell Johnson, personal interviews; Jon Uithol, email correspondence; Larzelere, *The Coast Guard at War*, 94; Swift Boat PCF-3 and PCF-4 crewmen names ENS Theodore Anthony Wright, RMSN Fred Raymond Read Jr., RM3 John Truman Richey, PCF-9 officer in charge LTJG Frederick Westco Bruns, and PCF-5 GMG3 George Cleveland Rekow appear on *Coastal Squadron One Swift Boat Crew Directory*, http://swiftboats.net/ PCF Group 1–9.

Chapter 9

1. Ed Hymoff, "Sea Raiders–US Navy Silver Star Commandos," *SAGA Magazine for Men*, March 1967, 8–11, 61–62, 64–65; *Coastal Squadron*

One Swift Boat Crew Directory, http://swiftboats.net/ PCF-26. "First Silver Star Presented Sailor," *Jackstaff News*, November 4, 1966, print.

2.   Ibid.

Chapter 10

1.   Ronald Rinehart, personal interview

2.   Saigon AP, "Officers Charge: Weather, Vietnamese Fire Endangers US Aircraft" *Michigan Daily*, vol. 77, April 6, 1967, 3. https://digital.bentley. umich.edu/midaily/mdp.39015071754183/687.

Chapter 12

1.   To read details about this incident, search "Monthly Historical Supplement Declassified Confidential Document," US Naval Forces Vietnam, March 14, 1967, 21. https://www.history.navy.mil/content/dam/nhhc/research/ archives/commander-naval-forces-vietnam/monthly-summaries-1967/ March1967.pdf; Charles P. Pfarrer Jr., Denis Baker, Dan Embree, Anthony R. Taylor, and Kenneth E. Gooding Jr., personal interviews; PCF-16 Underway Log #68, 13 March 1967, courtesy of Anthony R. Taylor personal collection.

2.   Ray Michilini personal interview.

3.   Fatigue Properties of Gun Barrel Materials, http://www.dtic.mil/dtic/tr/ fulltext/u2/738853.pdf.

4.   References to Bobby Don Carver taken from personal interviews with our engineman, Ronald "Porky" Rinehart, and our gunner, Bob Middleton. In addition, I met with Carver's sister, Patty Rae Carver Owens, in Leesville, LA for a personal interview.

Chapter 13

1.   Establishing and naming of Chu Lai: Robert Coram, *Brute: The Life of Victor Krulak, U.S. Marine* (Boston: Little, Brown, 2010).

2.   Personal interview via email with LTJG Lou Masterson, skipper of PCF-75.

3.   Robert K. Bolger, James Dennis Wiggins, personal interviews.

Chapter 14

1. "Historical Snapshot," http://www.boeing.com/history/products/c-47-skytrain.page; Cecil Brownlow, "AC-47 Broadens Viet Attack Envelope," *Aviation Week and Space Technology*, April 17, 1967; "Air Force Association Honors Captain Ronald W. Terry," *United States Air Force News Release*, March 25, 1966; Ronald W. Terry, "AC-47 Dragon Ships Improved with New Mini Guns," *United States Air Force News Release,* April 3, 1967.
2. Max Branscomb, Steve Netherby, Vern Jones, personal interviews.
3. Dave Payson, personal interview; July 11–15, 1967, Deck Log–USS *Wilhoite* (DER-397); National Archives, College Park, Maryland.
4. "USS *Gallup* (PG-85)," *Popular Mechanics*, September 1968, 71–73, 183.
5. Edward A. Knaup eyewitness account of trawler incident via postal service correspondence.
6. Victor G. Reiling Jr., personal interview.
7. Norman T. Saunders, personal interview.

Chapter 15

1. Rodney Bither, email correspondence.
2. Derald Smith, John Coates, David Ellingsworth, personal correspondence.
3. "The 60th Anniversary of the Ho Chi Minh Trail, By the Sea: Secret Stories Revealed for the First Time" [in Vietnamese]. https://vtv.vn/truyen-hinh/ky-tich-duong-ho-chi-minh-tren-bien-nhung-cau-chuyen-bi-mat-lan-dau-duoc-tiet-lo-20211023225420128.htm?fbclid=IwAR2t_I0WX_QfWx4 CTFcMdYH8rcmwImBJytuGH8V1StuEi-REou8pI3zdDU8. Segment 2 of the program: Vũng Rô in the Ho Chi Minh Trail, By Sea; timestamp 0:40:52 to 0:53:45; I first appear at timestamp 0:45:40.
4. GMG2 Eddie Knaup, email correspondence, "After Action Report, Trawler at Mui Batangan, Quang Ngai Province, Republic of Vietnam," July 25, 1967.

Chapter 16

1. Charles Black, "Trawler Runs Aground, Viet Cong Lose Weapons," *Columbus* (Georgia) *Ledger-Enquirer*, July 23, 1967.
2. Ken Weigand, Ron Seabolt, Tom Knapp, personal interviews.

Chapter 17

1. Anthony Chaplain Williams, personal interviews.
2. "The Fine Art of Building a Yabuta Junk," *All Hands Magazine*, September 1968, http://www.hullnumber.com/ALL-HANDS/the-fine-art-of-building-a-yabuta-junk; Tim Johnston, "Life with the Yabutas," http://www.warboats.org/yabuta.htm.

Chapter 19

1. "Monthly Historical Summary: Lost at Sea, PCF-87 Seaman Gunners Mate Alvin Lee Levan," *US Naval Forces Vietnam*, October 25, 1966, 46. *Coastal Squadron One Swift Boat Crew Directory*, PCF-87 listing, http://swift-boats.net/.
2. "Monthly Historical Summary: Perfume River Man Overboard, PCF-56," *US Naval Forces, Vietnam*, October 1966, 47; *Coastal Squadron One Swift Boat Crew Directory*, PCF-56 listing, http://swiftboats.net/.
3. PCF-77 capsized Perfume River mouth, November 15, 1966, three casualties: BM3 Harry Giles Brock, RMSN Bruce Allan Timmons, and MRC Willy Scott Baker, US Naval Forces, Vietnam, "Monthly Historical Summary," November 1966, 40–41; *Coastal Squadron One Swift Boat Crew Directory*, PCF-77 listing http://swiftboats.net/; David G. Wilbourne, "The Huế River," https://www.history.navy.mil/content/dam/nhhc/research/archives/commander-naval-forces-vietnam/monthly-summaries-1966/November1966.pdf; Anthony R. "Tony" Taylor, personal interview.
4. PCF-76 Capsize, November 6, 1967–US Naval Forces, Vietnam, "Monthly Historical Summary," November 1967, 2; Dan Daly, "Memories of Cửa Việt and the Loss of PCF-76," https://www.youtube.com/watch?v=e-e7VA0zeSH8; Dan Daly, Tom Jones, and Sterlin R. Harris, personal interviews; Dan Daly, White Water–Red Hot Lead (Havertown, PA: Casemate Publishers, 2017), 247–62; *Coastal Squadron One Swift Boat Crew Directory*, PCF-76 listing–http://swiftboats.net/.
5. Tony Snesko, email correspondence; B. Anthony "Tony" Snesko, "Swift Boat Rescue," *Vietnam Magazine*, April 2000; "PCF-14 Capsize," "Monthly Historical Summary," *US Naval Forces Vietnam*, November 1967, 4.

Chapter 20

1.   "Wandering Soul," PSYOPS Tape Recording, Operation Wandering Soul https://en.wikipedia.org/wiki/Operation_Wandering_Soul_(Vietnam_War)

2.   Patrick Henry Brady, *Dead Men Flying* (Brentwood, TN: Permuted Press, 2021), 5, 158; "The Buildup of 1967," US Army Medical Department (Office of Medical History), 56.

3.   Western Union Telegram to Mrs. Betty Ellen Carver, National Archives, College Park, MD.

4.   Edward Bergin's letter to Mrs. Betty Ellen Carver; copy of letter provided by Mrs. Carver's son, Kevin.

5.   Kevin Carver, personal correspondence with Ian Bailey, Commander Coastal Division. Twelve letters to Mrs. Betty Ellen Carver, National Archives, Maryland.

Chapter 21

1.   *Bob Hope Christmas Special 1967*, https://www.youtube.com/watch?v=8uqN5mXWHZM&t=2545s. The Chu Lai show begins at time-stamp at 24:41; Premier Nguyễn Cao Kỳ's Saigon Christmas message begins at 1:25:31.

2.   "Monthly Historical Summary: An Xuyen Province Trawler," *US Naval Forces, Vietnam: March 1968*, 3–4, Appendix I, 1–6; Larzelere, *The Coast Guard at War*, 130; Bernard Wolf, "North Vietnamese Trawler Incident," *Swift Current* 3, no. 4 (March 1968).

3.   "Monthly Historical Summary," *US Naval Forces Vietnam: March 1968*, 4–5, Appendix 1, 1–3, 4, 5.

4.   "Monthly Historical Summary," *US Naval Forces Vietnam: March 1968*, 7 and Appendix 1, 1–3.

5.   "Monthly Historical Summary," *US Naval Forces Vietnam: March 1968*, 5 and Appendix 1, 5; Americal Division Tactical Operations Center, Daily Staff Journal/Duty Officer's Log, March 1, 1968.

Author's Note

1.   Charles R. Stephan, "Trawler!" *US Naval Forces Vietnam Proceedings, March 14, 1967* (United States Naval Institute: September 1968), 60–71.

INDEX

Printed in the USA
CPSIA information can be obtained
at www.ICGtesting.com
LVHW091915041124
795688LV00034B/962